D0229375

£7

LOIRE
gastronomique

LOIRE
gastronomique

HILAIRE WALDEN

Foreword by ANNE WILLAN

Photography by MICHELLE GARRETT

Series Editor MARIE-PIERRE MOINE

CONRAN OCTOPUS

First published in
Great Britain in 1992 by
Conran Octopus Limited
37 Shelton Street
London WC2H 9HN

Text copyright ©
Hilaire Walden 1992
Design and layout copyright ©
Conran Octopus Limited 1992

All rights reserved. No part of this book may be reproduced, stored in a retrieval system, or transmitted in any form or by any means, electronic, electrostatic, magnetic tape, mechanical, photocopying, recording or otherwise without the prior permission in writing of the publisher.

The right of Hilaire Walden to be identified as Author of this Work has been asserted by her in accordance with the Copyright, Designs and Patents Act 1988.

British Library Cataloguing-in-Publication Data
A catalogue record for this book is available from the British Library
ISBN 1 85029 424 0

Researcher and French Liaison
SALLY ANNE SCOTT
Senior Editor SARAH PEARCE
Art Editor ALISTAIR PLUMB
Copy Editor LEWIS ESSON
Editorial Assistant ROD MACKENZIE
Production JILL MACEY
Typeset by Hunters Armley, Leeds
Printed in China

Page 1: Stained glass window at La Châtaigneraie
Page 2: Drying wild mushrooms, the Auvergne
Right: The characteristic flat-bottomed boat used on the Loire river
Page 6: Autumn in the Orléanais

NOTE ON RECIPES Both metric and imperial quantities are given. Use either all metric or all imperial, as the two are not interchangeable.

CONTENTS

Foreword 7
By Anne Willan

Introduction 8
Map of the Loire

THE YOUNG RIVER 14
The passage of the Loire from its Source through the Eastern Auvergne, Bourbonnais and Nivernais
Recipes 22

INTO THE VAL-DE-LOIRE 30
Past Berry to the Sologne and the Orléanais
Recipes 46

'THE ENCHANTED LAND' 60
Through Touraine, the heartlands of the Val-de-Loire
Recipes 76

LAND OF PLENTY 92
Through Anjou, Curnonsky's 'paradise for peaceful digestion'
Recipes 110

TO THE SEA 126
The final stretches of the river as it flows through the Pays Nantais to the Atlantic
Recipes 136

A Visitor's Guide 148

List of Recipes and Index 156

Acknowledgments 160

FOREWORD

BY ANNE WILLAN

The river Loire is full of surprises. The popular image of a lazy, sunlit waterway lined with grand Renaissance palaces built for the pleasure of the kings of France is just one of the many facets of this, the longest river in France. Westwards around Angers, the land flattens to the sandy, fertile soil of 'the garden of France', where fruits were developed such as Beurré pears, and the Reine Claude plums named for the wife of François I. But more than 500 kilometres (300 miles) upriver, the rugged Auvergne region where the Loire rises is no garden. Here cabbage and roots are the winter staples and cattle must be robust to survive in mountains covered with snow for a third of the year.

In between lies fine ground for growing almost every French gastronomic treat, and with the help of Michelle Garrett's evocative photographs, Hilaire Walden leads us on a connoisseur's tour of them all. With affection, she explains the history and the background of this most charismatic river. Cooks, bakers, growers, restaurateurs come to life, and so, more importantly, do their recipes. This is a book to take into the kitchen to tackle dishes like Rabbit and Herb Terrine, Pike with Hazelnut Sauce, and Raspberry Pancakes. My own particular favourite is Chicken with Lime Blossom, a delicious combination I had not come across before (we happen to have both in our own back yard in Burgundy).

Country cooking at its best – and it is no accident that the Loire remains so rural. The river is notoriously treacherous, liable to flash floods and full of shifting currents and sandbanks which make navigation chancey. As a result, its banks have escaped the clogging industry found along the Rhine and Rhône. Even today, environmentalists have defeated moves to dam the waters upstream, so that the Loire still flows untamed, dominating the countryside around it as it has for so many centuries. No wonder it has so much to offer in the way of fine food. And how lucky we are to have so knowledgeable a cook as Hilaire Walden to explore it for us!

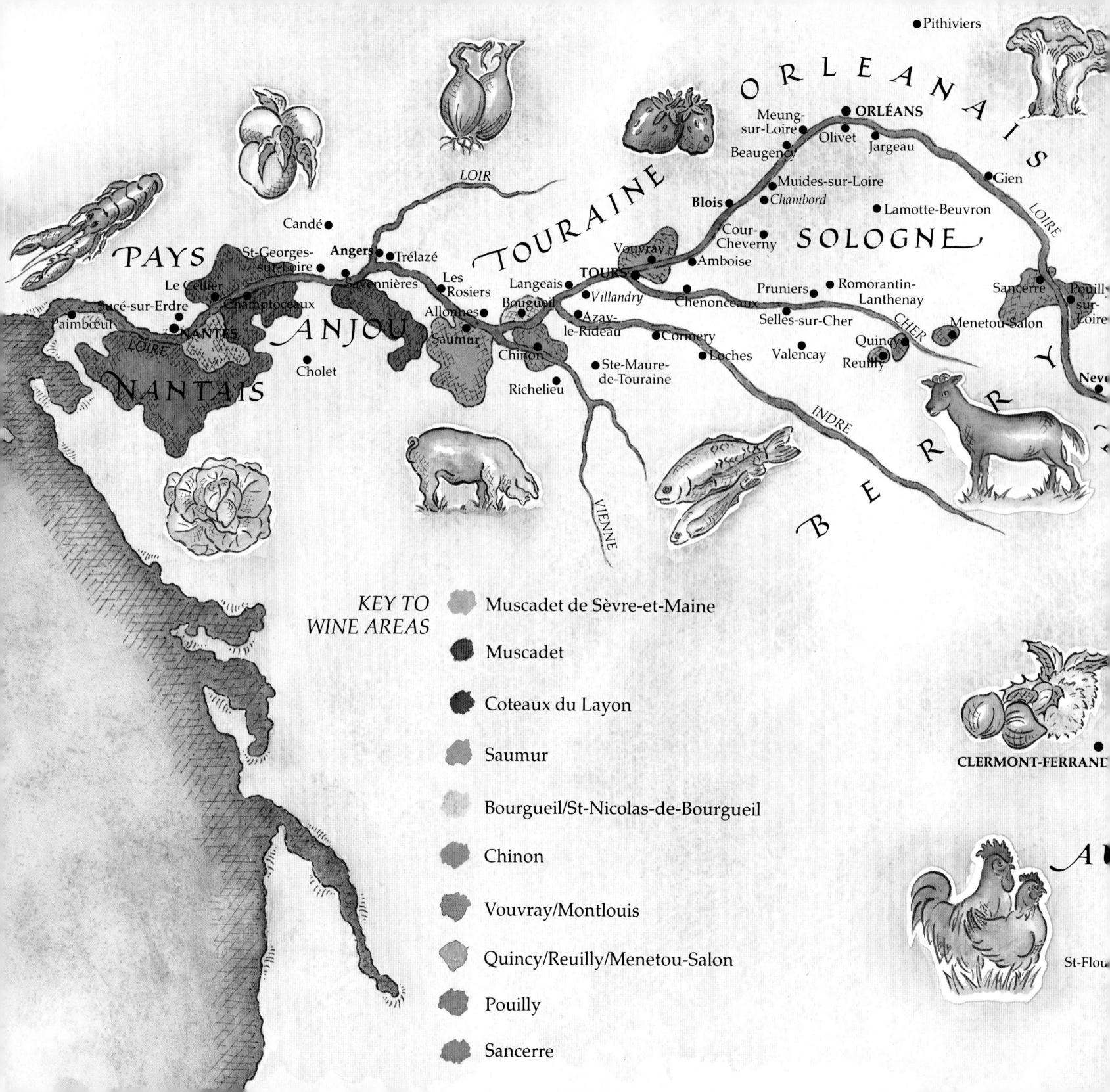
Pithiviers
ORLEANAIS
Meung-sur-Loire
ORLÉANS
Olivet
Jargeau
Beaugency
Muides-sur-Loire
Chambord
Gien
Blois
Lamotte-Beuvron
LOIR
LOIRE
Candé
Cour-Cheverny
SOLOGNE
PAYS
St-Georges-sur-Loire
Angers
Trélazé
TOURAINE
Vouvray
Amboise
Le Cellier
Savennières
Les Rosiers
Langeais
TOURS
Pruniers
Romorantin-Lanthenay
Sancerre
Pouilly-sur-Loire
Sucé-sur-Erdre
Champtoceaux
Bourgueil
Villandry
Chenonceaux
Paimbœuf
Allonnes
Azay-le-Rideau
Selles-sur-Cher
Menetou-Salon
NANTES
ANJOU
Saumur
Cornery
CHER
Quincy
LOIRE
Chinon
Loches
Valençay
Reuilly
Cholet
Ste-Maure-de-Touraine
Richelieu
NANTAIS
INDRE
BERRY
VIENNE
KEY TO WINE AREAS
Muscadet de Sèvre-et-Maine
Muscadet
Coteaux du Layon
Saumur
Bourgueil/St-Nicolas-de-Bourgueil
Chinon
Vouvray/Montlouis
Quincy/Reuilly/Menetou-Salon
Pouilly
Sancerre
CLERMONT-FERRAND
St-Flou

INTRODUCTION

THIS BOOK IS ABOUT THE FOOD AND WINE FOUND ALONG THE LENGTH OF FRANCE'S LONGEST RIVER. DURING ITS 1012-KILOMETRE (627-MILE) JOURNEY the character of the river changes, as do the soil, countryside and climate – and therefore the characters and ways of life of the people, along with the local foods and cooking. Great contrasts are discernible between the rocky terrain and peasant life-style of the Auvergne, with its rustic hearty cooking, the simple, unpretentious homely fare of the Nivernais, Bourbonnais and Berry, the gentle sophisticated bourgeois cooking of Touraine, and the combination of seafood and deeply regional fare of the two staunchly individual old cultures in Brittany and the Vendée. However, the differences happen gradually, with no abrupt changes, and many foods remain constant throughout – especially river fish, of course, although there are some subtle differences in the varieties, and wild mushrooms and game, both so beloved of the French.

The Loire rises out of a high plateau in the Auvergne, just below the rounded hump of Mont Gerbier-de-Jonc, 50 kilometres (30 miles) from Valence in the heart of the Rhône valley, and only 160 kilometres (100 miles) away from the Mediterranean. Its rivulet life begins at 1,400 metres (4,600 feet), and the stream sets off briskly southwards, towards the sun, before being diverted northwest by the massive presence of the Suc de Bauzon mountain, without which the Loire would have flowed into the Mediterranean. Instead, it forges through the cold and sparsely inhabited uplands of the eastern Auvergne, then works its way through the Loire gorge to Roanne. As it reaches the warmer, more hospitable lowlands, it gradually opens up and slows down. At Gien, the now mature river is deflected once more, this time by the hard rocks of the Beauce, so that instead of its destiny being the Seine, it begins to describe a great arc – with Orléans at its most northerly point – and ends up heading westwards.

The *fleuve royal* now flows gently, with an appropriate sedateness, through the broad fertile valley and benign climate of Touraine and Anjou, described by Flaubert in 1847 as 'varied without monotony, light, graceful, but it is a beauty which caresses without captivating, which charms without seducing and which, in a word, has more good sense than grandeur . . .'. This area was once the pleasure ground of French royalty and nobility and it is to them that we are indebted for many of the magnificent châteaux and for turning the valley into an architectural treasury. This stretch of the Loire has also been the birthplace of many famous literary and artistic figures, such as Rabelais and Balzac, and attracted many others who have lauded its praises, from Voltaire and Leonardo da Vinci to Oscar Wilde (who described the Loire as 'One of the most wonderful rivers in the world, mirroring from sea to source a hundred cities and five hundred towers').

With the sea in sight, the Loire bisects the port of Nantes, once the capital of Brittany, then washes the southern margin of Brittany's ancient granite rock, before finally dissipating itself ignominiously into the wide estuary at the Atlantic Ocean.

The Loire used to be the backbone of life and prosperity of the lands through which it wended its way, partly because it affected the climate and influenced the drainage of the soil – for both good and bad – but also because of its importance for carrying trade. This, in turn, spawned thriving ports, businesses and merchant classes as well as boatmen, and small hostelries to cater for them. There was even some traffic on the upper stretches, the most well-known being that of the wines taken to Orléans *en route* for Paris, but the main routes were downstream from Orléans to Nantes.

Cargoes going downstream included barrels of wine and vinegar, sacks of cereals, live fish in tanks, semi-ripe fruits, timber, wool, pottery, and slates from Anjou. Going upstream, there was salt, other fresh fish in tanks, dried seafish, cotton and other imports from the Americas and West Indies, such as spices, rum and sugar.

The Loire contains almost as much solid matter as water, and islands are apt to form suddenly, then disappear just as quickly. For this reason rivermen, known variously as *nautoniers* in the 15th century, *bateliers* in the 16th, 17th & 18th, and *mariniers* in the 19th, could be stuck on land at low water for long periods, and were often in danger of running aground in the shallows. A special type of boat was therefore devised for use on the Loire, with a flat bottom, a shallow draught, a raised bow, no keel or rudder, and lightweight so that it could easily be moved if it did run aground (see pages 4-5).

Mississippi-style steamboats were introduced in about 1829, and increased the traffic. However steam navigation flourished for only some 15 years. The almost simultaneous coming of the railways made the Loire easily accessible to Paris and her lucrative markets, but dealt a fatal blow to commercial traffic on the river, which had all but disappeared by the second decade of this century.

This has, however, helped keep the Loire far cleaner than comparable rivers in other industrialized countries. This cleanliness is further helped by the dearth of industrial complexes disfiguring its banks; the many tributaries are also uncontaminated.

Along its entire journey, the Loire crosses four main wine areas: Pouilly-sur-Loire, Sancerre and environs; Touraine; Anjou; and the Pays Nantais. In addition, there are other, lesser areas, such as St-Pourçain-sur-Sioule. Vines, mainly planted along the valley of the Loire and its tributaries like the Cher and the Layon, cover approximately 4,000 hectares (10,000 acres) accounting for 11% of France's vineyard area for *appellation d'origine contrôlée* (AOC) and Vin de Pays wines. About three-quarters of the output of the Loire vineyards is AOC, making it France's fourth largest AOC-producing region: whites account for 43% of the total, reds 40%, rosés 12% and sparkling wines 5%. Another 12.5% of the production is VDQS and 15% are Vin de Pays. The vineyards are divided between some 9,500 growers with an average holding of 5 hectares (12.5 acres). In the Pays Nantais area the norm is

1 *Roofscape, Auvergne.* **2** *The hills near Sancerre.* **3** *Café scene, Tours.* **4** *A goat farm at Muides-sur-Loire.* **5** *Château country: Saumur.* **6** *Harvesting produce for market, near Nantes.*

1 2
3 4
5 6

lower at 3.5 hectares (9 acres), compared with 7.5 hectares (19 acres) in Anjou (the smallest area of vines that can support a family of four is calculated to be 3.5-4 hectares).

As much as half of the wine produced comes from small growers, but in the last 10 years or so there have been considerable changes as the tradition of producing wine as part of a polyculture system is vanishing. The EC intervention policy had meant that there was no incentive to spend effort and money in producing good wine; so quality suffered and an unfortunate amount of mediocre wine was produced. With that let-out now removed, however, and increased competition from better quality wines from further south (as well as other countries, such as Spain, Italy and the New World) where improvements in the standards of the wines have been made, a Loire *vigneron* has to be dedicated and knowledgeable to survive.

There are now tufts of excellence thanks to some enthusiastic *vignerons*, often well-educated and having spent some time studying oenology. They are making considerable improvements in vinification techniques and experimenting with new ideas, such as giving both red and white wines some time in new oak. Most vineyards and businesses, however, have remained small, although there is a smattering of larger companies. Some change is also due to the fact that the French are generally beginning to drink more white wine.

Because of the differing climatic and soil conditions of the regions through which the Loire flows, different grape varieties are grown and varied styles of wine produced. In general, however (and this is one of those sweeping generalizations for which exceptions are not difficult to find), Loire wines are cool, aromatic and fresh: the whites are light to medium-bodied and crisp, ideal as aperitifs, especially during the summer months, or as accompaniments to seafood or river fish; the reds lightly fruity and enhanced by a brief sojourn in the refrigerator. The most notable exceptions are the wonderful, fragrant, sweet wines of Vouvray and the Coteaux du Layon, and some Chinon and Bourgueil, especially *vieilles vignes*, which have enough depth and complexity to make them excellent candidates for ageing.

In following the course of the Loire, I have strayed as far from the river as is thought both interesting and relevant. As a convenient and generally understood shorthand, I have used names such as Touraine and Anjou although the old provinces disappeared years ago. As they have no official standing, boundaries are generally fairly imprecise and variable, and so open to dispute.

You can eat extremely well all along the Loire, partly because of the ready access to good quality ingredients, particularly downstream from Orléans where the temperate climate and fertile soil result in an abundant and diverse range of excellent produce. As a testimony to the quality and variety of food in the region, in 1991 it gathered a total of over 40 Michelin stars. This does not mean that you can only eat well if you are willing to pay a lot of money, quite the reverse; it reflects the general attitude, style and value, and you can eat like the proverbial lord at the many excellent *fermes auberges*.

(Left)
A CORNUCOPIA OF PRODUCE
Fruits and nuts such as these are a common feature of the cooking in all the areas through which the Loire passes, because they are harvested in the autumn and can be stored to provide both staple food and variety during the winter.

THE YOUNG RIVER

THE PASSAGE OF THE LOIRE FROM ITS SOURCE THROUGH THE EASTERN AUVERGNE, BOURBONNAIS AND NIVERNAIS

THE LONGEST RIVER IN FRANCE STARTS ITS LIFE VERY UNPROMISINGLY AND INDISTINCTLY IN MARSHY GROUND AT THE EASTERN EDGE OF THE AUVERGNE. Remaining fairly inauspicious as it tumbles through its formative miles, not reaching true maturity until Nevers, the volcanic mountainous terrain through which it passes is, however, strikingly rugged and impressive. The landscape is interspersed with green valleys, deep rambling streams, *drailles* or drovers' routes, some over a thousand years old, by which cattle or sheep are taken to the summer pastures, and threads of convoluted roads. As the Loire flows northwards between the Bourbonnais and Nivernais, it widens and slows and the countryside becomes more gentle and open.

In the Eastern Auvergne the prevailing character is one of unique individualism, for the remoteness of this area, the long, bitingly cold winters with only short, hot summers, the land itself and the topography have given the peasant farmer desperately little return for his

(Left) Cockerels scratching in an Auvergnat farm.
(Above) The Loire river tumbling in its infancy through the hills of the Auvergne, enigmatic about its future length and glory.

PAGÈS
MARC D'AUVERGNE
DISTILLERIE DU VELAY
LE PUY en VELAY - FRANCE
50 cl
PAGÈS
MARC D'AUVERGNE
DISTILLERIE DU VELAY
LE PUY en VELAY - FRANCE
50 cl
TRIPOUX D'AUVERGNE
TRIPOUX D'AUVERGNE

labour. Moreover, it is not an area conducive to industrial and commercial progress and improvement, and has consequently suffered economic stagnation and depopulation. The exodus begun in the second half of the nineteenth century has continued since, although a steady growth in tourism and leisure activities in the last 30 years has brought a more positive outlook and rekindled wily Auvergnats' natural business talent, as the many very small producers who sell their first-class home-made produce demonstrate.

For centuries, Auvergnats have had to exist on food that could be found within walking distance of their door, though the clear mountain air has been an asset as it is ideal for drying wild mushrooms (a great buy in local markets) and hams and sausages. Crops and produce must be able to grow in poor soil and survive inclement weather, so staples such as potatoes and cabbages are most common. Livestock have to be hardy and really earn their keep. Sheep can live happily on sparse uplands and not only provide meat, but also milk both for drinking and making cheese, and wool for clothing; the same applies to goats. More or less every house had at least one pig as they are both undemanding and fruitful sources of food – to coin a phrase, everything but the squeak being used – which means a cornucopia of excellent *charcuterie*, given extra variety and distinction by the hams and sausages dried in the cold mountain air.

The most lush pastures are at an average altitude of 1000 metres (3300 feet), so snow comes early and disappears late, making it only possible for cattle to graze on them for 20 weeks a year. Traditionally, the cattle are driven from their winter quarters on 24th May and are brought down again on 13th October. On these days, the peace is broken by the 'transhumance' of cattle, dogs and men, and in the spring the occasion is made the more festive by the bunches of flowers tied between the horns of the cattle, or the flags attached to their bell collars. During their summer on the mountain the herdsmen used to live in small stone houses, or *burons*, and in these they would transform the rich, flavourful cows' milk into hard cheeses to provide valuable nourishment in the winter. The system of transhumance is not popular with the majority of today's farmers, but there are still some who follow it (after all, with modern transport, they are not as marooned on the mountain as they once were), and who make cheeses, such as Fourme du Cantal fermier, from unpasteurised milk in the specific, traditional way that creates its special character. It is a pressed cheese moulded into large cylinders; these are left to ripen for 3-6 months so the cheese is at its best in the late autumn or early winter when it has developed a delicious, nutty flavour redolent of the herb-rich pastures. When making traditional *aligot* and *truffade* (see page 20), the authentic version of Cantal to use is fresh, unpressed Cantal *tomme*, as it enriches them and makes them creamy rather than heavy or 'cheesey'.

The relatively squat Bleu d'Auvergne fermier was also made in the *burons* from raw summer milk and aged for 3-6 months. Although unpressed, it is firm to the touch and has a distinctive smell and flavour. Unfortunately, most Cantal and Bleu d'Auvergne are made commercially throughout the year in modern cheese factories. Such *laitier* cheeses are made

1 *Aperitifs and liqueurs are often based on wild herbs, flowers and medicinal plants, especially gentian and the slightly bitter vervain, which is a speciality of Le Puy.* **2** *Bleu d'Auvergne (left) and Fourme du Cantal were traditionally both made by shepherds in their* burons. **3** *A typical volcanic outcrop, a good vantage point for warding off invaders.* **4** *No good Auvergne home would be without their pigs.* **5** *Bilberry and strawberry sweets, specialities of the Auvergne.* **6** *Salers cattle were the preferred breed of the Auvergne, as they are strong, as weather-resistant as polar bears, very fertile – continuing to have calves up to an age equivalent to 80 in human terms – and give plenty of milk. Sadly, the handsome animals are a vanishing feature of the scenery.* **7** *A local fruit-studded cake made of brioche dough.* **8** Tripoux *characteristically puts to good use unlikely parts of an animal, in this case, tripe and pigs' trotters.* **9** *Fresh and dried wild flowers and herbs add a distinctive nuance to the foods of the region.*

1	**2**	**3**
4	**5**	**6**
7	**8**	**9**

LENTILLES VERTES DU PUY

Particularly around Le Puy, the air of the region coupled with the volcanic soil and local micro-climate are conducive to the growing, ripening and drying of the blue-green lentils for which Le Puy has become famous in the gastronomic world. Lentils have been cultivated here for a very long

time, but just how long is a matter of dispute. One theory is that they were brought by the Moors in the eighth century, others point to a Gallo-Roman vase which was found in the old city and is believed to have contained lentils. Lentilles vertes du Puy cook so well and have such a wonderful, refined yet distinctive, flavour that the use of the name has been protected by an appellation d'origine. So strongly do the growers, who still use traditional and entirely natural methods, feel about their lentils that they have also created a trademark.

from pasteurised lowland milk, are usually only about 2 months old, and lack the quality and calibre of the traditional, buron-made, versions.

In the mountains in early spring, the ground is resplendent with a natural carpet of a host of wild flowers and fragrant herbs, which change as the year progresses: daffodils, cowslips, irises, cornflowers, purple violets with giant scented heads, and *serpolet* or wild thyme. Not only are these lovely to look at and smell, but they provide a characteristic rich taste to the cooking of the region, giving flavour to the flesh of animals that feed upon such pasture as well as to their milk and cheese. Wild herbs and flowers are also a useful source of income: many are carefully spread out and dried with care in the warm dry mountain air, for sale in the local markets or shops. They find use in *tisanes*, in cooking and as medicines. At the Loire's first small town, Ste-Eulalie, an annual *Foire aux Violettes* is held on the Sunday following 12th July. The whole of the year's crop of violets will be sold in one day to a variety of buyers, who include confectioners as well as *parfumeurs* and pharmacists.

The alluvial soil in the lower valleys is very fertile and has the ability to intensify the flavour of the produce grown on it, so there are market gardens, and in sheltered sunny spots where it can become hot in summer it is worthwhile planting apple and pear trees, or even plums and cherries where there is very little risk of frost; in really favoured places, apricots can ripen. As the Loire flows northwards, one-man market gardens grow large enough to support additional staff, and fruit trees burgeon into full-scale orchards on propitious flatter stretches.

For free, from the wild, come fish. The many clear, cold, sparkling mountain streams that tumble and chatter into the Loire are home to some fine examples. Plump, shapely, well-flavoured brown trout are there for the 'tickling' or catching with a line and rod, however rudimentary. To have it really fresh and cooked in a simple, sympathetic way that enhances its succulence, and dressed with a sprinkling of local walnut oil, is one of life's great eating experiences. A few crayfish are still to be found in swift-running mountain streams, if you are lucky or know where to look. There is also some farming of crayfish.

On the ground there is a wealth of game, like the wild rabbits which become extra flavourful in the summer after they have fed on wild herbs and flowers. There are also hare, deer and wild boar for roasting over open fires, either in the open air or in the hearth, or reducing to melting tenderness by hours of cooking in a pot, helped along by local wine, albeit a rough one. Towards the north of the area, wild duck alight upon the lakes. In areas with grain fields, partridge may also occasionally be found.

Wander through the dappled woods in the summer, and if you are very attentive and lucky you may see, smell, and then taste delicate, delicious wild strawberries, mulberries, or even raspberries. In the Auvergne spring, which in reality is May, on the acid soils of the high shrubby heathlands where heather grows and the weather is not of the best, low, bright green bilberry bushes suddenly become speckled with small, semi-transluscent green-white flowers, flushed with pink, which are replaced by blue-black fruits lightly veiled in a silvery bloom in July and August. They will be scooped off the branches with ingenious shovel-shaped implements called *peignes à myrtilles*, and made into sweets and liqueurs for sale in local shops. Come the autumn, there are many kinds of wild mushrooms and nuts, which in a poor, isolated area such as this have an especially important role in the diet. Chestnuts, the fruit of what is known as the 'bread tree', are particularly important as they form the foundation and often the 'bulk' of soups, casseroles, pies, pâtés and stuffings, 'stretching' scarce meat. The nuts could also be ground into flour for breads and batters, the leaves spread as winter feed and litter for cattle, and the wood of felled trees used for furniture or burned as charcoal.

Whilst to us it might be gastronomic heaven to have a cache of *frais de bois* nearby, to pop out in the early morning to gather a basketful of wild mushrooms for breakfast or to have fresh, wild trout for lunch, and all for free, it is of little consequence to a man who has worked hard all day in the open mountain air in all weathers, and who needs strength to do it again tomorrow, and the next day, and the next, all through his life. Traditional dishes therefore had to be sustaining, economical, and easy for the housewife with little in the way of cooking facilities to prepare and cook. Frugality was a byword, and the cooking fortifying rather than refined. Soups, of course, were a mainstay. *Soupe aux choux* and *potée auvergnate* seem to be interchangeable names for basically the same dish, although the word *potée* tends to be used more around Clermont-Ferrand and *soupe* further south. The ingredients of both can vary, but the two invariable components are pork, usually salted, and cabbage. *Potée* is likely to be a more substantial dish, containing a greater variety of vegetables, especially carrots and potatoes, along with cured sausage and perhaps some beef or chicken (see page 24).

Dishes such as these were prepared in huge iron pots to last a week or more, being reheated and improving as the days went by. They were usually served as two courses. First the broth would be poured over bread in a bowl, then the meat and vegetables distributed as a main course. If there was any warm liquid left, it would be poured into the empty bowls with a dash or more of red wine – a custom called *faire chabrot*.

Bread, too, was a staple. I was told by a wiry Auvergnate of at least 80 years old, with a knowing shake of the head, that 'an empty stomach attracts illness' and 'in those days' (which were anything more than 20 years ago) they relied on bread, and plenty of it, to ensure that it never was. In the altitude and climate, rye was the normal grain, and when

DRYING MOUNTAIN HAMS

For his Jambons de Montagne, Alain Comte combines traditional 'artisanal' practices with the rules of the appellation contrôlée, which govern such things as hygiene and the pigs' diet. Based on the D590 west of Le Puy at 1000 metres (3300 feet) above sea level (where he also sells a range of other foods), he has found his ancient old barn to be better for drying hams and sausages than a new, purpose-built shed. Nevertheless, he is proud of his modern instruments for checking the development of the hams.

times were very hard, they would make do with chestnut or barley bread 'as dark and tough as tree bark'. A day was regularly set aside for baking and children would hover in the kitchen, waiting for the small ball of baked dough, known as a *michou*, which would be given to each of them as the bread came warm from the oven. From the frequent appearance of the term in house names, such as '*Notre Michou*', it must still have connotations of family togetherness. An affinity with bread and baking has obviously been absorbed into the genes of many Auvergnats, as the number of people selling baked products and their general quality are both high. The more astute bakers are now publicizing the organic nature of such ingredients as rye, nuts, herbs and cheese.

Of other baked products, the *fouasses* are exceptionally light and flavoured with orange flower water, a flavouring that can also be tasted in light brioche doughs, some of which are studded with candied fruits and baked in various crown shapes. The *pain d'épices* (see pages 41 and 57) tend to be more moist in this part of the world, and the lightest, most moist, best flavoured I have ever had I consumed in some quantity near Le Puy. Although the cake was not at all oversweet, I attributed its magnificence mainly to the excellent honey to be found in the locality. As well as a wide range of wonderfully flavoured honeys, the drink *hydromel* and dried pollen are also sold throughout the region.

Leaving the Auvergne, the Loire next flows between two of France's least known regions: the Nivernais on the right bank, the Bourbonnais on the left. Both are very rural with scattered populations.

Following the road along the eastern side of the Loire, the countryside of the Nivernais looks a trifle dishevelled in places, and unsophisticated although not run-down, untouched by progress. The landscape is open, with long straight roads and fields dotted with large creamy-white cows further distinguished by long curved horns, broad muzzle and short neck: for here is the home of Charolais cattle.

Charolais were introduced to the Nivernais in the eighteenth century and are now exported to 65 countries, the cattle being highly regarded for their lean meat and high ratio of flesh to carcass. The pedigree register is kept in a computer at Nevers, and includes the physical characteristics of each animal.

To the east of the region in the Morvan hills, pigs are reared on the by-products of the dairy industry to produce succulent and flavourful Morvan hams. For this reason, ham features particularly strongly in Nivernais cooking. Most frequently it is teamed with eggs, which nearly every home would have – more or less literally – on their doorstep. For *œufs au jambon*, very thin slices of air-dried Morvan ham are fried in farm butter and then eggs broken over the top and left to cook until lightly set so that when they are broken open the yolk flows over the ham. An *omelette nivernaise* contains lightly fried ham and herbs and is cooked in the same way as a pancake, so it is brown on both sides, and is served flat. Whole eggs in their shell may also be added to the pot along with the ham joint when it is being boiled, so they become impregnated with the flavour of the ham.

POTATOES

Potatoes are eaten extensively in the region and Auvergnats have some particularly delicious ways of cooking them.

They are often teamed with the region's delicious dairy products, as in aligot, truffade, criques, tapinaude (see page 26) and pommes de terre à la guerilla. The first of these is

probably the most famous: over heat, cheese and cream are beaten into mashed potatoes until long ribbons are formed as the spoon is lifted. For an autumnal gratin à l'auvergnate they are mixed with an equal amount of chestnuts.

Small round ratte potatoes (illustrated above), with their characteristic yellow skin and firm waxy yellow flesh, are shaken and rolled in earthenware poêlons along with good flavourful pork dripping, until crisp on the outside and tender in the centre.

Potatoes are also used in farcidure, dumplings or stuffing, and to bulk out pies.

Across the river the Bourbonnais is open, 'easy' land with grassy plains and wooded rolling hills which, in the south, occasionally rise sufficiently to be able to claim to be mountains. Elsewhere, there are many green fields, neat hedges, the odd hedgerow tree, and low hills crowned with small woods. Around Moulins, the market town of the Bourbonnais, there are green fields, wheat fields, market gardens and orchards. It is a well-watered landscape, with an abundance of lakes and rippling streams as well as the still pubescent Loire.

The food and cooking along this stretch of the river has the simplicity of many deeply pastoral areas in France, where people rely on products from their land and those garnered from the wild. 'Potager' vegetables of onions, potatoes and carrots as well as lettuce and peas, *produits fermiers* of milk, butter, cream and eggs, heavy bags of game from the abundant unspoilt countryside, and wild mushrooms and nuts are all used to make the straightforward 'homely' dishes that form a bridge between the hearty rustic mountain fare of the Auvergne, and the more diverse food of the Orléanais.

(Right)
VILLAGE STREET
Rural depopulation is a problem for the Auvergne.

POTIRONÉE AUX CHÂTAIGNES

Pumpkin and Chestnut Soup

(Illustrated opposite)

I am used to seeing the autumn countryside lit up by splashes of vibrant orange pumpkins squatting plumply on the ground. However, one day a sight caught my eye that caused me to get out of the car to take a closer look – pumpkin vines trained up a tree, with decorative patterns cut in the skins of the still-growing vegetables! I have also in my time come across a pumpkin farm and a book containing 138 recipes for the humble vegetable. This recipe was given to me by the aunt of a friend and she adamantly recommended that I should use the larger *potiron* type of pumpkin and not *citrouilles*.

SERVES 5-6
350g/12oz pumpkin flesh, cubed
175g/6oz peeled chestnuts
1 large onion, chopped
2 celery stalks, chopped
2 carrots, chopped
about 1l/1¾pt good chicken stock
4 tablespoons milk
salt and freshly ground black pepper
crème fraîche and chervil, to serve

Put the pumpkin, chestnuts and vegetables in a large pan and pour in 850ml/1½pt of the stock. Bring to the boil, then simmer for about 30 minutes, until tender. Allow to cool slightly, then purée along with the milk. Season to taste and add more stock if the soup is too thick. Return to the rinsed saucepan and reheat gently.

Serve with crème fraîche swirled in and chervil leaves strewn over the top.

CRÈME NIVERNAISE

Carrot Soup

SERVES 4
55g/2oz butter
350g/12oz young carrots, chopped
white of 1 slender young leek, thinly sliced
300ml/10fl oz vegetable stock
300ml/10fl oz milk
150ml/5fl oz crème fraîche
salt and freshly ground black pepper
chervil leaves or chopped parsley, to garnish

Melt the butter in a heavy-based saucepan over a low heat. Add the carrots and leek and cook gently, stirring occasionally, for 5-10 minutes. Add the stock and seasoning and simmer for about 15 minutes until the vegetables are tender.

Purée the vegetables and liquid, return to the pan and add the milk and cream. Heat through well without boiling.

Adjust the seasoning and serve sprinkled with chervil or parsley.

TERRINE DE LAPIN AUX HERBES

Rabbit and Herb Terrine

This is possibly the simplest of all terrines to make, and one of the lightest meat terrines I know.

SERVES 4
1 plump young wild rabbit, dressed, skinned and cut into small pieces
2 shallots, thinly sliced
2 tablespoons chopped parsley
2-3 sprigs of thyme, preferably wild
2-3 sprigs of tarragon
1 fresh bay leaf
350ml/12fl oz white Sancerre or Pouilly-Fumé
large piece of pork rind, blanched
115g/4oz piece of mild bacon, thinly sliced lengthwise
about 300ml/10fl oz rabbit or veal stock or water
freshly ground black pepper

Put the rabbit in a covered dish with the shallots, herbs and pepper and pour over the wine. Leave in a cool place for 48 hours, turning the rabbit over occasionally.

Preheat the oven to 130C/275F/gas1 (take care, oven thermostats are often inaccurate at low settings).

Line a terrine with the pork rind and half the bacon. Put in the rabbit along with the marinade, pressing the rabbit down well. Add sufficient boiling stock or water to cover the rabbit well, then cover with the remaining bacon. Cover the terrine tightly and seal the rim with foil. Cook in the oven for about 4½ hours, until the rabbit is very tender.

Strain the liquid off through muslin and re-cover the rabbit to keep it warm.

Remove any fat from the surface of the strained liquid, taste and adjust the seasoning with pepper. Pour a thin layer of this liquid into a dish or terrine.

Remove the bones from the rabbit, keeping the pieces of meat as large as possible. Place the pieces of rabbit and bacon, discarding the rind, in the dish or terrine and garnish with sprigs of fresh herbs, if liked. Pour over the remaining liquid, making sure it flows completely through the pieces of meat. Cover and chill for 12-24 hours.

(Right)
Pumpkin and Chestnut Soup (this page), with in the foreground Hare with Redcurrant Jelly (page 28).

La Marmite

61 rue des Lacs
St-Flour
Tel 71 60 03 06
See recipe on this page

If it were not for a board intriguingly packed with names of local dishes, such as *potée* (illustrated below), *tripoux* (see page 16), *aligot* and *pounti* (see opposite) standing by the doorway, La Marmite would be

easy to miss – or dismiss – as it is above a less than attractive bar (with pinball machines and video games), and approached by a not very inviting staircase. The *chef-patron* is M. Mourgues, so typically Auvergnat in appearance with dark hair and a dark moustache, but atypical in his friendliness, openness and generosity. The promise of the board on the street is amply fulfilled, for M. Mourgues offers a range of sound, wonderfully hearty, dishes on his menu, all served with no frills and no concession to gastronomic fashion.

(Above)
Made of ingredients that were once commonplace to local peasants, the omelette à l'Auvergnate *made by M. Mourgues of La Marmite in St-Flour (see left) sat on my plate like an invitingly plump and yielding golden-yellow bolster. As for the taste – exploding with pure natural straightforward flavours – it really showed what a difference is made by using good fresh butter, fresh free-range eggs and ham that has not been vacuum-packed or refrigerated. If only all 'designer dishes' in expensive restaurants tasted as good. The other secrets of re-creating such an omelette lie in adding one tablespoon of cold water to the eggs while you beat them, and in seasoning the mixture with freshly ground black pepper only (no salt) before cooking.*

Pounti

Egg and Vegetable Loaf

(Illustrated opposite)

Traditional *pounti* can vary widely in solidity. Some versions have a greater proportion of flour and correspondingly less milk, while others may have more meat.

Pounti is always substantial enough for a main course, but small portions can be served as a first course or as part of a buffet. I prefer it while it is still hot or warm, but others are quite happy to eat it cold and it is perfect for picnics.

This version is that of M. Mourgues of La Marmite in St-Flour (see left).

SERVES 6
2 leeks, finely chopped
about 20g/¾oz chopped parsley
115g/4oz green part of Swiss chard or spinach leaves, chopped
1 cabbage leaf, finely chopped
115g/4oz salt pork or green bacon, very finely chopped
85g/3oz plain flour
4 eggs, beaten
575ml/1pt milk
salt and freshly ground black pepper
butter, for greasing

Preheat the oven to 180C/350F/gas4. In a bowl, mix together the vegetables and pork or bacon.

Put the flour into another bowl and make a well in the centre. Gradually add the eggs and milk to make a smooth batter. Season and stir into the vegetable mixture. Pour into a buttered loaf pan about 23 x 28cm/9 x 11in in size and bake in the oven for 50-60 minutes, until just set in the centre.

ÉCREVISSES À LA NAGE

Crayfish in an Aromatic Broth

If you are lucky enough to find some wild crayfish, remove the black thread of intestine running down their backs: hold the fish firmly with your free hand (it is a good idea to wear rubber gloves for protection from nips), take hold of the central section of the tail, then twist and pull gently to draw out the intestine.

Putting stones in the bottom of the pan is an old trick to maintain the temperature of the water when the fish are added and thus help to ensure their rapid dispatch.

SERVES 4
2 small carrots, chopped
2 shallots, chopped
1 leek, sliced
1 bouquet garni
salt and freshly ground black pepper
about 700ml/1¼pt liquid, which could be all water or fish stock, or up to 425ml/15fl oz medium-bodied dry white wine substituted for the equivalent amount of water or stock
at least 300g/10oz crayfish per person (the actual number will depend on their size)

Put some largish clean stones, if available, in the bottom of a large saucepan. Add the carrots, shallots, leek, bouquet garni, seasoning and wine, if using, along with plenty of water (see above). Bring to the boil and simmer for 20 minutes.

Add the crayfish, return the liquid to the boil quickly, then reduce the heat and simmer for 4 minutes, or until they have changed to a beautiful deep carmine-pink.

Scoop out the crayfish into a large warmed bowl. Boil the cooking liquor until reduced and the flavour concentrated. Strain this over the crayfish and serve with plenty of bread to mop up the flavourful juices.

Alternatively, leave the crayfish to cool in the liquid, then lift them out and serve with a good, preferably home-made, mayonnaise. Reserve the liquid to use as a fish stock.

TAPINAUDE

Creamy Potatoes with Cheese

(Illustrated above)

Many recipes exist for this dish, but this one is an authentic old version used by M. Dray of La Renaissance (see opposite). It is less rich than some as it is made from half milk and half cream – which nearly replicates traditional creamy farmhouse milk – and does not include eggs, as in those versions in which the potatoes are baked in a custard. I have also made it successfully using all milk, for cooking the potato in the sauce seems to produce a result that is 'creamy' enough in itself. M. Dray serves *tapinaude* with simple main courses, but it can also be served as a first course, or as a light lunch or supper.

SERVES 4

25g/1oz unsalted butter, plus more for greasing
1 scant tablespoon plain flour
300ml/10fl oz milk
300ml/10fl oz crème fraîche
700g/1½lb potatoes, peeled and thinly sliced
115g/4oz Cantal or Gruyère cheese, grated
salt and freshly ground black pepper

Melt the butter in a saucepan, then stir in the flour. Over a very low heat, gradually stir in the milk and three-quarters of the crème fraîche, keeping the mixture smooth. Bring to the boil, stirring, and simmer for 5 minutes. Season.

Wash the potato slices and drain well. Place them in a saucepan, pour over the sauce and bring to the boil, stirring. Cover with buttered greaseproof paper and then the saucepan lid and leave to cook gently for 30 minutes; keep an eye on the potatoes to make sure that they do not 'catch' on the bottom of the pan.

Preheat the oven to about 180C/350F/gas4, or preheat a hot grill.

Transfer the contents of the saucepan to a gratin or ovenproof dish, pour over the remaining crème fraîche and sprinkle with the cheese. Place in the oven or under the grill for about 5-10 minutes, until the cheese is melted and golden.

LENTILLES VERTES DU PUY

Green Puy Lentils in the Auvergne Style

This is the basic recipe for lentils, to which can be added chunky farmhouse-style sausages, or raw ham in cubes or as a small joint, to make a typically Auvergnat dish – trencher-man fare but based on good ingredients and full of flavour.

SERVES 4

115g/4oz salted belly of pork or piece of bacon, cut across into strips
1 onion, finely chopped
1 carrot, finely chopped
1 leek, sliced
250g/9oz Puy lentils (see page 18)
500ml/18fl oz veal stock or water
a bouquet garni consisting of a large sprig of thyme, 1 bay leaf, 3 sprigs of parsley and a small sprig of rosemary
salt and freshly ground black pepper

Heat the pork or bacon fairly gently in a heavy flameproof casserole, stirring occasionally, until the fat runs.

Add the vegetables and cook, stirring occasionally, for about 3 minutes without allowing to colour. Stir in the lentils. After a few seconds, add the stock or water with the bouquet garni. Bring to the boil, then simmer gently for about 20 minutes, until the lentils are tender.

Discard the bouquet garni and adjust the seasoning to taste.

COQ AU VIN

Chicken in Red Wine

Slowly cooking a tough male bird in red wine to make it tender is so obvious that it must have been practised in many other parts of France, but I don't know of an area that can lay claim to such a good tale about the creation of the dish. The story is that during the Roman invasion of the Auvergne the Gauls were forced to retreat to the slopes of the Puy de Dôme where they were besieged by Caesar's troops. So far, this is true. One day the Gallic chief, symbolically thumbing his nose to Caesar, sent him an old, dried-up cockerel. Caesar decided that the insult could be turned to his advantage. He declared a truce and invited the Gallic chief to a dinner *à deux*. A wonderfully flavoured dish with a rich sauce was served, and the Gaul realized that his tough old cockerel, cooked long and slowly in the local wine by Caesar's chefs, had been transformed into a culinary masterpiece.

The nearest you may be able to get to a tough old cockerel may be a boiling fowl; failing that, use a large free-range chicken. You can marinate it in the wine overnight to give it a gamey flavour, although this will not much improve the tenderness.

This is a country recipe intended for good eating only – no mushrooms and bacon scattered artfully over, nor croûtons around the edge.

SERVES 4
25g/1oz unsalted butter
115g/4oz bacon, cut across into strips
2kg/4½lb chicken, any surplus fat removed from the cavity, and cut into joints
18-20 small white onions
1 carrot, chopped
225g/8oz mushrooms, preferably wild or chestnut or brown cap
450ml/15fl oz red wine
a good bouquet garni of fresh herbs, including thyme, bay leaf, parsley, tarragon and a little rosemary
salt and freshly ground black pepper
chopped parsley, to garnish

Heat the butter in a large, heavy casserole, add the bacon and fry until the fat runs. Remove and drain on a paper towel. Put in the chicken pieces, skin-side down, and cook over a medium heat until golden. Transfer to paper towels.

Stir in the onions and carrot, cook until lightly browned then transfer to paper towels. Add the mushrooms and cook, stirring, for 2-3 minutes.

Remove the mushrooms and pour the fat off from the casserole. Stir the wine into the casserole, add the onions and carrot and bring to the boil. Skim the surface, lower the heat slightly and add the chicken, bouquet garni and seasoning. Add water or stock, if the chicken is not covered. Adjust the heat so the liquid is barely moving, cover tightly and cook very slowly for about 1 hour, until the chicken is very tender, adding the mushrooms for the last 10 minutes or so.

Transfer the chicken and vegetables to a warmed dish and keep warm. Boil the cooking liquid until well reduced. Adjust the seasoning, and remove the bouquet garni. Return the chicken and vegetables to the sauce, garnish and serve.

LA RENAISSANCE **

Magny-Cours
nr Nevers
Tel 86 58 10 40
See recipe far left

Chef-patron Jean-Claude Dray has been cooking with old-fashioned generosity at La

Renaissance for over 30 years. Born in Nevers, he takes great pleasure in using local products and searching out old regional recipes. He then incorporates both into his repertoire, where they sit quite happily alongside dishes befitting a Michelin two-star restaurant.

Behind the restaurant is a large garden where M. Dray and a gardener between them grow nearly half of all the vegetables and herbs used in the restaurant. Plucking a leaf here, a sprig there, he showed me with great pride his specially selected varieties, such as the watercress that does not have to have its feet in water and which tastes milder and sweeter than usual.

BŒUF AUX HERBES

Beef and Vegetable Stew

At the beginning of the spring 'transhumance' (see page 17), a cow would be chosen from the herd, her horns adorned with an extra-special garland and she would be allowed to graze in whichever pastures she fancied until Midsummer's Day, 24 June. Her halcyon days were then over, her destiny to be simmered slowly in a large pot with plenty of wild mountain herbs and fresh early summer vegetables to provide a feast for the villagers.

SERVES 4-6
115g/4oz piece of lean green streaky bacon, cut across into strips
1.25kg/2½lb brisket of beef, cut into large cubes
450ml/15fl oz dry white wine
1 bouquet garni
8 baby carrots
4-6 baby turnips
3 small lettuces or lettuce hearts
150g/5oz small onions or shallots
150g/5oz shelled peas
salt and freshly ground black pepper

Heat the bacon in a large heavy casserole and cook slowly until the fat runs. Increase the heat, add the beef and brown.

In a separate pan, bring the wine to the boil with the bouquet garni. Pour this over the beef, season and add water just to cover. Bring to a simmer, cover tightly and cook slowly for about 2 hours.

Meanwhile, blanch the carrots and turnips for 5 minutes in boiling salted water. Drain. Blanch the lettuce for 2 minutes, drain well and cut into quarters.

Stir the carrots, turnips and onions into the beef, adding water if necessary. Cover and cook for 10 minutes. Add the peas and lettuce, cover and cook for 10 minutes, or until the vegetables are tender.

Check the seasoning and concentration of the cooking liquor. If it is too dilute, transfer the meat and vegetables to a warmed dish, and boil the liquid until reduced sufficiently. Return the meat and vegetables to the pot to serve.

FETCHOULETTE

Kid with Sorrel

In the spring, with only the odd lucky exception who will be kept for breeding, the young male goats are culled (in a culture where the *raison d'être* of animals is as food, they serve no other useful purpose). At this age they have none of the pungent 'goatiness' associated with older animals, but are delicately flavoured and tender. Breast of lamb or veal work well in this dish if kid is unavailable.

SERVES 4
25g/1oz butter
115g/4oz lean green streaky bacon, blanched and cut across into strips
700g/1½lb breast of kid, cut into cubes
1 tablespoon flour
200ml/7fl oz dry white wine
a bouquet garni consisting of a bay leaf, 2 sprigs of thyme and 2 sprigs of parsley
good bunch of young sorrel, trimmed and torn into shreds
salt and freshly ground black pepper

Melt half the butter in a flameproof casserole, add the meats and brown over a medium heat, stirring occasionally.

Reduce the heat, sprinkle over the flour and cook for a further 2-3 minutes. Stir in the wine and add sufficient water to cover. Add the bouquet garni and bring just to a simmer. Cover and cook very gently for about 40 minutes, stirring occasionally, until the kid is tender.

Meanwhile, gently cook the sorrel in the remaining butter for 2-3 minutes. Add to the veal, and continue to cook, uncovered, for about 10 minutes.

LIÈVRE À LA DUCHAMBAIS

Hare with Redcurrant Jelly

(Illustrated on page 23)

SERVES 2
1 saddle of hare
2 shallots, finely chopped
about 300ml/10fl oz crème fraîche
2 tablespoons white wine vinegar
1 tablespoon good redcurrant jelly
salt and freshly ground black pepper

Preheat the oven to 130C/275F/gas1.

Make sure the thin, silvery membrane which covers the saddle closely has been removed. Put the saddle into a heavy casserole that it just fits. Scatter the shallots over the hare. Stir together the crème fraîche, vinegar and seasoning and pour over the hare; it should just be covered. Cover the casserole tightly and cook in the oven for 1-1½ hours, until tender.

Lift the hare from the casserole, allowing excess sauce to drain off. Place the saddle on a warmed plate and keep warm.

Pour the sauce, which will look unattractively curdled, into a small saucepan, stir in the redcurrant jelly and boil hard until smooth, reduced and thickened. Season and stir in any juices from the hare.

Carve the saddle, including the fillet that is underneath, lengthwise into thin slices. Serve with the sauce.

CONFITURE DE MARRONS

Chestnut Conserve

(Illustrated below)

In France this would be served with crème fraîche and crisp biscuits for dessert.

MAKES ABOUT 1.3kg/2¾lb
1kg/2¼lb chestnuts
450g/1lb sugar
1 vanilla pod

With the point of a sharp knife, make an incision around the top of each chestnut. Drop them into boiling water for 5 minutes. Drain and allow to cool a little, then peel them.

Put the peeled chestnuts in a saucepan and add just enough water to cover. Cover the pan, bring to the boil and simmer for about 30 minutes.

Meanwhile, put the sugar into a small heavy-based pan with a small ladleful of water. Split the vanilla pod lengthwise and remove the seeds. Add both the pod and seeds to the sugar and heat gently, until all the sugar has dissolved, then boil for about 15 minutes.

Drain the chestnuts, reserving the cooking liquid, then purée them. Make the reserved liquid up to 500ml/18fl oz with water and blend this into the purée. Stir this mixture into the syrup and boil for about 10 minutes, stirring constantly.

Pour into warm, dry, sterilized jars or pots and cover tightly.

INTO THE VAL-DE-LOIRE

PAST BERRY TO THE SOLOGNE AND THE ORLÉANAIS

CONTINUING ITS JOURNEY NORTHWARDS TO ORLÉANS, THE LOIRE FLOWS PAST BERRY, HOME OF CROTTINS DE CHAVIGNOL CHEESE, AND THE VINEYARDS OF Sancerre with its twin wine Pouilly-Fumé across the river. Pouilly-sur-Loire is really just inside the last straggling outskirts of the Nivernais (see previous chapter), before it and the Berry merge imperceptibly into the Orléanais, with its *pains d'épices*, historic saffron and some of the best vinegar in the world.

The city of Orléans, on the northern bank of the Loire, sits at the point where the river is deflected westwards, forming a wide loop running through rich fertile soil surrounded by beautiful forests. Stretching into the Touraine south of the river, to the west of Berry and thus contained in this loop, lies the Sologne, country of *tarte Tatin*, superb asparagus and *confréries* by the dozen.

(Opposite) The Sologne is encased within the bend of the Loire. It is a little known region with a distinct character and plenty to interest the food lover, especially during the autumn and winter when game and wild mushrooms are available. (Above) There is some riding to hounds in the Sologne. The dogs at Château de Cheverny are a cross-breed of English hound for sturdiness, and Poitevin for 'nose'.

1 Neat stack of wood. **2** The restaurant at Auberge des Templiers, Les Bézards. **3** Stained glass window at Château de Cheverny, where there is also a hunting museum; in one room around 200 pairs of antlers from slaughtered stags are displayed. **4** The flat-bottomed Loire boats, known as chalands or gabares. **5** Collecting fishing bait from the river. **6** Walnuts. **7** Hunters with guns and dogs. **8** Cotignac is a quince paste or jelly well worth bringing home for yourself or as a gift, as it is (or should be) wonderfully flavoured with the powerful fragrance of the fruit. Many commercially-made cotignacs dilute the quinces with apples, so check the label before buying. Sometimes cut into shapes and rolled in sugar, cotignac is also sold set in round containers. **9** A country garden near Beaugency. **10** Gâteau de Pithiviers feuilletté (see page 57). **11** Milk churns at a goats' cheese-maker near Muides-sur-Loire; goats produce less milk than cows. **12** Romorantin-Lanthenay, the market town of the Sologne. **13** Cerises d'Olivet were once a local speciality.

1	**2**	**3**	**4**	
5	**6**	**7**	**8**	**9**
	10	**11**	**12**	**13**

Chocolatière Royale
à la Orange
COTIGNAC D'ORLEANS
Chocolatière Royale
à la Orange
COTIGNAC D'ORLEANS

ASPARAGUS

Asparagus is an important crop in a number of areas of the Sologne, chiefly centred around Contres and Soings-en-Sologne. But you will never actually see the prized vegetable growing as the thick-stemmed white asparagus is invariably cultivated so that it does not see the light of day. Harvesting is effected with a special tool looking like a carpenter's gouge. The pickers run this implement into the earth with

astonishing dexterity, probing for the asparagus stalk. The tool is then slid down the stalk, with the asparagus cradled in its convex side, and the stalk is cut off cleanly at the bottom with a deft slight twist of the wrist.

(Opposite)
CHÂTEAU DE CHEVERNY

The Sologne, labelled 'redoubtable' by many, is not homogeneous, and is often unjustly dismissed in its entirety as drear and inhospitable. Much of the area was once a fine oak forest, but indiscriminate deforestation in the Middle Ages reduced it to a sour wilderness, rather than the hoped-for arable land. Big trees are water pumps, and an acre of adult broad-leaved trees will normally pump thousands of litres of water a day out of the soil. If virtually all the trees are removed without provision for drainage, the soil will become waterlogged. This is especially true in an area such as the Sologne, where there is surface clay, a damp climate and an accumulation of water from the Massif Central. As a result of deforestation here, a survey in 1518 estimated there to be over 4,000 lakes, and reclaiming the land with hardwood forest proved impossible. Little success also resulted from other initiatives, such as that by Napoléon II in the mid-nineteenth century to construct many drainage channels, including the Canal de la Sauldre. Recent plantations of pine trees have been more successful in the job of reclamation, but these have done nothing for the landscape and have probably contributed to the unwelcoming image of the Sologne.

Physically, spiritually and temperamentally the Sologne is quite different to its neighbours – especially those further down the Loire – but it is not at all monotonous. True, in the east there are some uninspiring pine forests, but there is a fair bit of heathland, with a quiet, away-from-it-all openness that does have a certain beauty; it takes on a softer character when covered with sunny yellow broom, purple heather and ling.

What population the Sologne has is scattered in small villages and towns, many of which are interesting if isolated. With a frugal livelihood, the region has suffered from depopulation, although it is not as poor now as it once was.

In the western half of the region, where the soil is dry, horticulture is an important activity. Small enthusiastic producers are realizing the potential for a modest living from growing specialist fruit and vegetables, with asparagus and strawberries as the most lucrative.

Some of the finest asparagus in France is grown in the Sologne. It was first planted in the 1870s by a local man, Charles Depezay. He had been garrisoned near Argenteuil, north-west of Paris, and had spent long hours crouched in sandy fields where asparagus flourished. Noticing that the soil closely resembled that at home, he took some plants back with him. Now it is an established and important crop and one or two growers are even experimenting with green varieties, which traditionally the French have eschewed.

The Sologne is rich with culinary delights, for there are plenty of good natural ingredients and artisan producers who are all apparently flourishing. These are genuine concerns, proud of their craft and their products and not simply jumping on the nostalgia bandwagon using 'olde-worlde' packaging. Driving through the region is a heavenly experience for food lovers as there is plenty of evidence of small farms producing natural *produits fermiers*. As well as products like milk, cream, eggs and goats' cheese, these include duck (which is invariably turned into *confit*), goose (of which nearly every imaginable part is used: gizzards, neck, hearts, and livers for *foie gras*), poultry and guinea fowl, *rillettes* and other cooked dishes.

EAU-DE-VIE DE POIRE WILLIAMS

The most interesting tipples of the Orléanais, eaux-de-vie are produced from the orchards south of the city by the cooperative Covifruit. Pear is the most important, with 5–600 tonnes of Poires Williams being distilled annually between September and November and during January. The production of a litre (1¾ pints) of their 50% alcohol

eau-de-vie (10% higher than most others) requires a full kilogram (2lb) of pears. To produce the eau-de-vie with a pear in the bottle, special wide-shouldered bottles are slipped over the fruit while it is still growing on the trees in about May or June. Once mature, they are cut from the trees and the space in the bottles filled with neutral alcohol. This is replaced by pear eau-de-vie just prior to shipping.

(Above right)
QUIET SOLOGNE FARM

These are either sold from the producers' own premises or in shops in many of the local villages and towns, such as Jargeau, celebrated for the fine quality of its sausages and the other products to be found in its *charcuteries* (the Grand rue, or rue Gambetta, is well worth a detour for the number and quality of its food shops).

In Romorantin-Lanthenay, the capital of the Sologne, the annual *Journées Gastronomiques* are staged over the last weekend of October. Traffic is banished from the town and a public-address system festooning the streets keeps everyone informed of events in the three marquees where culinary competitions are held and hundreds of small producers exhibit, offering their products for tasting (fortunately there are not many wine-makers). The quality of the products is so high it has led to the establishment of a nationally known label of the collective trademark of the *Journées Gastronomiques de Sologne*. The region's innumerable *confréries* have a presence at the *Journées*, ranging from the 'Confrérie de Pâte de Citrouille' for those with an interest in pumpkins, to the 'Confrérie de Tastandouillettes de Menn'tou-sur-Cher' representing local sausage lovers, and the 'Confrérie de Mousses des Mangeux de Grenouilles' consisting of the many devoted aficionados of frogs' legs.

Because of the poor soil there are generally few cattle, although there is some grazing near the region's edges. Sheep are also rare, although in Fontaines-en-Sologne some of the old compact Solognote breed are reared, as they are renowned for the flavour and texture of their flesh. The region does boast a diverse selection of good *charcuterie*: fat juicy *boudins noirs* with cream and onions, with Gamay or even with wild mushrooms, whilst *boudins noirs* with chestnuts are a speciality of the village of Pruniers-en-Sologne, near Romorantin. There are also *boudins blancs Solognots*, *saucissons secs* and dried hams of wild boar, venison *saucissons* and *saucissons secs*, *rillettes* of wild rabbit and *rillons*.

Hunting, both on horseback and on foot with guns, is a favourite pastime and a good source of revenue as successful Parisian businessmen will pay large sums to take part in organized 'hospitality' shoots held at the hunting lodges where once the aristocracy gathered. Pheasants, deer and 'wild' boar are reared on farms and released just before these shoots, but some true wild game may still be found, especially rabbits and duck. Even so, during autumn and winter, game is the local restaurants' staple.

The many lakes, rivers, lazy canals, streams, gleaming ponds and *étangs* are a fisherman's paradise. They are increasingly used as a source of income, with '*élevage*' (rearing) of carp, trout and pike. Other catches include tench, gudgeon, barbel and bleak, and in winter eels make easy pickings when they cluster around the gates as the *étangs* are drained.

Honey from bees that have roamed the heathlands and pine forests is used in many of the local sweetmeats, such as *ruches de Salbris* (honey-glazed biscuits), *croquets Solognots* (almond biscuits), and a wonderful, tender, moist honey and pumpkin bread, made by Lebrun's in Romorantin, containing succulent tangy pieces of citron peel.

Other products to be found in *boulangeries* and *pâtisseries* include *galettes de pommes de terre* (see page 46) and *pâtes de pommes de terre*, which are made from mashed potato and *fromage blanc* mixed with flour to make a dough that is then rolled and folded three or four times, as in the making of puff pastry. *Pâte de fromage* is made in a similar way, replacing the potato with soft goats' cheese which is about 2 weeks old. *Bourprudinier* or *briprunelloise* are very long savouries of puff pastry filled with prized Prudiniers sausages. *Boudins de Prudinier aux pommes feuilletées* have potato incorporated into the pastry and the same filling is used for *fridules*, puff pastry triangles. *Pain sur Boulenc* is bread made by an *artisan boulanger* in the old-fashioned way using pure natural ingredients, *boules aux châtaignes* are rolls with chestnuts, and *pain de fromage* contains pieces of cheese mixed into the bread dough.

However, the Sologne's best-known pastry is the famous caramelized upside-down apple tart known as *tarte des demoiselles Tatin*. This is reputed to have first been made in the small town of Lamotte-Beuvron by the *sœurs Tatin*, who were local hoteliers. The sisters moved from the hotel in 1907, but it thrives today as the Hôtel Tatin, 5 ave de Vierzon, capitalizing on the name and the legend. The sisters' coal- and wood-burning, blue-tiled stove survives, but the present *chef-patron*, Gilles Caillé, who bought the hotel in 1968, uses a conventional gas oven to bake ten or so tarts a day. He is a member of

TARTE TATIN

During the 1850s two sisters, Stéphanie (Fanny) and Caroline, moved from a nearby village to Lamotte-Beuvron and built the sturdy stucco-fronted Hôtel-Terminus Tatin to cater for visiting hunters and travellers. According to a version of the legend, one day Caroline inadvertently put the apples she had cooked in butter and sugar for a tart into a pastryless pie

tin. Rather than tipping out the mixture so she could line the tin with pastry in the normal way, she placed the pastry over the apples and then inverted the pie after baking it to make a tarte renversée.

Another version simply says that such tartes renversées *had been made throughout France for years, but the Tatin sisters' recipe 'caught on' and became famous. The celebrated gastronome Curnonsky (see page 105) even came down from Paris by train to try the famous* tarte Tatin, *but his verdict is not recorded.*

La Confrérie des Lichonneaux de Tarte Tatin, and so makes his tarts according to the club's rules. *Pâte sucrée*, not puff pastry, is used, and the apples, butter and sugar are not caramelized on top of the stove before baking (see page 56).

Flowing north to Orléans, the Loire passes through land that has been a centre for the experimental cultivation of fruit and vegetables since the Middle Ages. In and around Olivet, right in the suburbs of Orléans, there still flourish small orchards and market gardens growing apples, especially Golden Delicious and Granny Smith but also some reinettes, and some old specialities of cherries and pears (Beurré Hardy and Bon Chrétien, so appreciated by Marcel Proust, have virtually disappeared but Williams remain). Sadly, with the temptation of high prices for the land for building, the acreage devoted to market gardening can only be expected to decline.

Here a still not-infrequent sight in sunny open places, or sheltering against a garden wall, are the crooked branches and dark green leaves of quince trees. In April and May they are at their prettiest, decked with white or rose-pink blossom. From late September, the leaves turn to bright autumnal tints and the downy golden fruit develop their powerful and unmistakable rich fragrance. The quinces are picked when they are golden, although they will still feel firm and will be too hard to eat raw. In fact, they are not particularly pleasant when raw, but when cooked they soften and release their heavenly luscious, honey-like flavour and aroma (see the recipe for Wild Duck with Quince on page 55).

Quinces are popular in tarts and are used to flavour *eaux-de-vie*. However, they are most usually associated with preserves, such as the lovely *gelée de coing* and the more coarsely textured *marmelade de coing*. *Cotignac* (see page 33) is a thick quince paste which can be cut into cubes or lozenge shapes and rolled in sugar, similar to *pâte des fruits*. Commercially the quince is invariably mixed with apples and this adulteration may also be practised domestically, apples being more widely available and easier to handle.

Orléans is at the most northerly point on the Loire, and grew up because of its proximity to the lucrative markets of Paris and its environs as well as its position at a crossroads between north and south, east and west; it made a natural loading point for produce going up and down the river. From the Middle Ages, Orléans was a very important grain market and boat-building centre, and when supplies of sugar cane started coming from the West Indies many refineries sprang up giving rise to several sweet specialities, such as the *bonblancs* that used to be sold by street sellers crying '*des bonblancs, tout chaud blancs . . . ces bonblancs*'.

Orléans also held an important position in the wine trade, being at the spot where cargoes of wine were unloaded for despatch by road to Paris. By the time wine reached Orléans, especially from upstream, much had often turned to vinegar, so an enterprising soul hit on the idea of using what would otherwise be wasted. By 1392, such was the reputation of the town's vinegar that it was recognized as a vinegar-making centre by Charles VI, and in 1580 Henri III created the Guild of Master Vinegar-Makers by letters patent.

The special gentle process used to make *vinaigre d'Orléans* (which is now protected by an *appellation contrôlée*) was developed in 1797 by a M. Pouret and a M. Martin (see right). The two joined forces in 1841 to establish Martin-Pouret, now the sole surviving company making Orléans vinegar, as opposed to making vinegar in Orléans. Unlike its forebears, the company does not nowadays buy in wine that has turned to vinegar, but wine that is surplus to production – and this only after it has been tasted by the company experts to make sure that it has a good flavour. About 60–70% of the wine comes from the Loire, the rest from the classic wine-making areas such as Bordeaux, Burgundy and Beaujolais.

North of the city are the rich, rolling, poppy-speckled grain lands of the Beauce and the Gâtinais, where larks soar invisibly into the wide, wide horizon, their merry song being the only indication of their presence. In the midst of the seemingly boundless fields snuggles the small town of Pithiviers, where there is a long tradition of baking – hardly surprising considering the surrounding abundant crops.

If local legend is to be believed, *pain d'épices* has been a speciality of Pithiviers since the end of the tenth century. About 992, an Armenian bishop, Gregory, began living as a hermit in a cave about 2 kilometres (1 mile) from the town. In 999, he realized he was dying and invited priests, ministers and secular pious people to visit him. To refresh their souls after the journey he offered canticles and hymns, but for their bodies he offered a spiced Armenian honey cake. As his guests tasted this, they thought they were enjoying the 'delights of Paradise'; and so was born the fame of the town's *pain d'épices*.

VINAIGRE D'ORLÉANS

Jean-François Martin, great-grandson of the original M. Martin, explained to me during our tour of his premises on the outskirts of Orléans that the vinegar process starts with the blending of the various wines to ensure a consistent base; then the wine is left in oak vaisseaux, or barrels, some of which are over 100 years old. Each barrel contains one part air and two parts wine/vinegar and the

procedure used is similar to the sherry solera system in that the barrels are never emptied; about half the wine/vinegar is pumped off and replaced by new wine. The barrels are placed on oak shelving in dark, temperature-controlled rooms to allow fermentation to take place. When there is no more alcohol, the vinegar is aged for six months to reduce the acidity and develop the aroma and bouquet.

(Opposite)
BOAT HOUSE NEAR OLIVET

(Opposite)
THE WHEATFIELDS OF THE BEAUCE
North of Orléans lie the productive agricultural lands of the Beauce. Unfortunately, due to the use of chemical sprays the welcoming, nostalgic sight of gay red poppies adding splashes of contrasting colour to the yellow, undulating sea of wheat is one almost of the past.

(Left)
PAIN D'ÉPICES
The small town of Pithiviers, north of Orléans, is so famed for its two eponymous gateaux that many do not realize that it has a third speciality, pain d'épices, *a honey and spice cake* (*see page 57*).

Most modern *pains d'épices* are rather dry and generally considered everyday food '*pour les enfants*', certainly not a prominent speciality in the numerous pâtisseries. In these establishments, pride of place is given to two eponymous gâteaux: one a double-crust, almond-filled free-form puff pastry pie, with a distinctive swirl pattern on top (see pages 32 and 57); the other a brioche-type dough studded with crystallized or glacé fruits and decorated with icing. There is also *pâté d'alouette* which should now be but a legend, as lark shooting was legally banned in 1982, but shops still claim to sell it (although how much lark is actually in their pies is debatable) and local people definitely do still make it at home.

In the Gâtinais, saffron was cultivated from the Middle Ages. The area became the world's centre for saffron production and whole families, even whole villages, were involved in growing the purple autumn-flowering *Crocus sativus*. At its height, annual output equalled that of the world today, about 60 tonnes. The Musée du Safran, in the tiny sleepy town of Boynes, displays artefacts such as a cloth sack of saffron dated 1772, and the trays in which the fine stamens (which had to be removed from each crocus by hand) were suspended over a fire to dry. What a wonderful aroma must have pervaded the vicinity at harvest time!

(Above)
GOAT FARM
Many small farmers have just a few of the brown Alpine breed of goat, which they keep for milk for cheese.

(Right)
OLIVET CHEESE
The small town of Olivet is today virtually a suburb of Orléans, so it seems strange that it should be the home of a cheese, and that the cheese should be one of the few made from cows' milk that are found along the whole of the Loire.

CHEESE

The famous Crottin de Chavignol is made from the milk of the goats of eastern Berry, around Sancerre. Mention goats' cheese to many people and the image conjured up will bear some resemblance to Crottin de Chavignol – small, usually hard, smelly and strong – and probably produce a turning up of the nose. At one time this reaction was perhaps justified as, until given the protection of an *appellation d'origine*, there were some poorly made, not very pleasant specimens masquerading as 'Crottins de Chavignol'. Now, however, the absence of the official seal reveals an interloper.

Chavignol cheese has a very long history, and similar cheeses have been made by local peasants since the sixteenth century. However, the name '*crottin*' was not used until 1829, and supposedly resulted from the resemblance of the blackened mature Chavignol cheese to a small oil lamp with that name. Traditionally, a Sancerrois farm worker would take a few hard *crottins* with him to the fields to nibble during the day.

There are many small producers of goats' cheese and some *fromage de brebis* producers in the Sologne. In the Orléanais, however, cows' milk is used for cheeses such as Olivet. There are four types of Olivet, all smallish discs. Simple Olivet is similar to Coulommiers, rich and supple in texture with a light, faintly sweet flavour and smooth, pale-yellow paste. Olivet au foin is a naturally made cheese which has been ripened in hay and wrapped in hay or leaves. Occasionally it is eaten fresh, or after half-ripening, that is for just 10–14 days. Olivet bleu is actually not a blue-veined cheese, but a smooth straw-yellow cheese with a rich supple texture and a natural blueish tinge to its quite bloomy rind, acquired during a month's curing in local chalk caves. It has a mildly fruity flavour which can sometimes be sharp. The best time for eating it is from spring to the end of the autumn. Olivet cendré is ripened in ash-filled casks for about 3 months so that its flavour deepens and becomes more savoury. This ageing time means it is available into the winter. Originally it was made when milk was plentiful, to preserve it for times of low milk yields or for when there was a demand for 'picnic' foods to take to the fields, as at haymaking and harvest time. Other Orléanais cows' milk cheeses include: Bondaroy au foin, a soft cheese with a tangy flavour which is cured in hay for 5 weeks; Frinault, a small richly flavoured disc of full-fat cows' milk cheese; Frinault cendré, and St-Benoit, or St-Benoist, a farm-made disc of partly skimmed milk cheese with a pale rind and fruity flavour.

Wines

The best-known wine of this whole area, white Sancerre, is produced in Berry. Because of the similarities to – and frequent association with – Pouilly-Fumé, which is made just across the river, I am going to cover the two together, although strictly speaking Pouilly-Fumé comes from the *département* of Nivernais.

Both Pouilly-Fumé and white Sancerre are made from the same grape variety, sauvignon, which gives them their pale green/yellow colour, their slightly smoky/musky/grassy bouquet and a flavour vibrant with crisp, lively, fruity tones, redolent of blackcurrant leaves and ripe gooseberries or perhaps redcurrants. If the weather is right, the wines have an acidity that sharpens up their flavour. However in warm years, such as 1989 and 1990 which were responsible for such marvellous sweet wines further downstream, the wines of Sancerre and Pouilly can lack crispness.

Sancerre and Pouilly do come from opposite sides of the river, so the soil, topography and micro-climates are different. The Pouilly area is on a gently rolling plateau with a chalky clay soil which is generally slightly heavier than that of the sometimes very steep slopes of the Sancerre vineyards. Pouilly-Fumé, which gets its name from the grey smoke-coloured bloom that forms on sauvignon grapes (not from the characteristic smell of gun-flints being struck, as is sometimes reported), therefore tends to have more roundness, weight and body and can age better than Sancerre.

On the whole, nothing is to be gained by keeping either wine, and both are generally drunk young for maximum freshness (1–2 years old for Sancerre, 2–3 for Pouilly-Fumé), although Pouilly can be good at 4 years and, in exceptional circumstances, can last up to 10. Drink them cool, at about 10–12°C (50–54°F), to bring out their aroma and taste; if they are too cold their characteristic bouquet and flavour are lost. Excellent aperitifs, they also make

DOMAINE VACHERON

Unusually for Sancerre, Domaine Vacheron is better known for its Sancerre Rouge than its white version. For in a reversal of the normal Sancerrois policy of reserving the best, south-facing slopes for

sauvignon vines – relegating the pinot noir to poor, north-facing plots – the late Jean Vacheron planted pinot noir vines on the choicest, sunniest slopes and lavished much time and effort on making wines with the capacity to age and evolve into complex wines of character. One feature of the vinification, only possible because of the amount of concentrated fruit in the wines, is the ageing in oak barrels, a proportion of which are new every year. The exact proportion and the ageing time are adjusted according to the style of each vintage.

DE LADOUCETTE
The stylish milestone outside the Château de Nozet explicitly encompasses the profile of Ladoucette wines. The family company owns about ten times the average Pouilly-Fumé vineyard holding of 6 hectares (15 acres), and sells about 40% of the *appellation's* output. Large-scale production does not mean low standards; all Ladoucette wines are made to the highest criteria using the best of modern oenological techniques to ensure they are not only of irreproachable quality but also consistent. In addition to de Ladoucette Pouilly-Fumé, a limited amount (about 100,000 bottles) of a prestige cuvée, *Baron de L*, is vinified from grapes grown on old vines on choice land.

(Opposite)
SANCERRE VINEYARDS

fine accompaniments to goats' cheeses (especially local *crottins*) and light summer dishes. The firmer-bodied, more steely wines have a good acidity, making them quite capable of standing up to light creamy sauces, and some Pouillys work well with chicken.

Only within the last 35 years or so have the wines of Sancerre and Pouilly-sur-Loire become very fashionable. Prices have inevitably risen and unfortunately the quality has begun to fall, with wines being sold too young and in a 'difficult' stage of their maturation. However, a new generation of 'serious' wine-makers are now investing time, energy, knowledge and a great deal of money in making respectable wines.

There is a second, lesser, white from Pouilly-sur-Loire, called Pouilly-sur-Loire and produced from the chasselas grape variety, although each year less and less chasselas are planted as they are more difficult to grow. Neither red nor rosé wines are made there, but before the vineyards were devastated by phylloxera, Sancerre was principally a red-wine producing area. Subsequently, however, it has been found that the soil and climate are better suited to white grape varieties, especially the sauvignon that now accounts for about 80% of hectares planted.

In recent years, *vignerons* have chosen to ignore this experience and have been planting pinot noir to cash in on the vogue for red Sancerre. This is a good example of price not corresponding to quality, for not only are the vines planted in inappropriate sites, but *vignerons* used only to making white wines often do not understand the subtleties of making good red wines. Consequently, the light charming fresh fruitiness of which such wines are capable is too frequently marred. Happily there are exceptions (see previous page).

Served cool, a red Sancerre can be a good summer partner for lamb, rabbit, veal and poultry, as well as light meat *pâtés*. The slightly salmon-pink Sancerre rosé is best served chilled as a thirst quencher.

South-west of Sancerre there are three small *appellations*, Quincy, Reuilly and Menetou-Salon, all growing sauvignon and making wines that are very dry, crisp and characteristically fruity and aromatic, although a trifle more muted than Sancerre (this applies to the price as well!). Each is delicious in its own right, and there are fascinating differences of nuance between them: for example, Quincy wines tend to be lighter. Menetou-Salon is a district on the way up – and worth following – and Reuilly produces some light reds and rosés.

Orléanais wines have to be sought out, for although Orléans once stood among vineyards, rows of more rewarding fruit trees have replaced the vines. The wines that are produced are light and not usually very memorable (the best only reach VDQS status), although some growers are beginning to make surprisingly drinkable wine from chardonnay, called auvergnat blanc locally. However, less than 10% of Vin d'Orléanais is white.

The best-known Orléanais wine is made from gris meunier, a red so pale it verges on being a rosé. Drunk when young and lightly chilled, its fresh, slightly earthy taste is pleasant enough for inconsequential quaffing. Other reds are made from the pinot noir and cabernet franc grapes, known locally as auvergnat rouge and moir dur respectively.

GALETTES DE POMMES DE TERRE

Potato Pastries

(Illustrated below)

This recipe is based on the first *galette de pommes de terre* I ever had, the crisp flaky savouriness of which immediately seduced me. I was to come across quite a few more, many of them severe disappointments, before I learned to reject on sight those that looked dense or greasy – unfortunately all too often the case with mass-produced or carelessly made examples. *Galettes* make excellent snack food, particularly good for picnics: fill them with cooked onions or mushrooms, sliced tomatoes, ham or *charcuterie*. Or serve them just as they are, perhaps with a salad.

MAKES 15-18
100g/3½oz potatoes, peeled and diced
200-225g/7-8oz plain flour
70g/2½oz chèvre fromage frais or very soft fresh goats' cheese
70g/2½oz unsalted butter, softened
1 egg yolk, beaten with 1 tablespoon water, for glazing

Steam the potatoes until tender, then mash them until very smooth. Leave until cold. Mix in just enough of the flour and one or two tablespoons of cold water, depending on the flouriness of the potatoes, to give a soft pliable dough.

Blend the cheese with the butter and form into a flat square. On a lightly floured surface, roll out the dough to a square about 3-5mm/⅛-¼in thick. Place the butter and cheese block in the centre and fold the long sides of the dough in over it. Then fold the bottom third up over the block and the top third down, as when making puff pastry. Seal the edges lightly with a rolling pin and turn the dough through 90 degrees so the closed seam is to your left, like the spine of a book. Cover and chill. Repeat the entire rolling and folding operation twice more, turning the block through 90 degrees each time and allowing the dough to rest, chilled, between each operation.

Preheat the oven to 190C/375F/gas 5.

Roll out the dough to a rectangle a generous 5mm/¼in thick. Using a large sharp knife, cut it into rectangular pieces about 4cm/1½in wide and 5cm/2in long, or as liked. Brush them with egg glaze.

Bake in the oven for about 20 minutes, until golden. Transfer to a wire rack. When cool, slit them open for a filling, if using, and eat while still warm or cold.

(Below)
Filled galettes de pommes de terre on sale in Romorantin in the Sologne.

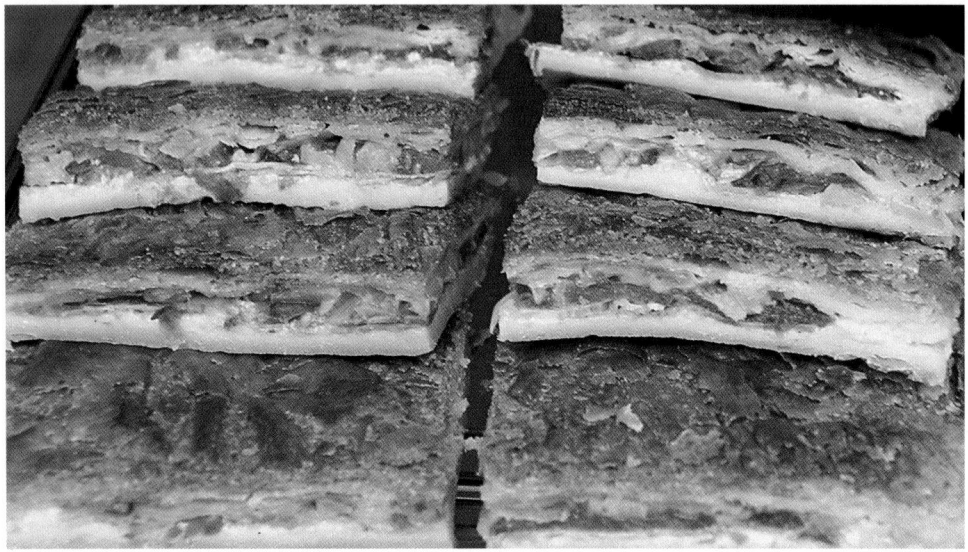

POMMES À LA FORESTIÈRE

Baked Jacket Potatoes with Wild Mushrooms

Usually *pommes à la forestière* is a baked dish of wild mushrooms interspersed with layers of sliced potatoes, but for an autumn barbecue – or indeed for a supper when sitting around the fire at home on a cold night – this recipe for individual jacket potatoes is unsurpassed. Serve them very hot and wrapped in clean napkins.

SERVES 4
4 baking potatoes
25g/1oz unsalted butter
½ small onion, finely chopped
thin slice of air-dried ham, chopped

115-150g/4-5oz wild or brown cap mushrooms, cleaned and chopped
about 3-4 tablespoons crème fraîche
freshly ground black pepper
chopped tarragon, chives or parsley, to serve

Bake the potatoes in the embers of an open fire, or in an oven preheated to 190C/375F/gas 5, for about 1¼ hours, or until tender.

Meanwhile, melt the butter in a frying pan over a medium heat. Add the onion and cook for 2-3 minutes. Stir in the mushrooms and cook for 3-4 minutes. Then stir in the ham, crème fraîche and black pepper and heat through.

Holding the potatoes in a cloth, cut a slice from the top and, using a teaspoon, press down the flesh to make a small well. Divide the mushrooms between the wells, slowly spooning over the juices so they soak down into the potatoes. Sprinkle with the chopped tarragon, chives or parsley and eat immediately.

PÂTÉ AU TRAUFFAUDE

Potato Pie

There are many versions of pie, called variously *pâté*, *tourtière* or *tourton*, containing potatoes. You may come across them locally as *trauffades*, *truffiats*, or *treuffes*. More simple recipes use stock instead of the crème fraîche or omit either the onion or bacon, or both; more robust, traditional versions make it in a *tourtière* – a type of deep flan dish much used in Berry. For any version, pâte brisée (which can be bound with milk instead of egg yolks and water; see page 77) may be used instead of puff pastry, and milk can replace the crème fraîche or cream.

SERVES 4
300g/10oz medium-sized waxy potatoes, peeled and thinly sliced
250g/9oz puff pastry
150g/5oz bacon, cut across into strips
2 tablespoons chopped parsley
1½ tablespoons chopped chervil
1 tablespoon chopped chives
1 onion, finely chopped
85ml/3fl oz crème fraîche or double cream, warmed gently until very hot

Preheat the oven to 200C/400F/gas 6.

Blanch the potatoes in boiling salted water for 5 minutes. Drain well.

On a lightly floured surface, roll out just over half of the pastry to about a 20cm/8in circle. Trim the edges and place on a dampened baking sheet. Roll out the remaining pastry to make a lid for the pie.

Arrange about one-third of the potato slices on the pastry, leaving the edges free, and sprinkle with about half of the bacon, herbs and onion. Repeat the layers, ending with a layer of potatoes. Dampen the edge of the pastry. Trim the edges from the pie lid and cover the pie. Seal the edges well, knock them up and scallop them. With the point of a sharp knife, either cut two large slashes in the top, or cut a large circle of pastry from the centre of the lid, but do not remove it.

Bake in the oven for 30 minutes. At the end of this time, ease off the central circle, if formed. Pour the very hot crème fraîche or cream into the pie through the space left by the circle of pastry, or through the slashes, making sure it flows evenly over and through the potato slices. Replace the circle if removed and return the pie to the oven for 10 minutes until the top is a rich brown and the potatoes tender.

Leave to stand in a warm place for 5-10 minutes before serving.

HARICOTS ROUGES AU VIN ROUGE

Red Haricot Beans in Young Red Wine

The young red wine used in this recipe would probably be similar to Beaujolais Nouveau as the same grape variety, gamay, is grown in the vicinity.

SERVES 4
55g/2oz unsalted butter
300g/10oz red haricot beans, soaked overnight, rinsed and drained
250ml/9fl oz young red wine
85g/3oz dried ham, such as Auvergne or Bayonne, chopped
1 onion, quartered
1 garlic clove, finely chopped
1 bouquet garni consisting of 1 sprig of thyme, 2 small sage leaves, 1 fresh bay leaf and several sprigs of parsley
70g/2½oz rillons (see page 76)
1 teaspoon mignonette pepper
salt
1 tablespoon chopped flat-leaved parsley

Melt half the butter in a large heavy-based saucepan. Stir in the beans until well coated with butter, then add the wine and 250ml/9fl oz water. Bring to the boil and skim off the scum.

Add the ham, onion, garlic and bouquet garni and boil for 10 minutes. Then cover and simmer for about 1½ hours, until the beans are tender, adding more water if necessary.

Sauté the *rillons* in the remaining butter until hot. Add these to the haricot beans with the mignonette pepper and plenty of salt and cook for a further 15 minutes.

Serve the beans with the chopped parsley scattered over the top.

LE GRAND HÔTEL DU LION D'OR**
69 rue Georges Clemenceau
Romorantin-Lanthenay
Tel 54 76 00 28
See recipes opposite and on page 58

M. and Mme Barrat have restored the Lion d'Or building and turned it into an extremely

luxurious hotel; but it is their daughter Marie-Christine and her talented chef husband Didier Clement, who have created the food for which the restaurant is famed. Marie-Christine studied medieval cooking at university and inspired Didier to experiment with herbs and spices used in those times. Some of these required painstaking research but now many are grown for them locally. Didier incorporates the old-fashioned flavours into his clean, simple style of cooking with innate skill and subtlety.

ÉCHALOTES D'ORLÉANS

Shallots with Vinegar and Honey

(Illustrated on page 50)

SERVES 4
55g/2oz unsalted butter
225g/8oz shallots, preferably grey
55ml/2fl oz white wine vinegar, preferably from Orléans
100ml/3½fl oz white wine
1 tablespoon honey
salt and freshly ground black pepper
chopped fresh thyme, to garnish

Melt the butter in a heavy-based pan over a low heat. Add the shallots and cook slowly, shaking the pan occasionally, until transparent and soft.

Stir in the vinegar and boil until it has almost completely evaporated. Stir in the wine and reduce by about two-thirds.

Stir in the honey and seasoning. Check the levels of sweetness and acidity and add more honey, vinegar or wine as necessary.

Serve sprinkled with thyme.

BROCHET AUX NOISETTES

Pike with Hazelnut Sauce

I first ate this dish when my spirits were not much brighter than the exceptionally drear late summer weather. The dish looked fresh and bright enough on the plate but I was still not very enthusiastic when I took the first bite. I immediately exercised my prerogative to change my mind, and devoured it with relish. The rich flavour and texture of the nut-butter sauce was a beautiful companion to the pike in this old Tourangeau recipe.

I have not yet quite been able to recapture that wonderful sauce, for that year's nuts had been unusually good. The ones used in my sauce had been picked after a period of warm sunshine, then spread out on sacking and left in a warm sunny place for a few days so that the husks came off easily. If you are lucky enough to find a hazelnut tree, you will have some truly fresh nuts with which to effect a proper re-creation.

SERVES 4
175g/6oz unsalted butter, softened, plus more for greasing
4 pike fillets
2-3 tablespoons dry Vouvray
1-2 tablespoons lemon juice
40g/1½oz shelled whole hazelnuts, lightly roasted, skinned and very finely chopped
1 egg yolk
salt and freshly ground black pepper

Melt 25g/1oz butter in a large pan. Add the pike, pour over the wine and lemon juice and season. Cover with buttered greaseproof paper and poach the fish until just cooked; about 5-7 minutes, depending on the size of the fillets. Remove the fish, cover and keep warm.

Put the nuts into a mortar and, using the pestle, work in the egg yolk. Gradually stir in the cooking juices to make a smooth sauce. Stir into the pan and gradually beat in the remaining butter.

Alternatively, chop the nuts very finely in a small blender or food processor without allowing them to 'oil'. Work in the egg yolk, then slowly pour in the cooking juices. Gradually add the remaining butter to give a smooth sauce.

Season the sauce and add lemon juice if necessary. Pour the sauce over the fish as it is, or first pass it through a sieve.

SAUMON DE LOIRE

Loire Salmon with Radish

(Illustrated right)

Because salmon is one of the fish most associated with the Loire it appears frequently on local menus. However, it does not follow that the salmon served is from the Loire and it certainly will not be if 'du Loire' is not mentioned, or if it is the autumn or winter. At Le Grand Hôtel du Lion d'Or (see opposite), Didier Clement would only use genuine local fish. He teams it perfectly with very thinly cut, peppery-sweet summer radishes and I have adapted his recipe slightly.

SERVES 1
6 red radishes
150g/5oz piece of wild salmon, sliced horizontally into 3
15g/½oz unsalted butter
juice of ½ lemon
100ml/3½fl oz crème fraîche
salt and freshly ground black pepper

Very thinly slice 4 of the radishes and use to cover the top of each slice of salmon.

Melt the butter in a frying pan over a medium heat. Add the salmon, radish-covered side uppermost, and cook for about 3-4 minutes, depending on the thickness of the salmon, and its temperature before the start of cooking.

Meanwhile, cut the remaining radishes in half vertically, then very thinly slice these halves. Arrange them on a plate.

Add the lemon juice to the crème fraîche and season to taste.

Reassemble the salmon into one piece, place it in the centre of the plate and spoon crème fraîche over and around it.

COLLIER D'AGNEAU MÈRE GIFFARD

Neck of Lamb with Beans and Mushrooms

(Illustrated far left)

This is the type of 'hearty, homely' fare so often associated with the damp, misty image of the Sologne. The characteristic elements that make this welcoming autumnal or winter dish so memorable are floury potatoes which collapse to make a thick sauce, *haricots demi-secs*, and chanterelles, which each give off their wonderful perfumes and flavours. In the absence of *haricots demi-secs*, use dried haricot beans and soak them overnight beforehand. If chanterelles are not available, use 225g/8oz chopped brown cap, or ordinary white, mushrooms with 25g/1oz dried ceps soaked in hot water for 20 minutes.

SERVES 4
25g/1oz pork fat or unsalted butter
1 large onion, chopped
4 carrots, quartered
2 starchy potatoes, quartered
200g/7oz haricot beans, preferably demi-sec
250g/9oz chanterelles, well washed
1 sprig of thyme
1 small sprig wild thyme
1 bay leaf
1 sprig of rosemary
4 good slices of neck, scrag end or breast of lamb
salt and freshly ground black pepper
chopped parsley, to garnish

(Opposite, left to right)
Neck of Lamb with Beans and Mushrooms (this page), with Shallots with Vinegar and Honey (page 48).

In a large heavy casserole, heat the pork fat or butter, add the onion and cook, stirring occasionally, until browned.

Stir in the carrots, potatoes, haricots, mushrooms and herbs. Place the lamb on top, add 500ml/18fl oz water and bring slowly to a simmer. Skim the surface, cover, then leave to cook very slowly for about 1¼-1½ hours, by which time the meat and beans should be tender and the potatoes collapsed to make a thick sauce. Check occasionally during the cooking and add more water if necessary.

At the end of the cooking time check and adjust the seasoning and the amount and consistency of the liquid: if necessary, spoon some off and boil it to reduce it. Serve garnished with parsley.

PÂTÉ DE PERDRIX EN CROÛTE

Partridge Pâté Baked in a Pastry Crust

(Recipe follows overleaf)

Orléans and the lands to the north have long been renowned for their game pâtés *en croûte*. This is hardly surprising considering the proximity of gently undulating wheatlands, which not only supplied an abundant golden harvest of grain, but also served as breeding grounds for partridges. These are not the greylegged species native to Britain, but the slightly larger and visually more interesting – though gastronomically less appealing – grey-legged 'Frenchmen'. Unfortunately, modern farming practices often involve removing hedgerows from the landscape and applying chemical pesticides and herbicides, with a consequent decline in the partridge population.

SERVES ABOUT 8
2 dressed partridges, livers and hearts reserved
3 tablespoons marc or brandy
3-4 tablespoons chopped mixed herbs
115g/4oz veal
115g/4oz lean pork
85g/3oz pork back fat
25g/1oz butter, plus more for greasing
2 shallots, chopped
about 55g/2oz chicken livers
85ml/3fl oz medium-bodied dry white wine
3 eggs, beaten
about 450g/1lb puff pastry
salt and freshly ground black pepper

Remove the flesh from the partridges. Cut the breasts lengthwise into strips, season and pour over half the marc or brandy, and sprinkle over a pinch of the herbs. Cover and leave in a cool place for about 4 hours, turning 2 or 3 times. Mince or very finely chop the remaining partridge flesh with the veal, pork and back fat.

Melt the butter in a sauté pan over a low heat, add the shallots, cover and cook gently until very soft but not coloured. Make up the partridge livers and hearts to 115g/4oz with chicken livers. Add to the pan and cook briskly for 2 minutes so they remain pink in the centre. Stir in the remaining marc or brandy, set alight then using a slotted spoon transfer the shallots and livers to a plate and leave until cold.

Stir the wine into the cooking juices, boil for a couple of minutes then cool. Mince the liver mixture, add to the other minced meats with the wine and seasoning, and leave overnight.

The next day, preheat the oven to 190C/375F/gas5.

Roll out three-quarters of the pastry and use to line a buttered hinged pâté mould about 23 x 12cm/9 x 5in in size, pressing it well into the angles and leaving 2cm/1in overhanging all round. Roll out the remaining pastry for a lid.

Add the remaining herbs and two of the eggs to the minced meats. Layer the terrine with half of the mixture, then arrange the partridge breast strips down the centre and cover with the remaining minced mixture, piling it in a dome.

Fold the overhanging pastry over the filling and put the pastry lid in place. Seal the edges well and brush with the remaining beaten egg. Make a small hole in the top and insert a foil 'chimney' to allow steam to escape.

Bake in the oven for 20 minutes, then reduce the temperature to 180C/350F/gas4 and cook for a further 45 minutes to 1 hour. Cover with foil or a double thickness of greaseproof paper if the pastry begins to brown too much.

Leave to cool before unmoulding. Keep in a cool place for a day before serving.

CHEVREUIL AU SANCERRE ROUGE

Venison in Red Sancerre

The most popular way of serving venison I have come across in all manner of restaurants in the region, from simple *fermes auberges* to high-class establishments, is the classic *grand veneur*. Done well it can indeed be a splendid dish 'fit for a king'. However, it is a very lengthy process so I am giving a simpler recipe, one that you are more likely to cook but which is sure to be enjoyed with just as much relish.

I like to cook venison, as well as other game, in a red Sancerre as it produces a lighter dish than those in which more traditional heavier wines are used. I use the same recipe for smaller cuts.

SERVES 8-10
85g/3oz piece of salt belly of pork or green bacon, cut across into strips
1 haunch of venison, weighing about 3.2-3.5kg/7-8lb
3 shallots, chopped
2 young carrots, chopped
1 celery stalk, chopped
a bouquet garni consisting of 1 bay leaf, 2 sprigs of thyme, 2 parsley sprigs and a sprig of rosemary
1 bottle of red Sancerre
55g/2oz good pork fat or unsalted butter
225ml/8fl oz game stock
salt and freshly ground black pepper

Using a sharp knife, make slits in the venison at intervals and insert the strips of pork or bacon. Place the haunch in a deep dish. Add the vegetables and herbs. Season and pour over half the wine. Cover and leave in a cool place for 24 hours, turning from time to time.

Preheat the oven to 200C/400F/gas6.

Remove the venison from the dish and pat dry. Strain the marinade and reserve the wine and vegetables.

In a roasting tin, heat the pork fat or butter and add the vegetables. Brown them quite quickly over a high heat, stirring frequently. Using a slotted spoon, remove them and reserve. Add the venison to the tin and brown it evenly. Lift it out, put the vegetables and herbs underneath, then lower the venison back again, and baste it with some more reserved wine.

Roast in the oven for about 15 minutes, then lower the temperature to 180C/350F/gas4 and roast for a total of 9 minutes per 450g/1lb, including the initial period at the higher temperature. Baste frequently with the reserved wine. Transfer the venison to a warmed plate, cover and keep warm. Stir the remaining wine into the cooking juices and boil until syrupy.

(Left)
The recipe for Pheasant with Ceps below is excellent for older birds, but a young tender one can be roasted. Here at the Hôtel St-Hubert on the road to Cherverny a young bird is nearly ready to be served with a sauce made from the cooking juices, stock and some local wine.

Stir in the stock and reduce until lightly syrupy. Add any juices that have collected on the plate with the venison.

Strain the sauce into a warmed jug and serve with the venison.

FAISAN AUX CÈPES

Pheasant with Ceps

Containing the spoils of much-loved hunting, this dish brings together two of the most popular autumnal foods, both of them eagerly sought wherever there is suitable terrain almost the whole length of the Loire. It is an ideal way of cooking older birds, or those of indeterminate age, to make a casserole good enough for the finest dinner party. Partridges are equally delicious cooked in this way.

SERVES 3-4
1 pheasant, dressed and cut into pieces
3 tablespoons oil
4 tablespoons red vinaigre d' Orléans
1 bay leaf
3 sprigs of thyme
a small sprig of rosemary
1 large onion, chopped
300ml/10fl oz red Sancerre
2 slices of bacon, chopped
225g/8oz ceps, trimmed and cleaned
350ml/12fl oz chicken stock
25g/1oz unsalted butter, diced
salt and freshly ground black pepper

Fit the pheasant pieces into a non-metallic dish. Pour over half the oil and half the vinegar. Scatter over the herbs, reserving 2 of the thyme sprigs, and half the onion. Pour in the wine and season lightly. Cover and leave in a cool place for 8 hours.

Remove the pheasant from the dish and pat dry. Reserve the marinade but discard the herbs from it.

Heat the remaining oil in a heavy flameproof dish into which the pheasant will fit snugly. Cook the bacon and remaining onion in it over a fairly low heat, stirring occasionally, until the onion has softened. Using a slotted spoon, transfer to a paper towel. Evenly brown the pheasant 2 pieces at a time. Transfer to paper towels. Cook the mushrooms in the casserole, stirring occasionally, then transfer to paper towels.

Stir the remaining vinegar into the cooking liquid, boil until well reduced, then stir in the reserved marinade. Allow to bubble for a few minutes. Add the stock, bring to the boil and skim.

Lower the heat and put half of the bacon mixture, half of the mushrooms and 1 reserved thyme sprig in the bottom of the casserole. Place the pheasant on top, then add the remaining bacon mixture, thyme sprig and mushrooms. Cover tightly and cook over a very low heat, or in the oven preheated to 170C/325F/gas3, for about 1½ hours.

Transfer the pheasant and mushrooms to a warmed dish. Boil the cooking juices until well reduced, adding any juice which collects on the serving plate from the pheasant. Over a low heat, gradually stir or whisk in the butter. Season to taste and pour or strain over the pheasant.

CANARD SAUVAGE AUX COINGS

Wild Duck with Quince

(Illustrated left)

This recipe is based on an evocative account of a dish described to me by an old French friend during wistful reminiscences of the wonderfully scented dishes his wife used to prepare when they were first married. She also made *eau-de-vie de coing* and he suspected that some of that was added to the marinade. Fragrant quinces are the key to success.

SERVES 4-6

1 large or 2 small-to-medium-sized ripe quince(s)
2 mallards, green glands removed
300ml/10fl oz medium-bodied dry white wine, such as a Chenin Blanc
85g/3oz unsalted butter
2 shallots, finely chopped
150ml/5fl oz chicken stock
salt and freshly ground black pepper
pinch of sugar
squeeze of lemon juice

Wipe the down from the surface of the fruit, then peel, core and slice them, reserving the trimmings.

Put the ducks into a heavy flameproof casserole and tuck the quince slices around them. Pour over the wine, cover and leave in a cool place for 8-12 hours, turning the birds occasionally.

Preheat the oven to 180C/350F/gas4.

Simmer the quince trimmings in 300ml/10fl oz water for 15 minutes. Strain and reserve the juice. Lift the birds and quince slices from the casserole and pour off the marinade. Season the ducks.

In the casserole, melt 25g/1oz of the butter, add one-third to three-quarters of the quince slices with the shallots and sauté them for about 3-4 minutes. Remove. Add another 15g/½oz butter to the casserole, then add the birds, breast-side down, and brown them lightly. Turn them over carefully and lightly brown the undersides too.

In a pan, bring the wine, strained quince juice and stock to the boil. Pour this over the duck, cover the casserole tightly and cook in the oven for about 45 minutes until the ducks are tender, turning them over halfway through.

In a frying pan, melt another 25g/1oz butter, add the remaining quince slices and fry them for about 10 minutes until golden and tender, turning them over halfway through to cook them all over.

Transfer the duck to a warmed plate. Purée the contents of the casserole and reheat. Lower the heat and swirl in the remaining butter. Taste and adjust the seasoning, adding a little sugar or a squeeze of lemon juice if necessary to lift the flavour. Serve the duck with the purée and the slices of quince.

LAPIN DE GARENNE À LA SOLOGNOTE

Stuffed Wild Rabbit

SERVES 4

1 wild rabbit, skinned, with the liver, kidneys and heart retained
a handful of mixed fresh herbs, including parsley, chives and chervil, chopped
300ml/10fl oz Loire Sauvignon
70g/2½oz unsalted butter
55g/2oz lightly smoked streaky bacon, chopped
1 small shallot, finely chopped
115g/4oz mushrooms, preferably wild or chestnut or brown cap, chopped
115g/4oz cooked Swiss chard or spinach leaves, chopped
2 small carrots, chopped
2 onions, quartered
115ml/4fl oz veal stock
1 bouquet garni
salt and freshly ground black pepper

Put the rabbit in a bowl and scatter some of the herbs over it. Pour the wine over, cover and leave in a cool place overnight.

Remove the rabbit from the marinade and wipe it dry, reserving the marinade. In a saucepan, melt half the butter, add the bacon and cook over a fairly low heat until the fat runs. Finely chop the rabbit liver, heart and kidneys, then add these to the pan with the shallot and mushrooms. Increase the heat slightly and cook for 3-4 minutes, stirring occasionally. Stir in the Swiss chard leaves or spinach, along with the remaining herbs and seasoning.

Place the rabbit on its back, spoon in this stuffing and fold the flesh of the sides over the stuffing. Sew up with thick thread or fine string, and truss with the legs neatly tucked in.

Heat three-quarters of the remaining butter in a flameproof casserole in which the rabbit will fit comfortably, add the rabbit and brown it lightly. Lift it out. Add the carrots and onions to the casserole, brown these lightly then place the rabbit on top. Pour in the stock, add the bouquet garni, cover and cook gently for about 1 hour, until the rabbit is tender.

Transfer the rabbit to a warmed plate and keep warm. Stir the reserved marinade into the cooking juices and boil until slightly syrupy. Lower the heat and gradually swirl in the remaining butter. Adjust the seasoning. Remove the stuffing and serve with the rabbit cut into pieces, and the sauce strained over.

(Top)
In Orléanais apple-growing is not especially intensive, but there are plenty around for such classics as tarte Tatin.

TARTE DES DEMOISELLES TATIN

Upside-down Apple Pie

(Illustrated left)

To make a true country-style *tarte Tatin* the apples should be cut into large chunks, not paper-thin slices. The sisters (see page 37) cooked their *tarte* in a metal 'oven' placed over charcoal and this produced the characteristic caramelization of the sweetened buttery apple. Modern gas and electric ovens will not produce the same effect so, nowadays, the apples, butter and sugar are usually browned over direct heat before being covered with pastry and baked. Our tart was photographed at the Hôtel St-Hubert near Cheverny. If using a baking tin, and especially if using gas, make sure the apples don't 'catch'.

SERVES 6-8
175g/6oz unsalted butter, diced
225g/8oz caster sugar
6 firm dessert apples, such as reine de reinette or Cox's, peeled, cored and halved or quartered
squeeze of lemon juice, optional
350g/12oz puff pastry or pâte sucrée (see page 90), chilled

Using about 50g/2oz of the butter, thickly butter the bottom and sides of a 23cm/9in tin-lined copper *tarte Tatin* mould about 5cm/2in deep, or a heavy frying or sauté pan that can go into the oven, or a thick-bottomed baking tin. (The buttering is easiest if the butter is diced.) Sprinkle over two-thirds of the sugar.

Arrange the apples in the tin or pan, and sprinkle over the remaining sugar and butter. Cook over a high heat for 15 minutes until the apples are tender and the butter and sugar thickened and golden brown. Remove from the heat, add the lemon juice and allow to cool, removing some liquid if there is too much.

On a lightly floured surface, roll the pastry out to a circle about 2cm/½in larger in diameter than your tin. Prick it with a fork, place it on a baking sheet, cover and chill for 30 minutes.

Preheat the oven to 220C/425F/gas7.

Cover the apples with the pastry, tucking it down the sides of the pan or tin.

If using puff pastry, bake for 12-15 minutes then lower the temperature to 180C/350F/gas4 and cook for 10-12 minutes until the pastry is risen and crisp. If using pâte sucrée, bake for 25 minutes.

Leave to cool for a few minutes then invert on to a warm plate and serve warm.

GÂTEAU DE PITHIVIERS

Almond-filled Pastry Cake

(Illustrated on page 32)

SERVES 6-8
450g/1lb puff pastry
1 egg yolk beaten with 1 teaspoon cold water, to glaze
icing sugar, for sifting
FOR THE FILLING
85g/3oz almonds, ground
85g/3oz caster sugar
85g/3oz unsalted butter, softened
2 egg yolks, beaten
2 tablespoons dark rum

Make the filling: using a pestle and mortar, pound the almonds with the sugar to make a paste. Spoon this into a bowl and work in the butter followed by the egg yolks and rum. Cover and chill very well.

Divide the pastry into two portions, one slightly larger than the other. On a lightly floured surface, roll the smaller portion out to a circle about 25cm/10in in diameter. Trim the edges and very carefully transfer to a baking sheet.

Roll out the other piece of pastry to a similar circle and trim the edges. Place the almond filling on the first circle, leaving a border of about 2cm/1in clear all the way round. Brush the border with beaten egg. Place the second circle of pastry centrally over the filling and press the pastry edges together to seal well. Make a scallop effect around the edge and a slit in the centre.

With the point of a sharp knife, starting at the centre and working to the edge, score the surface of the pastry in curved, half-moon-shaped lines to give the traditional appearance – but be careful not to cut right through. Brush the top with the egg glaze, avoiding the scored lines. Cover and chill for 30 minutes.

Preheat the oven to 220C/425F/gas7.

Bake the pie for about 20 minutes, then lower the oven temperature to 200C/420F/gas7 and bake for a further 15 minutes or so, until the pastry is risen and golden brown in colour.

Preheat a very hot grill. Sprinkle some sugar over the surface of the pastry and place it under the grill for a minute or two until the sugar has caramelized. Carefully transfer to a wire rack.

PAIN D'ÉPICES

Honey Spice Cake

(Illustrated on page 41)

Although it is not traditional, I like to eat *pain d'épices* spread with butter or *fromage blanc*.

MAKES 1 CAKE
225g/8oz plain flour
55g/2oz rye flour (or use all plain white flour)
2 tsp baking powder
1 tbsp ground cinnamon
½ tsp ground ginger
pinch of salt
2 eggs, beaten
225g/8oz honey, warmed until runny
1 tsp finely crushed aniseeds
butter, for greasing

Preheat the oven to 190C/375F/gas5 and butter an 11 x 23cm/5 x 9in cake tin.

Sift the flours, baking powder, spices except the aniseed, and salt into a bowl. Form a well in the centre and pour in the eggs and honey. Add the aniseed and gradually draw the dry ingredients into the liquid to make a smooth batter. Pour into the prepared tin and bake in the oven for 40 minutes, or until a skewer or thin knife inserted into the centre comes out clean.

Remove from the oven, leave to stand for about 5 minutes then turn out on a wire rack to cool.

FINANCIERS DE SULLY

Almond Cakes from Sully

Another version of this recipe coats the top with icing after cooking and cooling, but I find this additional sweetness spoils the moreish, chewy-nuttiness of *financiers*, rather than adds anything to them.

MAKES ABOUT 20
2 egg yolks
85g/3oz caster sugar
25g/1oz flour
25g/1oz ground almonds
55g/2oz unsalted butter, melted and cooled, plus more for greasing
about 40g/1½oz flaked almonds
icing sugar or icing (optional)

Preheat the oven to 180C/350F/gas4.

In a large bowl set in a *bain-marie* over a low heat, whisk the egg yolks with the sugar until very thick and mousse-like.

Sift the flour over the surface, then, using a large metal spoon, gently fold it in with the ground almonds and butter.

Coat the base of a buttered, 23 x 15cm (9 x 6in) baking tin with the flaked almonds. Evenly cover these with the almond mixture and sprinkle some more nuts over the surface.

Bake in the oven for about 30 minutes.

Cut into fingers and leave to cool slightly before turning on to a wire rack to cool. Sprinkle with icing sugar.

(Above)
With such a long history of an abundant variety of fruits, home-preservation is in the blood and many a larder will have a row of tempting bottles.

PANNEQUETS DE FRAMBOISES

Raspberry Pancakes

(Illustrated far right, with the restaurant's own pâte des fruits)

This is one of the most popular desserts served at Le Grand Hôtel du Lion d'Or (see page 48). Both pancakes and sauce may be made well in advance.

SERVES 4
150g/5oz plain flour
pinch of salt
3 eggs, beaten, plus 3 extra egg yolks
450ml/16fl oz milk
85g/3oz caster sugar, to taste
about 70g/2½oz unsalted butter, melted
450g/1lb raspberries
115ml/4fl oz crème fraîche
2 tablespoons icing sugar

Put 125g/4½oz of the flour into a bowl, stir in the salt and make a well. Add the eggs and then gradually stir in 250ml/9fl oz of the milk to make a smooth batter.

Whisk together the egg yolks and caster sugar. Blend a little of the remaining milk with the flour in a cup, then whisk into the egg yolk mixture. Heat the remaining milk to just on boiling point, then slowly stir into the egg yolks. Return to the rinsed pan and heat, stirring, until thickened, then cook gently for about 2 minutes, still stirring. Strain into a bowl and leave to cool, stirring occasionally.

Pass the raspberries through a non-metallic sieve to make a purée.

Stir 40g/1½oz of the melted butter into the batter. Heat the remaining butter in a crêpe pan or small frying pan, coat the pan then pour the excess into a bowl to use again. Add a small ladleful of batter, swirl it around, then cook quickly until lightly coloured on the underside. Turn the crêpe over and cook the other side. Remove and keep warm while making a total of 16 crêpes.

Just before serving, preheat a hot grill. Stir the crème fraîche into the crème pâtissière, and flavour with a little raspberry purée. Place a spoonful of this in the centre of each crêpe and fold into four.

Sprinkle the folded crêpes with icing sugar and place them under the hot grill until the sugar melts to a glaze.

Pour the remaining purée over 4 plates and arrange 4 crêpes on each.

'THE ENCHANTED LAND'

THROUGH TOURAINE, THE HEARTLANDS OF THE VAL-DE-LOIRE

TOURAINE IS A LAND OF SIMPLE ELEGANCE AND QUALITY. WARM BALMY DAYS AND EVENINGS AND WIDE BLUE HORIZONS GRACE A CALM COUNTRYSIDE OF meadows, fields and woods, dotted with châteaux and producing lush harvests of fruit and vegetables, fine goats' cheese and gentle wines.

The majority of the fruit, early vegetables and vines are planted on the rich, fertile and well-drained soil near the Loire, and along the valleys of its tributaries. To the south, there are rolling hills with yellow fields of giant sunflowers and corn. These hills open out after Loches to the plateau of Ste-Maure, with its quiet pastoral appeal. In summer, herds of sleek brown goats, looking like small deer, graze on the usually lush pastures to provide the rich milk for the region's many *fromages de chèvre*. There is also a wealth of good poultry and game, and more cattle than nearer the Loire.

(Opposite) The famous kitchen garden at Villandry features only produce available in the sixteenth century. Box hedges mark out the nine vegetable patches.
(Above) Baskets or plates displaying a variety of brightly coloured, sparkling pâte des fruits *are a frequent sight in* pâtisseries *all along the Loire. Made from local, sun-ripened fruit boiled down with sugar, they are quite delicious.*

LANGEAIS
Soirée
Dansante
Choisissez
y en a encore
un !

The Tourangeaux are polite, charmingly friendly and hospitable. They also quietly pride themselves on speaking the purest French. As Touraine has the highest concentration of popular châteaux along the Loire, tourists flock there and tourism is a major source of revenue. However, most stay in and around the châteaux towns, and if you move slightly away you will find tranquil beauty and unspoilt villages.

From the air, the land looks like a piece of lace. Weaving across its surface there are many small streams flowing into rivers which, in their turn, flow into the Loire. This network has its influence on the food, keeping the pastures well watered and providing bountiful catches for fishermen.

Along the Creuse, a tributary of the Vienne, local farmworkers moor their punts so they can supplement their income by spare-time fishing. As the river bed has ideal lurking places for big fish, there are pike and pike-perch. In summer, however, the particular prize are grey mullet which come all the way up from the Atlantic. A local fishermen told me that whereas shad stay in the Loire, the mullet prefers to fork right into the Vienne.

At La Chapelle, one of the tiny old river ports with a terraced stone *levée* sloping down to a quay, I spotted a few cabined punts. Investigation showed these to be owned by local fishermen who still earn a reasonable amount netting salmon in spring and catching eels, bleak and pike at other times. In Chaumont, I was introduced to the handful of locals, both young and old, who net or line-fish commercially from small punts. Their catch includes gudgeon,

1 *Decorative ironwork from a hotel window.* **2** *An early morning drink in a bar during the Sunday morning market in Langeais.* **3** *Apples piled up in the market in Tours.* **4** *Cakes on display in Maison Poirault, rue Nationale, Tours, where you can watch handmade sweets being made.* **5** *An architectural feature on the town hall building, Tours.* **6** *Tobacco plants are grown in sunny spots along the Loire and the Cher. The harvested leaves are hung in special sheds to dry, then supplied to the French National Tobacco Company.* **7** *Mural at Le Coq Hardi, Monnaie, north of Tours.* **8** *Artichokes on sale at Tours market. The vegetable was a favourite food with François I's court at Amboise; at a wedding feast in 1575, his daughter-in-law, Catherine de' Medici, ate them until she almost burst.* **9** *A selection of goats' cheeses on sale at Tours market, and including the famous log-shaped Ste-Maure. Not only are there many different goats' cheese producers, but also many different styles.*

1	**2**		**3**
	4	**5**	**6**
7	**8**	**9**	

bleak and roach for *Friture* (see page 114) in the spring, or large fish caught under licence from the bigger flat-bottomed boats called *toués*. These have cabins at the stern where fishermen used to live for weeks at a time.

In the gentle waters of the Indre gliding past Azay-le-Rideau, a few carp still lead the same leisurely existence as they did when Catherine de' Medici's chefs created *Carpe à la Chambord* (see page 81). Although carp caught in rivers do not get as fat as they do living an even more sedentary life in ponds, their flesh can have a fresher flavour.

Rarely mentioned in the same breath as salmon, shad and carp when talking of fish in the Loire area, perch are, however, prized in Touraine. Although handsome, the spines on the first dorsal fin can be quite unpleasant and the scales stubborn if not promptly removed. Their taste, especially that of smaller fish, is well worth the trouble, and certainly worth choosing on the rare occasions that perch appears on restaurant menus.

(*Above*)
BAR CHARLES VIII
The bar entrance at the Hosten et Restaurant Langeais.

The family pig has not yet vanished from the countryside, although it is now not necessary for a family to raise and fatten their own pig during the spring and summer to provide the household with food during the lean winter months. Those homes with a smallholding or allotment often still cosset and pamper their own pig until it is in prime condition for the ceremonial killing and ritual transformation into all manner of good things: some fresh for eating immediately, such as *boudins noirs*; some for keeping a few days; others to last for longer, packed in fat or cured with salt. These occasions were family affairs. Everyone would know their role, whether it was separating the rind from the fat, cutting up strips of back fat, filleting, mincing, or immersing meat in the salt bath. An enormous *fait-tout* slowly bubbled and steamed on the stove while the family got on with the business of making pâtés, *boudins*, *rillettes* and their crisp cousin *rillons* (or *rillauds* or *rillots*, as they are called in some places).

Rillettes are a cross between pâté, potted meat and a purée (see pages 66 and 76). They are made throughout the region, and in Anjou. Although many places, such as Tours, claim to be their 'home', or to make the *vrai* or best, the truth is probably that there is no one birthplace, and no one place where they are invariably better than elsewhere. They have been made since at least the fifteenth century, when the kitchens of large houses would have a circular depression formed in the brick floor for the fire, with an inner rim to support the huge *rillettes* cauldron. Cut out of one side was a step, so that the pot could be reached more comfortably during the long, laborious job of stirring a large batch.

The pork for *rillons*, described by Balzac as 'residue of pork fried in its own fat, resembling cooked truffles', is cut into large cubes and sometimes may be salted and left for

(Opposite)
FISHING ON THE RIVER
You may see this type of boat moored against a line of nets across the river. A long spar, a balancier, *is pivoted over the bow and a* carrelet, *a net resembling a square, upside-down umbrella, hangs from it, submerged. The fish swim along the nets to find a way through, only to pass over the* carrelet, *making it vibrate and so alert the fisherman. Experience allows him to differentiate between flotsam, small fish or big fish. If the latter, he quickly trips the balance so that the* carrelet, *with its fish, is whisked from the water.*

RILLETTES

The meat used in rillettes is usually pork, but it can also be duck, goose, rabbit or game, or a mixture of any of these with pork. The proportions of fat to lean can vary from half to almost equal parts, and flavourings can range from just salt to a small pinch of quatre-épices, a bouquet garni, or some chopped onion – which I was told by Gilbert, a portly prize-winning charcutier, is vital for the mixture's acidity.

Nearly every maker will have their own recipe, and make their own choice of what quality and cuts of meat to use. The appearance of the rillettes is a fairly good guide to quality; be very wary of factory-made examples, as the process and equipment used reduce the whole thing to an unpleasant homogeneous mass.

Rillettes are generally eaten with foods with contrasting textures or 'bite', like fresh crusty bread, a crisp salad, pickled walnuts or gherkins.

a few hours to pickle slightly before cooking. Often the bones are left in the meat to add flavour. The cubes are baked very slowly until the flesh is just tender – not soft – so most of the fat is expelled and they become crisp and crunchy (see page 76). The *rillons* are then packed into sterilized pots, the reserved fat poured around them, and left to set. *Rillons* are eaten hot with fried apple rings or a tangy apple sauce and puréed potatoes, or cold with a crisp salad, piquant mustard and a glass of chilled dry Vouvray.

If pigs' blood is available, *boudins noirs* will be made, but in Touraine *boudins blancs* are more often seen. Sitting in a *charcuterie*, usually on a white tray, *boudins blancs* look most uninspiring, and their appearance does not do justice to what has been dubbed the 'queen of sausages'. They are made from white meat, such as chicken or veal, enriched with pork back fat and crème fraîche and bound with eggs and breadcrumbs (an exception among French sausages). The traditional seasoning is delicate white pepper, perhaps with a little onion and some *quatre-épices*. Added champagne, brandy or *foie gras* are affectations happily not rife in the Loire. Here herbs are sometimes added to the *boudin* mixture, or the *boudins* rolled in them after initial cooking. *Boudins* may be eaten straight away, as they are poached by the *charcutier*, but it is more normal to reheat them by grilling or frying.

Andouillettes are about the same size as *boudins blancs* and are also bought ready cooked. Their base is pigs' innards, to which a wide variety of flavourings is added. Although basically made of the same ingredients as *andouilles*, they do contain more fat and are larger. They are usually brined and sometimes smoked, and sold in slices for eating cold. Vouvray is almost as well known locally for its *andouillettes* as it is for its wines.

In the south, the small town of Richelieu, named after the seventeenth-century cardinal and statesman, also acquired a reputation for the quality of its *charcuterie*, in particular its potentially confusingly termed *jambon de volaille*. This was not chicken cured in the manner of ham, as we now have turkey ham, but chicken legs boned, stuffed and cooked in white wine. Since the late 1980s, similar '*jambons*' of poultry have become fashionable.

Richelieu's royal master, Louis XIII, used to stay at the Château d'Amboise, north-east of Richelieu's own town, because of the proximity of the hunting in the popular Forêt d'Amboise. While at the Château, for some unknown reason, he had a penchant for cooking for himself – there is no evidence to suggest that he did this elsewhere. Either he only ever fancied something plain to eat or he had an extremely limited repertoire of dishes, as he usually made a simple onion omelette moistened with a little local red wine.

Charles VIII, an earlier occupant of the Château d'Amboise, played a much more pivotal role in the gastronomic history of the Loire, as he was responsible for the introduction of several products to the region. Among the many things which captivated him when he was in Italy, attempting to annex Lombardy, were their food and their gardens. In 1495, after one of his forays, he included many specimens of fruits, vegetables, seeds and plants in his convoy of treasures, scholars and experts. Among the latter was one who knew about breeding chicken in incubators, a practice then unknown in France. Not surprisingly, the vast train of 6,000 mules was ambushed and looted at Fornova. Fortunately many plants, such as artichokes, survived and later took to the favourable climate and well-watered fertile soil of their new home at Amboise. They grew well and quickly became popular, spreading throughout the whole region and into Anjou. The chicken expert also survived the ambush and his now-ubiquitous system was put into practice at Amboise in 1496.

With plenty of rich aristocrats in the great houses and châteaux, coupled with the presence of Tours and good transportation links to the lucrative markets of Paris, the industrious inhabitants of Touraine quickly saw the potential for growing rare vegetables and fruit. Nowadays we make a fuss about *primeurs* vegetables, but as long ago as the sixteenth century there were market gardeners, known locally as *bêcheux*, who specialized in them. As well as artichokes, superb thick white-stemmed asparagus is a particular speciality, with the region coming second only to the Gard in volume produced.

Celery is also a major commercial crop, although of little gastronomic significance. However, some of the rows of barren banks of earth which look as if they might be hiding celery heads may instead be concealing a crop of cardoons (see page 80), as these are grown like celery – the stems buried in banks of earth to keep them white and give them their delicate texture and delicious flavour. When harvested, cardoons look like prickly celery that has had an overdose of fertilizer. They belong, instead, to the thistle family and taste vaguely like their close relation the artichoke. The outer stalks and leaves of cardoons are removed before use, leaving the inner, more tender ones, and the hearts. The latter are sometimes referred to locally as *moelle végétale* and are served cut into rounds as a garnish. Confusingly, the classic recipe *cardons à la moelle* combines cardoons with a rich red wine sauce containing

(Below left)
THE FAMILY PIG
Even though Touraine is known for a number of pork products, such as rillettes and rillons, and pork dishes such as porc au pruneaux, and even though the need for a home supply of food throughout the winter no longer exists, an individual 'family' pig kept on a smallholding, or even in a back garden, is a far more likely sight than a large pig farm.

(Below right)
DRYING THE WASHING
Tea towels hanging on a line in a back garden near Villaines-les-Rochers.

(Top)
PLUM TART

(Above)
WILD MUSHROOMS
Many different types of wild mushrooms grow, each one in its own specific habitat.

(Right)
PEARS AND WALNUTS
Winter varieties of pears and fresh walnuts are often used together in cooking, particularly in fruit tarts, as they taste very good in partnership. These were photographed in the grounds of the château at Azay-le-Rideau.

beef marrow (*moelle*). This magnificent, silvery-white vegetable is sadly less popular today than it used to be – partly due to the poor monetary yield in relation to the space required to grow it.

Certain varieties of beans, such as *michelets*, are allowed to grow until they mature into full-sized haricot beans, ready for eating towards the end of summer. They are picked and sold in their shells. The fiddly job of shelling them is still considered worth the trouble, since they are creamier and more delicate than dried haricot beans, and can be cooked without pre-soaking.

Some full-sized haricot beans would have been preserved for the winter in a large stoneware pot, called a *potte* or *tinette*. The beans were peeled and washed then layered alternately with salt in the pot and covered with water and white vinegar, a plate placed on top to keep the beans submerged. The *potte* would then have been left in the cellar, or similar very cool place, to be dipped into when fresh vegetables were scarce. One of the few fresh regional winter vegetables was the black radish, which had the additional advantage of storing well for up to 4 months.

At one time, the larger coarser peas of the region were treated in the same way as beans, as they were more suited to eating dried than fresh. In the middle of the seventeenth century, however, the small tender green peas developed by Italian gardeners during the Renaissance were introduced, possibly by Catherine de' Medici's Italian chefs. The new variety were named *petits pois* in France to distinguish them from their fat cousins.

Italy was also the source of some of the virtual catalogue of fruits of which Touraine proudly boasts. For instance, Bon Chrétien pears arrived in the late fifteenth century at the Château de Plessis-les-Tours. The pear was introduced by Saint François de Paul. At the age of 70 he had been persuaded by the extremely ill Louis XI to leave Cantabria, in Italy, as the king believed the saint's prayers would improve his health. He was wrong, and he died in the saint's arms in 1483. However, the goodness of the saint's life was such that he was known as '*le bon chrétien*' (the good Christian), and the pear of which he was so fond was named after him.

In Blois, at the beginning of the sixteenth century, the greengage, or *reine-claude*, was also introduced from Italy and developed by Pierre Belon. It was originally known as the '*prune de la reine Claude*' (the plum of Queen Claude), because the first in France were served at the feast celebrating the wedding of locally born Claude, at the age of 15, to the future François I, and named in her honour. Later, in 1515, she became Queen of France and took the sweetly perfumed yellow-green, rose-flushed fruits to her heart. Not only did she have many trees planted herself, but she also encouraged others to grow them in warm sheltered sunny spots, and often even supplied the young saplings. There are other varieties of gages, such as the reine-claude de Bavay, bred by one of Napoleon Bonaparte's retired generals, which ripens later.

Ordinary plums arrived in the Loire much earlier than gages. Crusaders

Chocolat Poulain

The original chocolate factory was opened in Blois in 1848 by Auguste Poulain, in the days when its raw materials were brought up-river from Nantes. Poulain made a valiant attempt to

revive the shipping of the Loire as late as 1898. Only two battered chalands were still using the port, one selling pottery from Gien, the other bringing apples from Anjou. Poulain commissioned a special flat-bottomed, narrow-draught, 40 metre (130 foot) steam tug built at Nantes. For 10 years 'Fram' regularly chugged up and down to Nantes, bringing cocoa and sugar for the factory: seven tons in her own hold, seventy in the barge she towed.

No one else followed Poulain's example, and the company eventually had to revert to cheaper rail transport.

brought them back from Damascus, hence damascenes and damsons. The climate and soil were just right, and the trees flourished. Surplus fruit was dried and stored for winter use. The St-Catherine-de-Fierbois, also known as '*petit Damas*', was particularly popular for this purpose. By the sixteenth century, prunes from Touraine were much in demand in Paris, especially at Lent, and they were even mentioned by Rabelais.

However, growing plums and preparing prunes is not the most assured and profitable way of earning a living in an area where there is an easier livelihood to be gained from growing apples and pears. Long gone are the days when every country housewife gathered the plums from her own trees before sunrise, so they were still covered with dew, and then spread them on wicker trays to leave them in the sun to dry. The drying was completed by putting them each day in the dying heat of the old-style heavy ovens until they were '*demi-fraidi*', turning them from a plump rich purple to shiny, wrinkled and black. Small, golden, rose-flushed, juicy and tasty mirabelles were, and still are to a lesser extent, popular around Blois. They were at one time dried for sweetmeats called '*pistoles*'.

Melons were introduced into France somewhat earlier – by the Romans. The reputation of melons grown in the 'garden of France' began to take hold during the reign of Henry IV. This was perhaps due to the reputed practice of feeding the melons with honey-water! Langeais melons gained a reputation for themselves in Paris and elsewhere and they were given the nickname of '*sucrins*', derived from *sucre*. An entry in John Evelyn's diary, made during the summer of 1644 when he was staying at Tours, reads, 'We have now a store of those admirable melons, so much celebrated in France for the best in the kingdom.' Melons played such an important role within the community that three were incorporated into the town's coat-of-arms. Today, melons are grown on south-facing hillsides near Langeais, and you can buy them – still warm, succulent and sweet – from many roadside stalls or from local markets.

The traditional pastries of Touraine, *cordes* (small plaited discs), *russeroles* (fritters), *cassemuses* or *casse museaux* (muzzle breakers) – so called because of their hardness – and *fouaces*, date from the Middle Ages and the last two were mentioned by Rabelais. In one of his tales he tells of a confrontation between some *fouaciers* who were taking their wares to market in Parilly, near Chinon, just before the *vendange*, and some shepherds guarding the grapes against the depredations of birds. The shepherds tried to buy some of the *fouaces* but the *fouaciers* refused, very rudely, so a fight ensued. This won the shepherds their *fouaces* but resulted in a war.

Originally, *fouaces* were baked in the ashes in the hearth (*focus*, hence the name). Nowadays, they are baked in ovens, and basic recipes vary from characteristically Rabelaisian

(*Above*)
TUREENS, VOUVRAY
Chef-patron Bernard Copin of the *Auberge du Grand Vatel*, is President de la Touraine Gourmande, a group of restaurateurs whose aim it is to provide good quality local food.

(*Opposite*)
CHÂTEAU DE CHENONCEAU
When Catherine de' Medici took possession after the death of her husband, Henri II, her chefs introduced their own Italian ways and ingredients.

(Top and above)
GOATS' CHEESES
Ste-Maure (top) is the most well-known cheese of the region, helped in some large measure since 1974 by the efforts of members of the Commanderie de Ste-Maure de Touraine.

ingredients of butter, egg yolks, saffron and spices, to simple plain flat yeast cakes which are best eaten hot with butter or a rich soft cheese and, perhaps, some good home-made fruit *confiture*. *Fouaces* may be more interestingly flavoured with orange flower water, and I have also seen quite a number of 'fancy' yeast breads based on *fouace* dough.

In the heyday of the Loire river trade, because of the availability of the basic raw materials, several *chocolatiers* – including France's largest chocolate company, Poulain, whose advertising hoardings with their distinctive horse emblem will be familiar to anyone who has visited France – set up in business in Blois. To this day, the town is famous for its chocolate and chocolate confections and it still boasts several good *chocolatiers* and *pâtissiers*. Chocolate-lovers are particularly advised to take a stroll along the rue Denis-Papin. This road was named after a Blésois doctor and engineer who, realizing the potential of steam, created the pressure cooker. His '*marmite de Papin*' was originally intended as a means of extracting nourishment from bones by cooking them at temperatures above boiling point, but its full range of uses in cooking food developed later.

A local chemist, Jean-Antoine Chaptal, Comte de Chanteloup and one of Napoleon Bonaparte's ministers, developed the process of adding sugar to wine in order to strengthen it, and so immortalized his own name in the term 'chaptalization'. He also invented the process for extracting an inferior type of sugar from sugar beet when Napoleon's blockade of the West Indies resulted in shortages.

CHEESES

Driving through the region, especially in the south, the roadsides are dotted with signs announcing the sale of farm-made goats' cheese, leaving you in no doubt that Touraine is goats' cheese country. The cheeses can vary quite substantially, as can the farms. Some are very hygienic and organized; some milk by hand, others by machine; some keep the goats 'free-range', others house them under semi-intensive conditions in barns. Goats' cheese has been made here since at least the ninth century, when Charlemagne commented upon it, and later Rabelais recommended local '*talmouze aux fromages de bique*' while Balzac mentions the cheese of Ste-Maure. This town is still the centre of production, processing some 30,000 hectolitres (660,000 gallons) of goats' milk a year. Since the turn of the century, Friday has been the day local farm cheese-makers sell their products in its old market place. There is now also a cheese festival there during the first weekend in June.

Originally Ste-Maure cheese was made only on the Ste-Maure plateau in and around the town. Later it was also produced in Anjou, Charente and Poitou, with a resultant debasing of the quality and name. Since July 1990, however, it has been protected by an *appellation d'origine contrôlée* limiting its area of production. Produced both on farms and in factories, Ste-Maure is a log-shaped cheese, about 15 centimetres (6 inches) long and 3.5 centimetres (1½ inches) in diameter, with a typical, very white paste. The characteristic straw running lengthwise through each cheese was intended to prevent them from breaking up. Made from lightly salted fresh whole milk, it may be eaten fresh, after just 10 days, when it is soft and moist. It is '*demi-affiné*' after about three weeks maturing, or once it has developed a white downy surface; it then has a light texture and pleasantly mild flavour which is not at all goaty. Ste-Maures with a greyish rind are more mature cheeses, about 2 months old, and have a stronger, more distinctly goaty flavour. The logs may also be rolled in wood ash for Ste-Maure cendré.

Selles-sur-Cher is also protected by an AOC, but the area of permitted production extends beyond the small town after which it is named. Even so, it is quite strictly limited. The cheese is made in a disc, about 10 centimetres (4 inches) across and 3 centimetres (1¼ inches) high, and has a soft, light texture and an attractive mild fresh flavour. The cendré version is aged for longer and is a little smaller as a result (water is lost during storage). It has a firmer texture and a more pronounced taste. Valençay is a different shape again – a low truncated pyramid – and it has a richer texture and stronger flavour than Selles-sur-Cher.

Pouligny-St-Pierre is another farm-made *appellation contrôlée* cheese, pyramid-shaped. When young, the cheeses have a clean, slightly salty taste, with a hint of straw, but the flavour can become quite distinctive as they mature.

There are many more cheeses in various shapes – logs, cones, discs and drums – usually quite small, fresh and light-textured. They are produced in small quantities, as and when there is milk or when it is convenient to do so. Many farms make no attempt to sell their cheeses beyond displaying a roadside sign, so almost every time you buy goats' cheese or try some in a restaurant, you will have a completely new selection to choose from and wonderful new flavours to savour.

Wines

There are about 8-10,000 hectares (20-25,000 acres) of vines in Touraine, with wines from only about one-third to a half of this area entitled to the simple *appellation* 'Touraine'. They are generally light fruity wines, for serving chilled and quaffing on a warm summer's day. More red than white is made, although the latter is generally better. Most important, and usually most enjoyable, are the white sauvignon wines. Flowery, fresh, and at its best distinctly aromatic, Touraine Sauvignon can make a reasonable alternative to Sancerre and

PAUL BUISSE

Through four generations and for nearly 90 years, the fathers and sons of the Buisse family have been *négociants* in Touraine. The highly regarded company is concerned about quality, restricting their portfolio to the Loire and specializing in AOC wines.

Young wines are bought from selected independent *vignerons* and stored in tufa cellars. For the core *Cuvées Prestiges* range, hundreds of samples of wines are rigorously analysed and tasted by six professionals. The prides of the range, for which Paul Buisse has been responsible, are his *Cristal*, a very fine Sauvignon, and Chinon and Bourgueil *vieilli sous bois* (matured in old oak casks). These two demonstrate the ageing potential of good red Touraine wines.

CHÂTEAU DE MONCONTOUR
To produce clean, fresh tasting young white wines, cool, even temperatures and stainless steel vats (stainless steel is inert) are both necessary. At Château de Moncontour very large vats have recently been installed in the tufa caves, where the right conditions exist naturally.

Pouilly-Fumé, at a more affordable price. The red equivalent is Gamay de Touraine. Made from the same grape as Beaujolais, good examples can be equally fruity, but more sensibly priced. Chilled, they make good summer quaffing wines or accompaniments to casual summer foods and light meat or poultry dishes.

There is also a Touraine *appellation* for sparkling wine, both white and rosé, but many producers prefer to follow the stricter specifications required for Crémant de Loire, and so reap a greater profit.

The sites for the higher *appellation* red and white wines are divided by Tours, with red wines to the west and white wines to the east. Vouvray, the most famous white Touraine wine, comes from vineyards on the north bank of the Loire, and these produce some truly delicious wines – unfortunately, there are also some not very good ones.

The vines grow on limestone and tufa plateaux, which form such thick strata in places that not only are there wine cellars hewn out of the cliffs, but also three- and four-storey dwellings. In 1644, the diarist John Evelyn observed with amusement that he had seen plumes of smoke billowing from chimneys among the vines.

All Vouvray wines are made from chenin blanc, so have the characteristic fruity, flowery flavour underlined with an acidity that prevents them being cloying and gives them the ability to last and mature beautifully for many decades. However, Vouvray is made in every style, still and sparkling, from dry through several shades of sweetness to, in exceptional years, luscious sweet dessert (*moelleux*) wines. The degree of ripeness determines the potential style, but which style is made also depends on the wine-maker. *Moelleux* wines are labour-intensive, so costly to make, and, despite their high quality, have only a limited market. So only *vignerons* with an established reputation find them a commercial proposition.

Vouvray is served cool rather than heavily chilled, and the degree of sweetness usually governs the age at which it is drunk. Dry Vouvray can be drunk young, as an aperitif or first-course wine; medium-dry Vouvray about 3-4 years after the vintage, as an accompaniment to rich fish, such as salmon, and lightly creamy dishes. Sweet Vouvray, on the other hand, improves on keeping, maturing to a golden hue and developing the rich scent of quince and cooked plums that makes it delicious with fruit desserts, or sipped on its own. Sparkling Vouvray is made by the *méthode champenoise*, as is the slightly effervescent *pétillant*. Montlouis, on the opposite river bank, produces similar but lighter wines.

The best-known red wines of Touraine – indeed of the Loire – are produced west of Tours from the vineyards of Bourgueil, St-Nicolas-de-Bourgueil, and Chinon. They are made principally from cabernet franc, but up to 2% cabernet sauvignon is permitted. These three areas produce light, fruity red wines, in which some people claim to be able to detect nuances of raspberries, currants, wild strawberries and violets (although these attributes are only discernible in mature, well-made wines of good vintages).

Bourgueil wines have a tendency towards austerity, which makes them a little difficult to enjoy when young. Although sometimes drunk a year or two after the vintage, they are usually better if left for 5 years or more to allow them to soften to a more delicate fruitiness. St-Nicolas-de-Bourgueil wines are usually somewhat lighter, especially when young, although the subtle bouquet can develop with age.

There are two styles of Chinon, and both have greater finesse than either of the Bourgueils. On the hillside, the porous tufa subsoil produces firm, full-bodied wine which benefits from 3-4 years ageing and can last for up to 10; while the mixture of sand and gravel on the plain yields lighter wines ready for drinking sooner. With their balance of tannin and fruit, I find Chinon red wines particularly good for cooking. Beef and game dishes, for example, are lighter made with them than with Burgundy or claret-style wines.

Bourgueil, St-Nicolas-de-Bourgueil and Chinon also all produce dry rosés, and from Chinon there is also a rare white wine.

(*Below and below left*)
GASTON HUET

I have been drinking Gaston Huet's wines longer than any other Loire wines, as I knew early on that they could be superlative. Now with the assistance of his son-in-law Noel Pinguet, M. Huet makes all styles of Vouvray. Although all are excellent, he is particularly lauded for his sweet wines, especially the ambrosial *moelleux* wines made only in great years. Vouvray and Touraine wines generally owe Gaston Huet (the 't' is pronounced) a big vote of thanks, as he has travelled

tirelessly promoting them at the same time as his own wines. Moreover, the other wines must have benefited from the high calibre of his products. Now nearer 90 than 80, he has relinquished the post of Mayor of Vouvray he held for many years and does not jet across the Atlantic quite so often, but still lives life more fully and happily than many younger men.

SALADE DE RILLONS

(Illustrated above)

A mention of *rillons* never fails to have one of two effects on me: either sending me into a reverie as my mind flies to memories of Tourangeau days; or making me voluble, as I recount to anyone at hand the innumerable joys of the region.

As La Cave Martin (see opposite) is right in the heart of Touraine, it is not surprising that they know that the best way to serve *rillons* is on a bed of salad, accompanied by a crisp dry Touraine Sauvignon.

SERVES 4
55g/2oz pork fat or good-quality lard, diced
900g/2lb belly of pork, cut into chunks
6 allspice berries
1 bay leaf
1 sprig of thyme
4 tbsp light olive oil
1½ tbsp white wine vinegar
1 large pinch of chopped fresh herbs
1 tsp Dijon mustard
salt and freshly ground black pepper
a generous selection of well-flavoured salad leaves, to serve

Preheat the oven to 150C/300F/gas2.

Melt the pork fat or lard in an ovenproof dish large enough to hold the pork in a single layer. Add the pork and turn the pieces to coat them in the fat. Tuck in the allspice, bay leaf and thyme, and season. Pour in water to a depth of 5mm/¼in, cover the dish with foil and bake in the oven for about 3 hours, basting occasionally, until the pork is very tender.

Drain off the liquid (this can be strained and the fat separated from the water for use in cooking). Increase the oven temperature to 220C/425F/gas7 and return the pork to the oven until lightly browned. Remove it from the oven.

Make a dressing by whisking together the oil, vinegar, herbs and mustard and season well. Arrange the salad leaves on a large serving plate, place the *rillons* on top and trickle over the dressing.

RILLETTES

(Illustrated on page 66)

Rillettes are very easy to make at home. If sealed tightly with fat, they may be kept in the refrigerator for serving as a snack, as a first course or for a light lunch. Crisp dry Loire Sauvignon wines or dry Vouvrays are ideal accompaniments as they counterbalance the fattiness of the *rillettes* and add a contrasting fruitiness. The *rillettes* I make do not have as high a fat content as many found in France.

SERVES 6
115g/4oz pork back fat, chopped
1kg/2¼lb blade bone or belly of pork, plus some bones
1 shallot, chopped
1 sprig of thyme

1 bay leaf
pinch of quatre-épices
salt and freshly ground black pepper

Preheat the oven to 130C/275F/gas1. Put the fat into a heavy pot and place it in the oven until melted.

Cut the pork into small pieces then add to the fat with the bones, shallot, herbs, spices and seasoning and about 5 tablespoons of water. Leave to cook very slowly (the fat must not bubble) in the oven for about 4 hours, stirring occasionally, until the meat is almost falling apart. Add more water if it appears to get too dry.

Remove the bones and herbs. Strain the meat in a sieve and reserve the fat. Using a fork, tear the meat into fine shreds. Pack these into sterilized stoneware pots, leaving a little room for a sealing layer of fat.

Remove the reserved fat which will have settled out from the juices. Heat and pour over the *rillettes* to seal out the air.

Store in a cool place but bring to room temperature to serve.

TARTE TOURANGELLE

Rillettes Tart

The idea of a quiche-type flan containing *rillettes* was not one that immediately appealed to me as it seemed to have all the ingredients for a fatty but fairly flavourless mouthful. I avoided examples that looked as if they would live up to my expectations. However, when I saw Daniel Poirer's *tarte Tourangelle* in the covered market in Tours, I snapped up a portion and was very glad that I did, for it was well flavoured, light, and not at all greasy. The secret, of course, lies in the quality of the *rillettes*.

SERVES 4-6

FOR THE PÂTE BRISÉE

175g/6oz plain flour
115g/4oz unsalted butter, softened and chopped
2 egg yolks
salt

FOR THE FILLING

2 large eggs, beaten
85ml/3fl oz crème fraîche
100ml/3½fl oz milk
1½ tablespoons chopped parsley
2 teaspoons chopped chives
115g/4oz rillettes, *see left*
salt and freshly ground black pepper

Sift the flour and salt on to a work surface and form a well in the centre. Put in the butter and egg yolks, and quickly blend them together using the fingertips until the mixture looks like rough scrambled egg. Draw in the flour, chopping it through with a round-bladed knife. Draw it into a ball and knead. Then cover and chill for approximately 30 minutes.

On a lightly floured surface, roll out the pastry and use it to line a 20cm/8in flan tin. Prick the base and chill for a further 30 minutes.

Preheat the oven to 190C/375F/gas5 with a baking sheet inside it. Place the lined flan tin on the sheet and bake in the oven for 15 minutes.

Remove the flan tin from the oven. Lower the oven temperature to 180C/350F/gas4. Leave the pastry to cool down.

Beat together the eggs, crème fraîche, milk, herbs and seasoning. Roughly dot the *rillettes* over the bottom of the pastry case and spread them out. Place the flan tin on the hot baking sheet again. Pour over the egg mixture, then bake for 25-30 minutes, until just set in the centre.

Serve warm or at room temperature, but not chilled.

LA CAVE MARTIN

La Vallée Coquette
Vouvray
Tel 47 52 62 18
See recipe far left

La Cave Martin is tucked away on the hillside behind Vouvray, but signs from the N152 on the way to Tours show the way up the winding country lanes. Although Edith and Philippe Bellanger had no restaurant experience before they bought the *ferme auberge* in the early

1980s (they both worked in offices), their accomplished cooking of regional dishes, such as *andouillettes au Vouvray* and *rillons*, have made them firm favourites with local *vignerons*. The couple have an unusual working partnership – he cooks the main courses, while she does the first courses and desserts. Of note for the summer is a good-sized terrace outside.

BOUDINS BLANCS, POMMES EN L'AIR

White Sausages with Apple Slices

(Illustrated far right)

Boudins blancs are the classic white sausages found all over the Loire region. The recipe that follows serves them on a bed of glistening, golden apple slices that have been literally tossed 'in the air' – to prevent them from absorbing too much butter whilst they are fried. This is traditionally served as a first course, but it also makes an excellent light lunch.

MAKES ABOUT 14 10cm/4in SAUSAGES
55g/2oz crustless pain de campagne or similar white bread (not pre-sliced steam-baked bread), torn into pieces
115ml/4fl oz crème fraîche
1 grey or ordinary shallot or ½ a smallish onion, finely chopped
225g/8oz skinned chicken breast
175g/6oz pork back fat or skinned streaky pork
225g/8oz lean veal or pork, such as fillet end of leg
2 egg whites, lightly beaten
1 tablespoon chopped parsley
leaves from 2 sprigs of thyme, chopped
leaves from 2 sprigs of marjoram, chopped
1½ teaspoons chopped chives
pinch of quatre-épices or ground mace
salt and freshly ground black pepper
about 3.5m/3½yd of 225g/8oz sausage casings
milk, for poaching (optional)
unsalted butter, for frying
3 reinette apples, or Cox's Orange Pippins, peeled, cored and sliced

Soak the bread in the crème fraîche until thick and then beat until smooth. Mince the meats and fat together. Mix in the shallot or onion, the bread mixture, the egg whites, herbs and seasoning. Leave to stand in a cool place for about 3-4 hours then chill well.

Fill the sausage casings with the meat mixture, taking care not to over-fill them. Twist and tie at intervals of about 10cm/4in. Knot the ends.

To cook the sausages, bring to the boil a large saucepan of water or a mixture of 2 parts water to one part milk. Lower the heat so that the water is just simmering, add the *boudins* and gently poach for about 10-12 minutes. Prick carefully with the point of a needle as they rise to the surface. Drain well and cool quickly.

Next day, separate them into individual sausages, brush with melted butter and grill, turning frequently, until heated through; or fry in butter until an even light golden brown. Transfer to a warmed plate, cover and keep warm.

If you have fried the sausages you can use the same pan to fry the apples, although you may need to add more butter; if you have grilled them, melt some butter in a frying pan. When hot, add the apple slices and cook quite briskly until light golden brown on one side. Turn them over and cook on the other side.

Transfer the apple slices to a serving plate or dish. Either place the sausages on top of the apples, or serve them separately.

(Right)
White Sausages served with Apple Slices (this page), and Brioches au Fromage Frais de Chèvre *(page 91). In a region where there seem to be more goats than cows, fresh goats' cheese may replace the butter usually used in the making of brioche. With a slight savouriness and light delicate crumb, the result is quite delicious.*

FÈVES À LA TOURANGELLE

Broad Beans with Ham

(Illustrated on page 87)

Some versions of this dish use a glass of white Touraine wine instead of the bean cooking water, but if you are using the fresh young beans for which this recipe is intended, I think the wine detracts from the flavour of the vegetables.

Serve this dish as an accompaniment to plainly cooked meats or poultry, as a first course or for a light supper dish with good buttered bread.

SERVES 4
225g/8oz shelled young broad beans
70g/2½oz unsalted butter
150g/5oz belly of pork or piece of streaky bacon, diced
24 small onions
2 egg yolks, beaten
1 tablespoon chopped mixed summer savory, chervil and parsley
salt and freshly ground black pepper

Boil the beans in salted water for 5 minutes. Drain, reserving the liquor.

Meanwhile, melt the butter in a large heavy-based pan over a low heat. Add the pork or bacon and the onions and cook gently, shaking the pan occasionally, for about 10 minutes without allowing the onions to colour. Add the beans and enough of their cooking liquor almost to cover, reserving the rest, and simmer gently until the vegetables are just tender and most of the liquid evaporated.

Blend 2 tablespoons of reserved bean liquid into the egg yolks. Over a low heat, stir this mixture into the beans. Cook gently, stirring, until lightly thickened. Stir in the herbs and adjust the seasoning.

CARDONS TOURANGEAUX AU GRATIN

Cardoons with Mushrooms

After initial boiling to make them tender, cardoons are usually finished in some other way, such as simply sautéing them in butter for 10-15 minutes, perhaps with a final sprinkling of herbs, or dressing them with a béchamel sauce. They may also be cooked, as here, layered with mushrooms – a vegetable with which they have an affinity. I always serve this as a simple light meal, but it can be a vegetable accompaniment to fish or meat.

SERVES 4-5
1kg/2¼lb cardoons
juice of 1 lemon
150g/5oz large mushrooms, preferably chestnut or brown cap, finely chopped
3-4 tablespoons dry breadcrumbs
115g/¼lb unsalted butter
salt and freshly ground black pepper

Discard the coarse outer leaves and 'strings' from the cardoons. Separate the outer stems from the heart. Cut the stalks into 5-8cm/2-3in lengths.

Cook the pieces of cardoon in lightly salted water acidulated with some of the lemon juice for about 25 minutes. Drain and refresh under cold running water.

Preheat the oven to 180C/350F/gas4.

Chop some of the outer stalks finely and mix together with the chopped mushrooms and seasoning. Layer this mixture with the remaining cardoons in a buttered ovenproof dish. Cover with breadcrumbs.

Melt the butter with a little lemon juice, pour over the breadcrumbs and put into the oven for about 25 minutes until lightly browned and crisp.

CÔTES DE BLETTE AU GRATIN

Swiss Chard Ribs with Eggs and Cheese

Swiss chard, or *blettes* or *côtes de blettes*, is popular locally. An old Tourangeau name is *poirée à carde*, which refers to the preferred rib section of the leaf, without its green ruff. Here tangy *chèvre* cheese transforms it into a rich first course, or an accompaniment for plainly cooked meats.

SERVES 4
900g/2lb Swiss chard
2 egg yolks
300ml/10fl oz crème fraîche
40g/1½oz unsalted butter
85g/3oz soft goats' cheese, chopped
salt and freshly ground black pepper

Strip the green leaves from the chard ribs and keep for another dish (see page 55, or use them in place of spinach). Remove the strings and the white covering skin from the ribs. Slice the ribs into 4-5cm/1½-2in lengths.

Blend the egg yolks with 1 tablespoon of crème fraîche.

Melt the butter in a casserole, add the chard ribs, cover and cook gently for 15 minutes, then add the remaining crème fraîche and cook for a further 10 minutes, uncovered. Add the cheese and heat gently until the cheese has just melted into the crème fraîche.

Preheat a hot grill. Remove the casserole from the heat and immediately stir in the egg yolk mixture gently. Season, using little salt but plenty of black pepper. Transfer to a gratin dish and place under the hot grill until lightly browned.

CARPE À LA CHAMBORD

Carp with Red Wine

Carpe à la Chambord is a dish of the classic French culinary repertoire. It was devised by Catherine de' Medici's Italian chefs in the kitchens at the Château de Chambord to moisten the compact flesh of the locally abundant carp, and to introduce flavour, for carp, although it can be insipid, does absorb other flavours well.

The dish involves stuffing a carp with veal or whiting forcemeat, larding the fish with bacon and braising it in red wine with herbs and a *mirepoix*. A sauce is then made from the cooking liquid to accompany the fish. However, if you see *carpe à la Chambord* on a menu nowadays it is unlikely to be the classic dish. It will probably be a portion of carp simply served with a red wine sauce, *beurre rouge* (*beurre blanc* made with red wine instead of white), or perhaps braised in red wine. If a stuffing is included, it will probably be the same type of mixture as that used in *quenelles*, a light fish and cream mousse. *Saumon à la Chambord* usually means portions of salmon, such as steaks, served with a red wine sauce; the fish may also, perhaps, have been cooked in red wine.

This version of *carpe á la Chambord* is a successful compromise for modern tastes and practicalities.

SERVES 4

1 carp, weighing about 1.5kg/3½lb, cleaned, trimmed and scaled
1 piece of bacon weighing about 85g/3oz, cut across into strips
150g/5oz unsalted butter, diced
85g/3oz mixed diced vegetables, including carrots, shallots and leeks
425ml/15fl oz Gamay de Touraine
1 bouquet garni
salt and freshly ground black pepper

Using the point of a sharp knife, make small incisions in the flesh of the fish. Then insert a piece of bacon into each cut. Sprinkle the fish with freshly ground black pepper.

In a heavy-based pan or flameproof casserole large enough to hold the fish, melt 25g/1oz of the butter. Add the vegetables and cook slowly for about 4 minutes until softened.

Stir in the wine, bring to the boil then adjust the heat so the liquid is barely simmering. Add the carp, bouquet garni and more black pepper and cook the carp gently for about 25 minutes, or until the flesh near the bone just flakes when tested with the point of a sharp knife. Carefully transfer the fish to a warmed plate and keep warm. Bring the liquid to the boil, skim the surface, then boil until reduced by about one-third.

Strain, then reheat but do not boil, and gradually whisk in the remaining butter. Taste and adjust the seasoning, then serve with the carp.

(Left)
Usually rainfall is adequate to ensure that fruit and vegetables thrive, but in drought years artificial watering may be needed. Successive dry summers can leave the Loire itself dismally low.

(Above)
Serious fishing is still a reality and can bring in a pleasurable income, as Loire fish are highly prized in the region and much in demand, with top restaurants willing to pay top prices to be able to add the captivating words 'du Loire' after the fish on their menus.

FILETS DE PERCHE À LA PURÉE D'ORTIES

Perch Fillets with Nettle Purée

Having a late picnic breakfast one clear spring morning, I absent-mindedly watched a fisherman casting into the Cher, but didn't take much notice. After making one catch, he pulled on a glove, wandered to some clumps of young nettles in the hedges near the river bank, and very carefully selected small leaves from the tops of young shoots. Obviously they were not for feeding to an animal. He returned to his fishing.

Intrigued, I ambled up and wheedled my way into idle conversation. The nettles were to make a sauce to accompany the perch he had just caught. His grandmother always prepared a similar sauce in the spring because she maintained that nettles were a good spring-time tonic, being rich in vitamins and minerals. He liked to wait until perch came back into season, because he thought the salty, tangy flavour of the nettles made such a good combination with the flavour of the fish.

When tiny flowers start to appear on the nettles the flavour changes and they no longer make good eating.

SERVES 4
40g/1½oz unsalted butter
2 small shallots, finely chopped
55g/2oz tender young nettle leaves, finely chopped
55ml/2fl oz medium-bodied dry white wine
55ml/2fl oz fish stock
150ml/5fl oz crème fraîche
800g/1¾lb perch fillets, skinned and carefully boned
salt and freshly ground black pepper

Melt half the butter in a heavy-based saucepan over a low heat, add the shallots and cook gently, stirring occasionally, until softened. Add the nettles and continue to cook gently for 1 minute.

Stir in the wine and stock and boil until reduced by half. Add the crème fraîche and reduce until lightly thickened.

Purée, strain if liked, and season. Reheat gently.

Melt the remaining butter in a frying pan over a medium heat, add the perch and cook for 1 minute on each side. Season, place on warmed plates and pour the sauce over.

COURGETTES FLEURS FARCIES

Stuffed Courgette Flowers

(Illustrated opposite)

Tours is a very busy university city, with a fast link to Paris (1 hour 40 minutes by TGV), yet it is possible to bask in clear warm sunshine on the terrace of Jean Bardet's restaurant (see page 84) eating vegetables grown within a few yards and packed with bright flavours. To devise this recipe for pike-perch, he needed to look no further than his own garden for home-grown courgette plants, vegetables and beautiful sun-ripened tomatoes. In my city garden the air is so smog-filtered that my tomatoes and herbs never develop much flavour.

SERVES 6

about 450-550g/1-1¼lb wild pike-perch or salmon fillet, cut into 18 pieces
18 courgette flowers, stamens removed
100g/3½oz unsalted butter
100g/3½oz carrots, finely chopped
100g/3½oz onions, finely chopped
100g/3½oz white part of leek, finely chopped
100g/3½oz celery, finely chopped
175ml/6fl oz white wine or fish stock
12 slim courgettes, halved
salt and freshly ground black pepper
peeled tomatoes, to garnish

Season the fish and place a piece carefully inside each courgette flower.

Melt 25g/1oz of the butter in a sauté pan, add all the vegetables except the courgettes, and cook, stirring occasionally, until softened but not coloured.

Add the wine or stock and boil until reduced by half. Pass through a fine sieve. Return to the clean pan. Heat to just below a simmer, carefully add the courgette flowers and cook gently for about 3 minutes. Transfer to warmed plates.

Meanwhile, blanch the courgettes in boiling salted water. Drain, refresh under cold running water, drain well again and thinly slice lengthwise, cutting almost through to the end. Melt 40g/1½oz of the butter in a frying pan, add the courgettes and heat through. Fan out on the plates with the flowers. Swirl the remaining butter into the juices in the sauté pan then pour this sauce over the plates.

Garnish with peeled tomatoes.

JEAN BARDET **

57 rue Groison, Tours
Tel 47 41 41 11
See recipes on page 82-3 and right

Jean Bardet, with his engaging and unpretentious enthusiasm,

so obviously appreciates the good things in life. Although he comes from Charente, he loves living and working in Touraine, because of the wide range of excellent local produce and wines available.

Since 1989 he has turned his attention to the garden that surrounds his hotel and restaurant in the middle of Tours. He and his three gardeners have successfully grown over 60 different herbs and many varieties of vegetables and fruits. Eels and carp are stocked in one of the ponds and wildfowl swim on another. He also keeps a pig and some plump chickens and geese. He serves his *amuse-bouches* (above) on spoons as an *hors d'œuvre*.

BROCHET RÔTI AU FOUR, AU VIN DE NOIX

Roast Pike with Walnuts

(Illustrated left)

Jean Bardet of the eponymous restaurant in Tours (see far left) cooks the potatoes for this dish in goose fat, giving them a particularly rich flavour which complements the leanness of the pike; failing that use duck or good pork back fat. He also uses *eau-de-noix des Pères Chartreux*, a deliciously versatile drink well worth adding to the shopping list when in France. A similar home-made liqueur can be prepared by steeping 12 fresh peeled walnuts in 450ml/16fl oz brandy for 2 months. At the end of this time, add 175g/6oz sugar, leave for a further month, then strain and re-bottle.

SERVES 4

85g/3oz goose fat, duck fat or pork back fat
550g/1¼lb potatoes, sliced, rinsed and dried
1 onion, finely chopped
2 fresh small bay leaves, cut into strips
salt and freshly ground black pepper
55g/2oz unsalted butter
4 pike fillets
350ml/12fl oz fish stock
about 3 tablespoons eau-de-noix
45g/1½oz walnuts, chopped
lemon juice
fresh bay leaves, to garnish

Preheat the oven to 180C/350F/gas4.

Heat 55g/2oz of the fat in a flameproof dish, add the potatoes, onion and bay leaves. Season, place a knob of butter in the centre then brown in the oven.

Heat the remaining fat in a frying pan over a medium heat, add the pike and cook for about 2 minutes on each side until lightly golden. Season, place on the potatoes and cook in the oven for a further 10 minutes.

Meanwhile, melt 25g/1oz butter in a heavy-based saucepan, add the nuts and cook for 1-2 minutes. Pour in the stock and boil until reduced by about half. Add *eau-de-noix* to taste and boil briefly to obtain a light sauce. Over a low heat, swirl in the remaining butter. Season and add lemon juice to 'lift' the flavour.

Transfer the potatoes and fish to 4 warmed plates, then pour the sauce over. Garnish with the fresh bay leaves.

MATELOTE

Fish in Wine

Matelotes are found all along the Loire and date from the days when it was an important commercial route. They were originally served to the Loire boatmen (*matelot* means sailor or mariner) when they tied up in the small ports or at the many riverside hotels and restaurants.

A *matelote* is not a soup. It is more like a stew in that the liquid should be concentrated and full of flavour; but the fish should be lightly cooked, not 'stewed'.

Matelotes are most often associated with eels, but they may contain almost any freshwater fish; they may even contain veal, as in *Matelote des Tonneliers*, (page 118). The wine will be that produced locally, so it may be red or white, crisp, or full and fruity, with each type changing the character of the *matelote*. Additional ingredients may simply be onions and mushrooms, there may also be bacon, and sometimes prunes are popped in, usually if eel is the fish; if the wine is red, this variation is sometimes called *bouilleture*.

SERVES 4

1.35kg/3lb mixed freshwater fish such as young eel, carp, tench, perch and trout
85g/3oz unsalted butter
1 onion, sliced
1 carrot, sliced
450ml/15fl oz dry Vouvray
bouquet garni consisting of 2 sprigs each of parsley and thyme, a sprig of tarragon and 1 bay leaf
about 85g/3oz button mushrooms
salt and freshly ground black pepper
chopped chervil or parsley, to garnish

Fillet, trim, scale and gut the fish. Cut them into 4cm/1½in pieces, reserving the bones, skins and heads. Melt 55g/2oz of the butter in a wide, shallow pan. Add the onion and carrot and cook over a fairly low heat, stirring occasionally, until the onion has softened.

Stir in the fish bones, skins and heads to coat them with butter, then add the wine, herbs, seasoning and 300ml/10fl oz water. Bring to the boil, skim, then simmer until reduced and well flavoured (no more than 20 minutes at the most!). Remove the fish heads, skins and bones.

Adjust the heat so bubbles are just breaking on the surface of the liquid, then add the fish in the order given, allowing the liquid to return to its original temperature before adding the next fish. Cook gently for about 8-10 minutes, until the flesh just flakes easily.

Meanwhile, melt the remaining butter in another pan, add the mushrooms and cook, tossing occasionally, for 4 minutes.

Discard the bouquet garni from the *matelote*. Serve in warmed wide bowls, with the mushrooms and chervil or parsley scattered over the top.

If liked, the *matelote* can be finished by swirling in some extra diced butter, or crème fraîche, just before serving.

POULET AU TILLEUL

Chicken with Lime Blossom

Among my collection of 'heavenly memories' is that of wandering in the late spring in eastern Touraine through country lanes lined with smooth-barked lime trees, the sun dappling through the widely spreading branches and teasing the rich fragrance from the greeny-yellowish flowers. We gathered the winged flowers (*tilleul*), which were then at their sweetest, and took them home. Some were used immediately to make lightly honeyed *tisanes*, the rest were spread out on a wire rack covered with muslin (thick paper or cardboard may be used instead) and left in the warm dry air during 2 or 3 weeks of perfect weather until they rustled.

They were then popped into a paper bag and placed inside a polythene bag to be taken back home for re-creations of the subtly flavoured chicken dish we had eaten 'on the spot'.

SERVES 4-5

3 or 4 large handfuls of dried lime blossom, weighing about 55g/2oz
1 traditional free-range chicken, dressed weight about 1.8kg/4lb

Put the lime blossom into a heavy saucepan or flameproof casserole large enough to hold the chicken. Place the chicken, breast-side down, on the flowers then add enough water to cover.

Bring just to a simmer. Adjust the heat so the liquid is only just on the point of bubbling, cover tightly and poach gently for 15 minutes.

Remove the pan or casserole from the heat and leave to cool completely. Don't worry: the chicken will be cooked through. In fact, it should be ready to eat after about 1¾ hours but I think it is most delicious when served cold.

Lift the chicken from the liquor, tipping any juices out of the bird's cavity. Cover and put in a cool place. Pour the cooking liquid into a wide frying pan or roasting tin and boil hard until well reduced. Pour into a shallow container and leave to cool. Then place in the refrigerator to set to a light jelly, which may be broken up and served with the chicken.

VARIATION

Sometimes, I use the jelly in a delicate, light-textured sauce to complement the chicken. When about 85ml/3fl oz of the reduced liquid is just on the point of setting, add it to 85ml/3fl oz lightly whipped crème fraîche along with 2 tablespoons mild but high quality mayonnaise. Whip lightly, cover, and chill slightly.

GÉLINE LOCHOISE

Poached Chicken

(Illustrated far right)

Géline is the old Tourangeaux name for an old-fashioned breed of small, black, highly prized chicken. They now seem to have disappeared and the *patte noire* has taken over in the area as the chicken to choose for flesh that is particularly fine and white.

This recipe from Loches, in which the chicken is poached in milk, is ideal as it preserves the colour and delicate flavour of the flesh. A little fresh tarragon added with the crème fraîche adds a charming nuance, and button mushrooms give greater complexity.

SERVES 4

40g/1½oz unsalted butter
1 chicken, dressed weight about 1.5kg/3½lb, cut into pieces
1 small onion, finely chopped
about 700ml/1¼pt milk
about 700ml/1¼pt chicken stock
a bouquet garni consisting of 1 sprig of thyme, 1 sprig of parsley and 1 small bay leaf
3 tablespoons crème fraîche or double cream
salt and freshly ground white pepper

Melt the butter in a heavy flameproof casserole into which the chicken will just fit when packed in. Add the onion and cook over a low heat, stirring occasionally, until softened but not browned. Stir in the milk, increase the heat and boil quite hard for 4-5 minutes. Add 225ml/8fl oz of the stock and return to the boil.

Season the chicken portions, and add to the casserole with the bouquet garni and just enough stock to cover the chicken. Adjust the heat to very low, so the liquid barely moves, and cook gently for about 45 minutes until the chicken is very tender.

Remove the chicken from the casserole and keep warm. Discard the bouquet garni. Strain the cooking liquid, if liked, and press the onion through a sieve back into the liquid. Boil it hard until reduced to about 225ml/8fl oz.

Stir the crème fraîche into the cooking liquid and bring to the boil. Simmer until slightly thickened. Adjust the seasoning. Coat the chicken with the sauce to serve.

(Right, left to right)
Broad Beans with Ham (page 80), and Poached Chicken (this page).

LE FIG
premier quotidien
URSS
Gorbatchev

PÊCHES TOURANGELLES À LA ROYALE

Poached Peaches with Raspberry Sauce

(Illustrated right)

Sun-ripened peaches and sweet raspberries from Touraine's fertile soil and long summer days give the true regional flavour to this dish. Recipes specifying raspberry jam or redcurrant jelly, instead of fresh berries, are 'interlopers' from elsewhere or appropriate to other seasons.

SERVES 4
4 ripe peaches
about 225g/8oz vanilla sugar
strip of lemon peel
450-550g/1-1¼lb fresh raspberries
55ml/2fl oz crème fraîche

Pour boiling water over the peaches and leave for about 10-20 seconds. Lift the fruit from the water and peel off the skins. Cut the fruit in half and remove the stones.

Put the peach halves in a saucepan and add just enough water to cover them. Add 85g/3oz sugar for every 575ml/1pt of water, and the lemon peel. Bring to a simmer and poach the peach halves in this syrup for 5 minutes until tender. Using a slotted spoon, remove the peaches and allow them to cool. Then place them in a dish, cover and chill.

Press the raspberries through a non-metallic sieve, reserving a few whole for garnish. Whip the crème fraîche until it stands in soft peaks, then add vanilla sugar to taste. Stir in the raspberry purée. Add more sugar, if necessary.

Serve the peaches with the sauce poured over. Garnish with the reserved raspberries.

MACARONS DE CORMERY

Macaroons

(Illustrated right)

Macaroons are of course made in many places, but those of Cormery, or, more specifically, the abbey there, are legendary. A hot ember that jumped from the fire and burned a hole in the cook-monk's habit, exposing his navel, was read by the abbot as a sign from Saint Paul to help him distinguish the abbey's macaroons from those of local bakers who were cashing in on their popularity. From then on, the abbey's macaroons were distinguished by a swirl in the centre.

MAKES 20-25
115g/4oz almonds, blanched and ground
175g/6oz vanilla caster sugar
½ teaspoon rice flour or cornflour
2 egg whites
sheets of rice paper

Preheat the oven to 190C/375F/gas5.

Mix the almonds, sugar and rice flour or cornflour in a bowl. Add the egg whites and, using a wooden spoon, mix all the ingredients together. Leave for a few minutes, then beat again briefly.

Lay sheets of rice paper, rough side down, on baking sheets. Using a teaspoon, place small mounds of the almond mixture on the rice paper, allowing plenty of room between them. Mark a small swirl in the top of each mound.

Bake in the oven for 15-20 minutes, until light and dry on the outside but still slightly tacky in the centre.

Carefully remove each macaroon from the rice paper. Leave to cool on a wire rack. Serve with cool crème fraîche or *fromage blanc* and fresh juicy strawberries.

TARTE AUX POIRES

Pear Tart

(Illustrated right)

There are innumerable versions of pear tart: large, small, round, rectangular; some with sliced fruit, others using halved pears; some with a cushion of custard beneath the pears, others with the fruit sitting directly on the pastry. They may even be embedded in a luscious almond mixture, as here. To make a tart which is more easily divided into smaller portions, slice the pears after poaching and before sprinkling with the alcohol, and then arrange the slices in even concentric rows on the pastry.

SERVES 8-10

FOR THE PÂTE SUCRÉE

200g/7oz plain flour
25g/1oz vanilla icing sugar
2 egg yolks
100g/3½oz unsalted butter, softened and chopped

FOR THE FILLING

1 egg white, beaten
240g/8½oz vanilla caster sugar
2 ripe but firm Williams or Comice pears
3 tbsp eau-de-vie de poire Williams
150g/5oz unsalted butter, softened
4 egg yolks
115g/4oz blanched almonds, ground
2½ tbsp plain flour

Sift the flour and sugar on to a work surface and form a well in the centre. Put in the butter and egg yolks, and quickly blend them together using the fingertips until the mixture looks something like rough scrambled egg. Draw in the flour, chopping it through with a round-bladed knife. Draw it into a ball and knead. Cover and chill for 30 minutes.

On a lightly floured surface, roll out the pastry and use to line a 25cm/10in flan ring. Prick the base of the pastry case and chill for a further 15-30 minutes.

Preheat the oven to 200C/400F/gas6, with a baking sheet inside. Place the flan tin on the hot baking sheet and bake blind in the oven for 15 minutes. Remove the paper, brush the pastry with the egg white and leave to cool. Reduce the oven temperature to 180C/350F/gas4.

Meanwhile, gently heat 115g/4oz sugar in 850ml/1½pt water, stirring occasionally until dissolved, then bring to the boil. While the syrup is coming to the boil, peel, halve and core the pears. Lower them into the boiling syrup and poach them for about 5 minutes. Using a slotted spoon, transfer the pears to a bowl and sprinkle over the *poire Williams*. Leave to cool.

Beat together the butter and remaining sugar until light and fluffy, then gradually beat in the egg yolks. Lightly fold in the ground almonds and flour. Drain the liquor from the pears and stir 1½ tablespoons of it into the almond mixture. Pour this into the pastry case, reserving the remaining liquor. Arrange the pears on the almond mixture and press them down well. Bake in the oven for about 15-20 minutes until the filling is lightly set and browned. When cooked, sprinkle over the reserved pear liquor and serve the tart warm or cold.

Brioche au Fromage Frais de Chèvre

(Illustrated on page 79)

SERVES 6-8
350g/12oz strong plain flour
pinch of salt
1 packet easy-blend yeast
1-1½ tablespoons milk
175g/6oz fresh goats' cheese or well-drained fromage blanc
3 eggs, beaten
oil, for greasing
butter, for greasing

Stir together the flour, salt and yeast. Form a well in the centre. Gradually stir the milk into the goats' cheese or *fromage blanc*, followed by the eggs. Then add this to the well in the flour and gradually draw the ingredients together. Turn out on a work surface and knead until you have a firm and elastic dough.

Place in a lightly oiled bowl, cover and leave to rise until doubled in volume. Turn out on a lightly floured surface and punch down.

Break off a quarter of the dough and form it into a ball. Form the larger piece into a ball as well, place this in a buttered brioche tin, and sit the smaller ball firmly on top of it; or you can put the dough into the tin in one piece. Leave to rise again, until the dough has doubled in volume.

Preheat the oven to 190C/375F/gas5. Bake the brioche in the oven for about 30 minutes, until the brioche is golden on top and sounds hollow when tapped. Leave in the tin for a few minutes to cool, then turn out on a wire rack.

LAND OF PLENTY

THROUGH ANJOU, CURNONSKY'S 'PARADISE FOR PEACEFUL DIGESTION'

TOURAINE ALMOST IMPERCEPTIBLY BECOMES ANJOU: IN MANY WAYS, ESPECIALLY WHERE THE TWO REGIONS MERGE INTO EACH OTHER, ANJOU SEEMS LIKE A continuation of Touraine. It has a similar gentle climate and lovely green country, and is well endowed with orchards, market gardens and vineyards. However, there are differences in the country, people and the food, and each region has its own identity.

The Loire broadens as it approaches the end of its journey. Downstream from Angers, which is not actually on the Loire proper but on the Maine just before it flows into the Loire, one is aware that the sea is not too far away. On the uplands, away from the Loire, the landscape opens into wide lush green fields, and the sight of brown, brown-and-white and black-and-white cows grazing contentedly serves to remind the visitor of the importance of cattle-raising to the economy of region.

(Opposite) A wonderful, lazy way to spend a day – whether fishing on the boat itself, or idly watching from the bank.
(Above) Apples have been an important crop in Anjou for centuries, and are now big business, for in recent years new pruning and cultivation techniques have considerably increased yields.

1 Flowers grown for cutting near Saumur. **2** Many small farms rear ducks for making foie gras and products such as confits. **3** Decorative ironwork on a gate near Saumur. **4** A hay barn on the road to Doué-la-Fontaine. **5** A hard-working country couple, still following the life-style of their forebears. **6** Painted panels in a boulangerie/pâtisserie in Angers. **7** The sight of many varieties of cabbages growing is a common one in Anjou, whilst a repertoire of magnificent cabbage dishes grace every table, from the humblest to the grandest. **8** Signs directing the way to home-made foie gras et ses dérivés can be seen around the countryside. **9** Strawberries are a lucrative crop in the Val-de-Loire. Sadly for the look of the countryside, they are often now grown under glass or plastic tunnels. **10** Many Angevins consider shallots to be an essential flavouring in many a truly traditional regional recipe. **11** Apples on a market stall.

1	**2**	**3**	**4**	**5**
6	**7**	**8**		
		9	**10**	**11**

(Overleaf)
NAPKINS
A restaurant's napkins are hung out to dry against a background of sunflowers.

FOIE GRAS
et ses dérivés
Ici
L. Maudet
LA PETITE FERME

Nearer the river, the fields are smaller and surrounded by low walls of the characteristic white, soft, chalky, volcanic tufa, and the houses are topped by slated roofs. Slate was originally worked by open-cast methods from the sixteenth century onwards. It was first mined in 1830, from subterranean galleries some 350 metres (1,000 feet) underground. Trélazé, near Angers, was once a world centre of the slate industry.

Angevins are easy-going, with a relaxed attitude to time which can take a little getting used to – a '*quart d'heure Angevin*' is generally considered to last at least 30 minutes. As Anjou generally has a touch less culture than Touraine, and is not quite as sophisticated, the cooking is more homely and rural.

The Loire in Anjou also has its tributaries, although they are smaller than those in Touraine. To the north, there are the Oudon, the Mayenne, the Sarthe and the Loir, which unite to form the Maine. To the south there are the Layon, the Thouet and the Dive, which join together south of Saumur. There are also some differences between the fish of the two regions. For example, perch, bream and carp are Tourangeaux fish, while pike and shad are said to be better in Anjou than Touraine. As they are nearer the sea and thus plumper (they do not feed on their way upstream), salmon fished from the Loire as it flows through Anjou are often considered to be superior to those caught in Tourangeaux waters.

Pike is gastronomically important in the Loire, and the most likely places to find it are the slack areas of the Loir, Thouet and Aubance, and off the many small islands found in the Loire. Although an angler's favourite, its popularity with eaters has declined because of the multitude of small bones and the occasional muddy taste which occurs if the fish has been feeding in slow-moving or unclear waters and has not been flushed through thoroughly before cooking. Summer visitors should not expect too much if they try the local *brochet*, as it is at its best in the autumn and early winter. At these times, the flavour of the lean firm flesh can be good, although it may be a little dry and dull if the fish is large. For this reason, it is often puréed with cream to make *quenelles*, or served with rich sauces.

Unable to sleep one warm starry night, I took a stroll by the Loire and almost literally stumbled across a fisherman. I am not sure which of us was more surprised, but he was the more loquacious as he gave vent to his irritation in a barely suppressed whisper. Realizing that the clumsy intruder was an Englishwoman interested in what he was doing – and in food – the other side of the true Frenchman took over and I was treated to a lengthy explanation of fishing together with a glass of his wine. Apparently fishing is not just the daytime activity I believed it to be, for it is not uncommon for local fishermen, along almost all of the region's rivers, to spend their nights peering through the darkness in quest of a shoal of the small fish that are the prey of the highly regarded pike-perch, or zander. As pike-perch can be farmed, do ask about its origins if you want to be certain of having the genuine Loire fish – the flavour of farmed fish lacks the distinction of that of the wild type.

In the spring, shad swim up the Loire from the sea to spawn. This is the time when the fish is most often served, as the roe is full and the time spent in fresh water has converted its

FRUIT TARTS
With a wide range of fruits, fillings, glazes and recipes for pastry, and the innumerable computations of these, the number of different fruit tarts is legion.

flesh from being relatively ordinary to being plump and moist, with a delicious fine flavour. Shad is a member of the herring family, albeit a somewhat superior one. Indeed its firm white flesh has such a fine flavour that it is known as the 'king of herrings'. Shad does have two of the characteristics of herring which some people consider drawbacks: it is quite a rich fish (but these days we are being urged to eat oily fish for the sake of our hearts), and it contains a large number of small bones. The tradition of marrying shad with sorrel, either in the form of a purée or a stuffing, helps to negate both these problems. Sorrel has the ability to dissolve small bones, and its acidity counterbalances the fish's richness.

Spring is also the time to enjoy the eels which swim up the Loire, and along just about every other river in the area. Eels feed at any time of day or night on almost every kind of aquatic creature, including fish. With a little cunning, therefore, it is relatively easy to catch one without a rod and line, although a fully grown eel is quite a handful. The canny Angevin practice is either to look carefully in likely places such as roots of weed beds, overhanging clumps of weeds, twigs and dead leaves, or to build an obstruction of twigs and weeds which will contain aquatic insects and encourage shoals of small fish to form. The obstruction is then lifted out of the water, and eels come with it. They are quickly extricated and placed on a sheet of newspaper spread out in expectation – this is the surest way of keeping eels still, the sticky adhesive effect of their mucous covering discouraging movement.

In the 4,000 kilometres (2,600 miles) of Angevin rivers there are also plenty of small fry, such as gudgeon and bleak, for the fisherman's line and the cook's frying pan.

Grown in the fertile land that stretches a mile or two on either side of the rivers are the fruits and vegetables which form the heart of Anjou cuisine. Both have become big business – but fruit is particularly successful. Some large companies are involved, and many growers have formed themselves into cooperatives. Much money and effort is put into tailoring the cultivation of fruit to the most appropriate areas, researching new varieties and crosses, reducing disease susceptibility and improving handling and storage.

For a reminder that the fruit trade here is not a recent phenomenon, visit the village of Le Thoureil, near Gennes. This was once a river port from where locally grown apples were shipped, and the church tower had a light that guided the boats ashore on dark evenings.

Traditional standard trees have largely been replaced by espaliers as they make far better sense commercially. I don't think they make such an impressive sight when they are in bloom. Nevertheless, Anjou in the spring is glorious – there are even some signposted 'blossom routes'. Walking by the orchards, observing the differing shades, shapes and densities of blossom is one of the most relaxing and revitalizing experiences I know. Throughout the season, there is a succession of colours, hues and types of blossom, as different fruits and different varieties don their frilly spring outfits. This may be seen not only in the regimented orchards but in the hedgerows, which are dotted with white wild cherry, red hazelnut and occasional pink almond blossom.

The traditional Angevin *Prunus* fruits, such as plums, cherries, peaches and apricots, are now not grown to the extent they were, as a greater, less troublesome and more assured income can be gained from growing apples and pears, especially the former. *Prunus* flower early, so the buds are vulnerable to the late frosts which dog the region as late as the end of April; so where the trees are grown they tend either to be planted on slopes so the cold air will fall away, or trained in fans against a wall. The cold, dormant period every winter works to the benefit of the fruit, which has a good flavour as a result, even if it is fragile to handle.

Apples flower later than pears, and the risk of late frost has been one of the reasons why apples have become the dominant fruit. Now it is hard to get away from late-flowering, heavy-cropping Golden Delicious ('Goldie') and Granny Smith ('Granny'). One autumn when driving down to the Loire after about three years' absence, I saw a large hoarding

POMMES TAPEES

The process used today for preparing pommes tapées *is the same as that used a century ago. The apples are peeled mechanically: about 40,000 cranks of the handle are needed to peel the 140 kilograms (311 lb) that constitutes one oven load. The apples are laid out on large flat wicker baskets, which are immersed in the Loire overnight to prevent them drying out too much during the 5 days of drying in*

the ovens. Once dried, each apple is placed in a special mould and tapped with a purpose-built hammer about 20,000 times. Then they are sealed in jars. Pommes tapées *are usually eaten poached as a dessert, but they also go well with duck.*

(Above)
CHARENTAIS MELONS
Technology is being used increasingly in the production, packaging and maturity testing of melons, but the crop still has to be harvested by hand. Although there are now new strains of canteloupe melons, and other internationally tested varieties available, Charentais still retains pride of place for the excellence of its quality.

(Opposite)
STRAWBERRIES FOR DESSERT
Luscious, sun-ripened and reddened Angevin strawberries need no fancy accompaniments.

proclaiming a fair for 'Granny and Goldie'; it took a little while before it dawned on me what the true subject of the weekend-long celebration was to be! Some of the easy-to-cultivate red varieties from the USA, such as Idared, are also being grown.

A honing down of varieties is also occurring with pears, with early-flowering and otherwise 'difficult' varieties being phased out. One of these is the yellow, red-blushed Doyenné du Comice. It is a particular shame that this is disappearing; not only is it one of the best eating pears – with sweet juicy 'buttery' flesh with a hint of spiciness and a harmonious blend of sweetness and acidity – but it originated in Angers. There is a gold-lettered plaque of Trélazé slate on a wall on the boulevard du Roi René to mark the site of the old garden of the nineteenth-century Comices Horticoles which reads: 'In this garden/ was raised in 1849-50/the celebrated pear Doyenné du Comice/ by the gardener/ Dhommé and by Millet de la/Turtaudière/President of the Comices Horticoles.' M. Millet de la Turtaudière had researched and worked very hard with single-minded dedication for years to produce the ultimate pear, Doyenné du Comice.

The Bon Chrétien pear (see page 69), which we usually know as Williams and which is called Bartlett in the USA, is easier to grow than Comice, but flowers earlier. The fruit is the first main variety to appear and can be eaten straight from the tree. It is large, golden-yellow with a dash of russet, and its flesh is white, sweet and juicy, with a musky note to the taste.

'Winter' pears (so called because they can be stored for a few months and are generally best for eating or cooking after storage) flower later than summer pears. They are more popular, with growers at least, and the region is the third largest producer in France. As well as Comice, varieties include the traditional plump, juicy and sweet Beurré Hardy (named after a nineteenth-century director of the Luxembourg Gardens), the flesh of which, as the name implies, has a butter quality. It also has an intriguing faint scent of rose-water. Like so many of the old favourites, however, the variety is being superseded by one preferred by growers – in this case, Passe-crassane. Fortunately, this is not the pear equivalent of Golden Delicious, and is a fat, juicy, rounded pear with a good flavour.

Such winter pears, and apples, would have been kept in well-ventilated cool dry cellars, individually wrapped in wax paper. Alternatively they were made into *poires* or *pommes tapées* (see page 99) – specially processed whole dried fruit which were at first made domestically, but small-scale commercial production began in the mid-1880s after phylloxera created havoc in the vineyards, and *vignerons* needed an alternative source of income. A small group of them built special large ovens in the tufa caves at Turquant, on the banks of the Loire east

MARKET GARDENS
The favourable soil and climate makes small-scale vegetable and fruit growing on smallholdings and allotments very rewarding. For those who sell their produce to local restaurants, it can also be profitable.

of Saumur. Production continued quite happily until around the turn of the century, then it began to decline and eventually died out. However, the practice was still carried out domestically in country areas until quite recently, and I have been told of people who still do prepare *pommes tapées* in their own homes.

Today it is possible to see the process in a refurbished troglodyte cave carved out of the tufa just east of Saumur. Alain Sylviane explained to me how he and his wife, Sylvie, discovered some caves containing some of the old ovens in their large garden. They decided to revive the old custom and set about researching the method.

The region is also known for other fruits, such as strawberries. The light soil along the northern bank of the Loire between Saumur and Angers is particularly famed for its luscious, warmly flavoured berries. There is both quantity and quality in the region (it lies fourth in the league table of producers). Most are grown in open fields, but in response to fierce competition increasing areas are being covered by glass or plastic tunnels, and new varieties of berries are being developed more with an eye to the colour and handling and storage characteristics than flavour. However, fruit bursting with legendary old-fashioned flavour can be bought from small producers. There are also melons and raspberries, and blackcurrants are grown alongside other crops as their season is so short, lasting just for the month of July. The currants tend to be exported to other regions of France, or used for liqueurs such as *crème de cassis* or *eau-de-vie*, or to make *pâte de cassis*.

The kitchen gardens and smallholdings producing vegetables have grown into increasingly larger market gardens, as growers and businessmen capitalize on the mild climate and fertile alluvial soil, coupled with good transport links and the proximity of lucrative Paris markets. This latter consideration has resulted in an emphasis on *primeurs*, which are grown particularly in the especially fertile stretch of land between the Loire and the Authion, just east of Angers – land which was drained, reclaimed, remodelled and redistributed for cultivation between 1824 and 1832.

Asparagus is also an important crop. As in the Sologne, it thrives in a similar area to strawberries. Some of the country's best spears are grown in the light soil between Saumur and Angers, on the Angers side of the river, with Candé being a particularly famed site. Excellent artichokes also grow in the same general vicinity; as do fashionably slim *haricots verts*, although different varieties of beans have been grown hereabouts for many years. These were not cooked *al dente* and served in neat bundles on elegant plates: instead, they were dried, or half-dried, to provide a staple vegetable in winter. Around Saumur, *grenots* were – and still are – a particularly prized variety.

Cabbages are generally more in evidence, and Angevins are known affectionately in the local patois as '*piochoux*' (little cabbages). The region boasts arguably both the greatest number of recipes and the most varieties of cabbage, from the large *choux pommées*, down to small green *piochoux* or *piochons*. Not only do Angevins generally know how to cook cabbage to great advantage, but they can also cook each variety in the most suitable way. *Choux pommées* are blanched, then cooked slowly in a *cocotte* with sausages; while *piochons* are cooked in their own steam in a closed pot with just a little lightly salted butter. Butter is a favourite companion for cabbage, as in *fricassée de choux verts* and the local version of *chouée* (see page 138), which here is made from *piochons*, and may be called *darée de choux verts* – served with *beurre blanc* (see page 136) instead of plain butter, this really raises the profile of the humble cabbage. Butter also adds the final flourish to the simply delicious dish of *trompe-bonhomme*: made from floury potatoes cooked in their skins (in the embers of the fire to be truly authentic), the peeled flesh is heaped on warm plates and eaten with plenty of good fresh lightly salted butter, chopped shallot and parsley.

Small white onions are also a feature of Angevin savoury dishes, but the area is perhaps better known for its shallots. These are generally highly esteemed for their quality,

MUSHROOMS

Three-quarters of the nation's mushrooms come from Anjou's tufa caves, although more go to industrial processing than to market. The atmosphere and steady cool temperature of the caves are ideal for growing mushrooms while the growers also benefit from low overheads. Around Saumur, the growers have an extra advantage in the proximity of the National School of Equitation which provides manure on which to grow the mushrooms. The mushrooms grown are psalliotes, *or more familiarly*

champignons de Paris, *a relative of the common cultivated mushroom. I found the Loire mushrooms to have more flavour than most; for, characteristically in the Loire, a tastier type of* psalliote *is grown, the particular growing medium contributes greatly to the flavour, the mushrooms are left to grow a little longer so they develop a more mature taste, and the 'root' is usually included when they are picked.*

especially the fairly small grey-brownish-skinned *échalote grise*. Anjou is, in fact, France's second largest producer of shallots, after only highly specialized and highly organized Brittany. Towards the west of the region, and more particularly where *primeurs* are grown, carrots, potatoes, leeks and turnips begin to make an appearance.

In restaurants and private homes, I have frequently had the luck to be offered local fruit and nut *eaux-de-vie* and liqueurs. If these were home-made, they would usually be brought out of a cupboard with great pride; and no matter how nonchalantly the host drank his glassful I knew my verdict was keenly awaited. Without exception, they have been good – often very good, with a quality that betrays years of experience. This is only to be expected in any self-respecting area blessed with such an abundance of fruits and nuts; making alcoholic drinks is a most admirable way of using surpluses!

A record dating from 1693-1696 shows just how long *eaux-de-vie* and liqueurs have been produced in the area. It details a number of local *cabaretiers* (owners of bars where there was also entertainment) authorized to have a copper still for distillation in their house and to sell the *eau-de-vie* by 'pot' (jug, tankard or flagon). *Eaux-de-vie* were also sold by apothecaries and, illicitly, by *crieurs d'eau-de-vie* who went from door to door in the early morning, offering their services. They would set up their tables at street corners, complete with portable stills fuelled by hand-lanterns, pewter flagons and their tills. Everyone, including the authorities, knew this went on, but turned a blind eye. Sharp practices inevitably crept in, and one *eau-de-vie de poire* has gone down in local folklore for being 'reinforced' with vitriol.

Religious orders were also allowed to use stills, and in the first half of the seventeenth century the Benedictine *Sœurs de Fidelité de Notre Dame du Bon Conseil* at Angers started producing what was to become a nationally renowned tipple. This was Guignolet, an *eau-de-vie* made from a number of cherries, such as wild, sour *griottes*, *merises*, and the small tart *guigne noir*: this was the indispensable element, as it gave the unique sharpness to the otherwise sweet drink. Each year the sisters made and sold many thousands of bottles.

After the disappearance of the priory in 1791, the making of Guignolet passed into the hands of *confiseurs*. Local peasants who picked the wild *guignes noirs* and sold them at their local market became known as *guignolets*. Production of the liqueur reached its peak in the nineteenth century, but tailed off towards the middle of this century. For some time now, the Anjou-based firm of Cointreau has been the only company producing it, and that in only a very small amount. Although *guignes noir* make very good *eau-de-vie* and liqueurs, being sharp they are not very good to eat, and many of the trees have been felled. However, some magnificent old trees remain, so it is worth keeping an eye open for the cherries. If you find some, prick them with a darning needle, pop them into a bottle, add caster sugar to come a quarter to a third of the way up, pour in enough brandy to cover the fruit, seal firmly and leave in a cool dark place for at least six months – preferably much longer.

Angers was the birthplace, in 1872, of the man who was given the title of the 'prince of gastronomes'. His real name was Maurice Edmond Sailland, but when he first started out in

COINTREAU

The now-international liqueur firm of Cointreau has its roots in Angers. It was founded in 1849 by two brothers, Edouard and Adolphe Cointreau, who were confectioners and began experimenting with ways of using the abundant local fruit and alcohol. They also tried using the bitter orange peel arriving at Nantes from the West Indies, and hit on the combination of this and matured spirit, which they distilled

and mixed with sugar syrup. Today, a mixture of dry bitter orange peels and fresh sweet peels, beet sugar and alcohol is used – pure and simple, with nothing else added. Production is still carried out at Angers, in new premises on the outskirts, although the company's head office is in Paris.

journalism he wanted a pen-name to use for his articles. A friend suggested a Russian-sounding Latin name, 'Cur-non-sky' (why-not-sky), which he adopted. He wrote copiously and intelligently on all culinary subjects, founded a monthly food-and-wine magazine, and set up the *Académie des Gastronomes*. Perhaps more than anyone else, he was also responsible for the great revival of interest in regional French food after the Great War. A friend of writers and fashionable people, an epicure and a great host, fêted and feared by restaurateurs throughout France, he grew to weigh nearly 130 kilograms (286 lb) and lived until he was 84. Until the end, he remained in love with his local cuisine and wines, but did not attempt to credit them with qualities that they did not possess. His words best sum up the food of the region: '. . . direct, reasonable, upright dishes which do not strive for effect'. Anjou, he added, 'is paradise for peaceful digestion'.

VARNISHING THE BOATS
Traditional Loire boats are light and have a shallow draft – so they can easily be manoeuvred off should they run aground on a recently formed shoal – and raised bows so they slide over obstructions in the riverbed.

(Opposite, left)
AUTOMATIC REMUAGE
Wines made by the méthode champenoise undergo a second fermentation in the bottle. The bottles are rotated so the sediment produced moves down to the cork. This remuage used to be done manually, but machines, such as this one at Buvet-Ladubay, have taken over.

(Below)
FOIE GRAS FARM

CHEESES

Anjou does not have any cheeses of great – or indeed lesser – renown, except to a very local public. Nevertheless, visit a local market, such as the excellent Saturday morning market at Saumur, and you will see a mouthwatering range of local goats' cheeses of varying sizes, shades, aromas, textures and degrees of firmness. Frustratingly, they are also usually nameless. The reason for this anonymity is the number of very small goats' cheese producers. The cheeses they make, like most goats' cheeses, will also be small.

Almost every rural family, even on really tiny properties, used to have one or two goats, as they are far more practical than a cow for a small plot of land, needing less space and being easier to manage. As goats produce less milk, there was little left over for cheese. The Loire's atmosphere and mild climate are also not ideal for keeping cheeses for any time, so they would usually be of a size that could be eaten at one sitting.

Many local residents will either have a favourite producer they visit in person (for some town dwellers, usually younger and more affluent, this is almost akin to the way in which many British families make their ritual Sunday pilgrimage to the countryside), or they will regularly visit the same stall at a market. A cheese so young and fresh that it is barely more than coagulated curds drained in a muslin bag in a cool airy place for a few hours, may perhaps be bought for eating the same day; for the next day, they may buy a slightly older and firmer cheese that has been given longer draining in *faisselles*, or other small moulds. Older and firmer still are those cheeses that have been turned out of the moulds and placed on straw or leaves on a cellar shelf and left for just 2-4 weeks; goats' cheeses lose moisture quickly, their flavour becoming more concentrated. Cheeses that are *cendré* are coated in the ashes of burned vine prunings. This coating slows down the maturation process and the cheese is slightly softer than an untreated version of the same age. Vine or nut leaves are also used occasionally.

WINES

There are some 1,000 *vignerons* in the region who depend entirely on the vine for their livelihood, and there are about 3,000 who may have just a few rows of vines as part of their overall farming, or other, activity.

Although wines of a wide range of styles and quality are produced, to the public at large Anjou is best known for the light, sweetish, pink wines which account for about half of the region's wine production. There are, in fact, three types of Anjou rosé. The most usual version is the medium-sweet Rosé d'Anjou. This is closely followed by Cabernet d'Anjou, also medium-sweet; as it is made from more 'noble' grape varieties (cabernet franc and cabernet sauvignon), and production is more strictly controlled, it can age well. In 1974 the *appellation* Rosé de Loire was created to try to meet the demand for dry rosés, and these pale, salmon-coloured, light wines can make pleasantly refreshing summer drinking when chilled.

However, production of the rosés is falling, especially that of the sweet 'pop' style. In contrast, during the last ten years the production of red wines has almost tripled and now equals the same 15% proportion of the total volume as sparkling wine. Anjou has some of the most dynamic and forward-looking *vignerons* of the Loire. Straight Anjou rouge can be made from gamay or from the regionally more exciting cabernet franc. Whereas this latter grape variety is used on its own in Touraine, in Anjou it is combined with cabernet sauvignon to add backbone, structure and finesse to the charming fruity flavours of the cabernet franc. The new generation of wine-makers are experimenting with the use of higher proportions of cabernet sauvignon, with the most up-to-date vinification techniques, and with ageing wines in new oak casks (*fûts de chêne neuf*). Some will juggle with all of these practices; others will be more selective, so as to retain more of the wines' *typicité*. The enthusiastic œnocrats are also more likely to make more of selling their *vieilles vignes* wines (wines made from old vines), and even to use the ploy of separately vinifying and labelling their wines from young vines, and so by implication claiming a superiority.

The only place with a named red wine of any note is Saumur. The *appellation* Saumur rouge embraces quite a wide area, but the vineyards lying within the more closely delimited area of Saumur-Champigny, to the east of the town, yield a wine with greater class. The chalk soil of Saumur is suited to cabernet franc, but here produces lighter wines with more immediate charm than those of a few miles away in Bourgueil and Chinon. Indeed, a good Saumur-Champigny can be one of the most lightly charming, eminently drinkable wines. Serve it chilled for ideal summer drinking, either on its own or as the perfect partner to most of the food of the region.

Reflecting the general trend in wine consumption, the move with ordinary Anjou blanc is now towards vinifying dry wines; 20 years ago medium-sweet was the

GRATIEN & MEYER

Alfred Gratien founded his company in Saumur in 1864, at the same time as he formed Alfred Gratien Champagne in Epernay. Jean Meyer joined the company six years later. Although many sparkling Saumur houses are now owned by Champagne houses, Gratien & Meyer is the only one to have maintained unbroken links between the two districts for over 100 years. Also uniquely, it is entirely family-owned and owns its own vineyards in the

best *crus* above Saumur, yielding about 10% of the company's needs, the balance being bought in from nearby.

Gratien & Meyer produce only sparkling Saumur, using the same method as for Champagne. However, ebullient and charming Alain Seydoux, Export Director and direct descendant of Jean Meyer, believes that the way forward for sparkling Saumur producers is to market their wines as quality products in their own right, and so dispel the consumer perception of them as a poor man's Champagne.

vogue. Although the wines must contain at least 80% chenin blanc (locally known as pineau de la Loire), with the balance made up of chardonnay or sauvignon, they are not the best examples of what the grape can produce. A far better impression can be gained by tasting sparkling Saumur, the region's best-known white wine. It is produced in and around Saumur, using the *méthode champenoise*, although it will be illegal to put this on the label. It will, instead, be labelled 'Saumur d'Origine'. It is not really meaningful to equate sparkling Saumur to Champagne because they are made from two distinct grape varieties grown on different soils in dissimilar climatic conditions, and so will have quite unique flavours and styles. As with nearly every *appellation* of wine, there are good and bad examples of both. A good sparkling Saumur will have an elegant, 'feminine' flowery-fruitiness, typical of the chenin blanc from which it is made. It may not just be white and dry, as sweet and red sparkling Saumur are also produced. An *appellation* for still white Saumur also exists.

The small area of Savennières, north of the Loire, is justly famous for its superb dry – occasionally semi-dry – white wines. Made from chenin blanc to specifications of low yield and high natural alcohol, the wines from the thin slatey soil are complex and not usually very attractive when young; they are therefore not wines for beginners. Given time (2-5 years), however, the elements marry together and the wines blossom to a refined, elegant smoothness. They develop the characteristic chenin blanc bouquet, with its subtle charming nuance of honey and flowers. There are two Savennières *crus*. Coulée de Serrant (see right) is the oldest, and has been planted with vines for six centuries, during which time its wines have often been highly praised. Curnonsky ranked it alongside Château d'Yquem. The other *cru* is La Roche-aux-Moines. The best vintages from each can last quite happily for up to 50 years.

It will probably come as a surprise to all but the most well-informed wine drinkers to know that some of the Loire's – even, some claim, the world's – best sweet wines can be made in Anjou, when the weather has been kind in the summer and autumn. They are produced from chenin blanc vines on the south-facing slopes in the Layon valley, so have the characteristic soft, fruity, floral-honeysuckle taste. They are also underpinned with quality-making acidity, which not only adds freshness to the flavour, but enables them to require a decade or more before they are ready for drinking.

The generic name for the sweet white AOC wines of the area is Coteaux du Layon. These are rarely really lusciously sweet, so can accompany fish and poultry rather than sweet desserts. The best wines for this sort of use come from two *crus*. Quarts-de-Chaume, a small plot of just 50 hectares (125 acres) has the lowest permitted yield per hectare in France. When blessed with the right weather during the growing season, the reward for successive selective pickings of only the ripest grapes is a sumptuous gold wine, tasting of apricots, peaches, quinces and honey. Bonnezeaux is a similar wine, but perhaps does not achieve quite the same heights.

Clos de Coulée de Serrant

The small *appellation* of Coulée de Serrant was bought in 1960 by Madame Joly, who has worked extremely hard at re-establishing the quality and reputation of her wines. The vineyard has been managed according to the 'biodynamic' system since 1985. This rejects the use of chemicals, and also advises against the use of clonally bred vines. In addition the Joly's wines are vinified completely naturally. Add to

this restrictive programme the low yield permitted under AOC regulations, and one can see why Coulée de Serrant wines are never cheap.

(*Left*)
Anjou Vineyards near the River Layon

SOUPE DES PÊCHEURS

Fishermen's Soup

SERVES 6

1.8kg/4lb mixed freshwater fish, such as pike, tench, perch, gudgeon, bleak etc.
a bouquet garni consisting of 4 sprigs of parsley, 2 sprigs of thyme, 1 small bay leaf, 3 sprigs of chervil and 2 sprigs of tarragon
1 onion, sliced
2 carrots, chopped
2 leeks, sliced
450ml/15fl oz dry white Loire wine
3 egg yolks
200ml/7fl oz crème fraîche
salt and freshly ground black pepper
finely chopped fresh herbs, to garnish

Scale and gut the fish, reserving the heads and tails. Put these trimmings into a large pan with the herbs, vegetables, wine and 450ml/15fl oz water. Bring to the boil, skim the scum from the surface then simmer for 20 minutes, skimming occasionally.

Cut the fish into 4cm/1½in pieces.

Strain the stock and season. In a clean pan, gently heat the stock just to a simmer. Add the fish in the order given, allowing the liquid to return to a simmer between each addition. Poach the fish for 10 minutes, or until just tender. Using a slotted spoon, transfer the fish to a warmed soup tureen and keep warm. Boil the cooking liquid until reduced by half.

Blend together the egg yolks and crème fraîche, then stir a little of the cooking liquid into it. Pour this mixture back into the saucepan and heat very gently, stirring, until slightly thickened; do not allow to boil. Test the seasoning then pour over the fish. Garnish with the herbs.

TARTE À LA TOMATE

Tomato Tart

(Illustrated left)

This is an adaptation of Mme Harrault's delicious tart from Le Chapy (see far right). Its special appeal depends on plump, juicy and well-flavoured tomatoes, which need no greengrocer's sign proclaiming them 'freshly picked' as their smell makes this all too obvious.

SERVES 8

FOR THE PÂTE BRISÉE

225g/8oz plain flour
115g/4oz butter
2 egg yolks

FOR THE FILLING

2 egg yolks, beaten, plus egg white for brushing
55g/2oz unsalted butter, diced
2 large onions, chopped
150ml/5fl oz crème fraîche
2-3 tsp chopped fresh herbs
6 large well-flavoured ripe but firm tomatoes, skinned if wished and sliced
70g/2½oz Cantal cheese, grated
salt and freshly ground black pepper

Make the *pâte brisée* with the flour, butter, egg yolks and 4 tablespoons of water as on page 77, and chill for 30 minutes.

Roll out the pastry and use it to line a 30 x 23cm/12 x 9in tart tin or baking dish. Chill again for 30 minutes.

Preheat the oven to 200C/400F/gas6, with a baking sheet inside. Prick the base of the pastry, place on the hot baking sheet and bake blind in the oven for about 15 minutes. Remove from the oven, brush with the egg white and leave to cool. Reduce the oven temperature to 180C/350F/gas4. Melt the butter in a frying pan over a low heat. Add the onions and cook very gently, stirring occasionally, until very soft. Using a slotted spoon, transfer the onions to a bowl to cool. Stir together the egg yolks, crème fraîche and seasoning. Stir in the onions and herbs then pour this mixture into the pastry case. Arrange the tomato slices over the top. Sprinkle with the cheese and bake for about 20-25 minutes.

Serve warm or cold.

SALADE DE GRENOTS À L'HUILE DE NOIX

Haricot Beans with Walnut Oil

There are many wild walnut trees in the Anjou area. The tufa soil gives a very special taste to the walnuts, and therefore to the oil made from them. This is an old family recipe of the 150-year-old firm Huilerie Croix-Verte in Saumur.

SERVES 4
350g/12oz grenots or haricot beans, soaked overnight
1 bouquet garni
15g/½oz unsalted butter
2 shallots, preferably grey, chopped
about 4 tablespoons walnut oil
salt and freshly ground black pepper
chopped parsley, to garnish

Drain the beans and rinse them in fresh water. Put them in a pot, add the bouquet garni, cover with water and bring to the boil. Boil for 10 minutes then cover and simmer for 60-90 minutes, depending on the freshness of the beans (the fresher the beans, the shorter the cooking time). Make sure there is adequate water.

Meanwhile, melt the butter in a sauté pan, add the shallots and cook for 2-3 minutes only: they should retain some crunch. Drain the beans, discard the bouquet garni and stir in the shallots. Toss with the walnut oil to taste.

Sprinkle with the chopped parsley garnish and serve warm.

ŒUFS POCHÉS SAUMUROIS

Poached Eggs in White Wine

SERVES 4
55g/2oz unsalted butter
125g/4½oz mushrooms, chopped
125g/4½oz onions, chopped
300ml/10fl oz dry white Saumur
175ml/6fl oz stock
1 sprig of tarragon
4 eggs
salt and freshly ground black pepper
4 slices of hot toasted country bread, buttered, to serve

Melt 25g/1oz butter in a heavy-based saucepan. Add the mushrooms and onions and cook over a very low heat for about 10 minutes, until softened, without allowing to colour. Add the dry white wine, stock and tarragon and leave to simmer for 10 minutes. Strain off the liquid, reserve it in a bowl, and keep the mushroom mixture warm.

Return the liquid to the pan, reheat to just below simmering point, add the eggs and poach until the yolks are set almost to the required degree. Using a slotted spoon, remove the eggs and dry them briefly on paper towels. Keep warm.

Boil the liquid until slightly syrupy. Lower the heat and gradually whisk in the remaining butter. Season. Place the mushroom mixture on the toast, place the eggs on top and pour the sauce over.

LE CHAPY
Allonnes
Tel 41 52 02 63
See recipe opposite

Annick and Jean-Claude Harrault have farmed their land 4km from Allonnes close to Saumur for 25 years. More rural it couldn't be, with free-range ducks and chickens, sheep, and a huge area for growing vegetables and fruit, including tomatoes, beans, strawberries, raspberries, melons, potatoes and sweetcorn. In 1985 Mme Harrault opened Le Chapy, inspired by years of praise for her cooking from friends, and putting into practice all the knowledge learnt from her grandmother and mother. Don't be fooled by the rather rustic-looking signs to Le Chapy: they greatly belie the quality of the *cuisine familiale* found there.

POIS À LA MODE DE L'ABBAYE FONTEVRAUD

Peas with Lettuce Hearts and Cream

At the side of Fontevraud Abbey there is a curious squat structure built on a *quadratum* of 4 corner towers with a large central tower, all topped by pepper-pot roofs. These towers are the chimneys for the five separate hearths in the kitchen beneath, where the food was cooked for the Abbey's 500 or so residents.

When cooking peas this way I like to reflect upon the tranquillity of the Abbey's interesting old vegetable garden; I can imagine the frugal cooks devising a recipe that works just as well for old peas as young ones, and wrapping the just shelled peas in a damp napkin to keep them fresh.

SERVES 4-6
450g/1lb shelled peas
1 round-head lettuce, outside leaves removed
1 sprig of summer savory (optional)
115-225g/4-8oz unsalted butter
1 egg yolk
175ml/6fl oz crème fraîche
salt and freshly ground white pepper
pinch of caster sugar (optional)

Wrap the peas in a damp napkin. Open out the lettuce and place the sprig of summer savory, if used, between the leaves. Tie up the lettuce and put it in a casserole with the peas, a pinch of salt, the butter and about 85ml/3fl oz water. Simmer until the peas are just tender.

Blend the egg yolk with the crème fraîche, pepper and caster sugar, if used.

Remove the lettuce from the casserole. Blend the cream mixture into the peas and heat gently; do not allow to boil.

RAGOÛT D'ARTICHAUTS SAUMUROIS

Artichokes with Mushrooms

(Illustrated opposite, left)

This dish brings together two of the area's most well-known foods: artichokes are clearly visible for all to see, while the area's mushrooms are hidden away in tufa caves (see page 103). The flavour of the result belies the simplicity of the recipe. Possible additions include tender sweet young peas or broad beans added after 15 or 12 minutes cooking respectively, or cooked fresh prawns, stirred in at the end and allowed just to heat through.

SERVES 4
4-8 globe artichokes, depending on size
juice of 1 large lemon
1 tablespoon white wine vinegar
25g/1oz unsalted butter
4 tablespoons dry white non-sparkling Saumur
115g/4oz ceps, fairly thinly sliced
salt and freshly ground black pepper
few sprigs of chervil, chopped, to serve

Break off the artichoke stems close to their bases.

Pull away and discard the first few outer layers of leaves from one artichoke. Using a large sharp stainless steel knife, cut across this artichoke about halfway down. Using a small sharp stainless steel knife, trim away all the leaves, cut or pull away the inner leaves and pull away the hairy choke, leaving just the tender base.

Brush the base with lemon juice then put it into water acidulated with the wine vinegar while preparing the remaining artichokes in the same way.

Take the artichokes out one by one and cut each base into quarters, sixths or eighths, depending on size. Brush the cut surfaces with lemon juice.

Melt the butter in a saucepan, add the artichokes and wine. Season lightly, partially cover and cook over a low heat for about 20 minutes, tossing frequently, until the artichokes are nearly tender. Add the mushrooms and cook for a further 5 minutes. Check the seasoning.

Transfer to a warmed serving dish and sprinkle with chervil.

CHOU AU BEURRE

Buttered Cabbage

(Illustrated opposite, right)

This is quite unlike the usual British concept of cabbage with butter – over-boiled cabbage with a knob of butter on top. It takes time to do the buttering, but it is worth every minute. The cabbage retains its bright green colour and reduces considerably to delicious result.

SERVES 4
1 small Savoy or other green cabbage
55g/2oz unsalted butter, diced
salt and freshly ground black pepper

Cut the cabbage into strips and remove the core. Boil in salted water for 7-8 minutes until just tender. Drain very thoroughly.

Melt half the butter in the same pan, return the cabbage to it and stir over a low heat. As the liquid from the cabbage is produced and re-absorbed, gradually add the remaining butter, stirring gently.

When the cabbage is thoroughly coated with butter, and there is no remaining liquid, add plenty of black pepper, but not too much salt. Serve immediately.

SANDRE FARCI, SAUCE À L'ANJOU ROUGE

Stuffed Pike-perch with a Sauce of Red Anjou Wine

Paul Le Quéré of Pavillon Paul Le Quéré (see page 117), kindly gave me this recipe.

SERVES 6
1 tablespoon olive oil
½ smallish fennel bulb, chopped
150g/5oz mushrooms, finely chopped
about 150g/5oz sorrel, trimmed
6 thick slices of pike-perch fillet
175g/6oz unsalted butter, chopped
3 shallots, preferably grey, finely chopped
400ml/14fl oz red Anjou wine
salt and freshly ground black pepper
melted butter for brushing

(Above)
Slices of pike-perch as served in red wine sauce at the Pavillon Paul Le Quéré, with a garnish of courgettes and other seasonal vegetables, and with onion leaves slowly cooked in red Anjou wine sweetened with honey.

Heat the olive oil in a frying pan over a low heat and gently cook the fennel in it until softened. Add the mushrooms and sorrel and cook over a low heat, stirring occasionally, for 10 minutes. Season then leave until cold.

Cut horizontally through each piece of fish fillet, and place the sorrel stuffing in between the two layers.

Melt 25g/1oz of the butter in a heavy-based saucepan over a low heat and cook the shallots in it, stirring occasionally, until softened. Add the wine and simmer until reduced to about 6 tablespoons. Over a low heat, gradually whisk in the remaining butter. Season to taste. Keep warm over a very low heat, but do not allow to boil.

Season the top of each piece of fish, and brush with melted butter. In a non-stick frying pan over a moderate to high heat, cook for 2 minutes on each side, turning the fish pieces over carefully. Transfer to 6 warmed plates, and spoon the sauce over.

FRITURE

Deep-fried Small Fish

(Illustrated right)

Friture was a popular dish with boatmen along the Loire, and is still sold in small cafés and restaurants along the banks of the river. The best *friture* will be found in establishments supplied with freshly caught small fish. In spring, these fish would include gudgeon and smelts, which swarm into fresh water to spawn, small perch (*perchettes*) and bleak, abundant in the Loire and its tributaries. In some popular places, *friture* may be no more than what would elsewhere be termed *goujons*, or strips of fish, rather than small fishes.

The fish are coated in milk and flour then dipped twice in hot oil: the first time to cook the fish, the second to crisp it up. They should be eaten very soon after the second cooking, while they are very hot and 'crackling'. The fish will lose their crispness quite quickly, so it is best not to cook for too many people eating at the same time. Fried parsley is traditionally tossed with the fish, and you must work quickly if everything is to be at its delicious best. At Notre Dame (see page

118), where this photograph was taken, M. Choupin served the *friture* with sliced tomatoes and chopped shallots mixed with the parsley.

The following recipe makes a light main course or delightful first course, and the crisp, dry style that typifies white Loire wines is the ideal vinous accompaniment.

SERVES 4

700g/1½lb very fresh small fish, cleaned and gutted
about 150-175ml/5-6fl oz milk
flour, for coating
clean flavourless oil, for deep-frying
small handful of fine parsley sprigs
salt and freshly ground black pepper
lemon wedges, to serve

Heat a good depth of oil to 180C/350F. Season some flour with salt and pepper. Dip the fish in milk, allowing the excess to drain off. Then toss a few at a time in a bag containing the seasoned flour, to coat them lightly and evenly. Keep the different types of fish separate.

Carefully lower a few fish at a time into the hot oil and cook briefly until it is lightly coloured. Keep the cooked fish warm while cooking the remaining fish, and keep an eye on the temperature of the oil to make sure that it does not drop.

When all the fish have been cooked once, reheat the oil, and plunge the fish back in it to crisp them up and become golden. Remove the fish from the oil and the pan from the heat. Tip the fish out on to paper towels to drain.

Using a slotted spoon, lower the parsley sprigs into the oil and fry for about 8-10 seconds. Then scoop them out with the spoon and drain on paper towels.

Sprinkle the fish with salt, toss with the parsley and serve with lemon wedges.

FRICASSÉE DE POULET ANGEVINE

Chicken in White Anjou Wine

SERVES 4
1.5kg/3½lb free-range chicken, cut into 4 portions
55g/2oz unsalted butter
16 small onions
200ml/7fl oz chicken stock
200ml/7fl oz dry white Anjou wine
1 small bouquet garni
salt and freshly ground white pepper
12 medium-sized mushrooms, halved
2 egg yolks
juice of ½ lemon

In a heavy flameproof casserole, melt the butter over a medium heat. Add the onions and the chicken, skin-side down, and cook for about 10 minutes without allowing to colour, turning the chicken halfway. Remove and reserve the onions. Add the stock, wine, bouquet garni and seasoning to the chicken. Cover and cook over a low heat for 20 minutes. Add the onions and cook for another 20 minutes, until the chicken is just cooked. Add the mushrooms and cook for 10 minutes.

Remove the chicken, mushrooms and onions from the casserole, cover and keep warm. Skim excess fat from the surface of the cooking liquid then boil it until reduced by about a quarter.

Remove a ladleful of this liquid and leave it to cool slightly. Stir it into the egg yolks, then pour back into the casserole and heat, stirring constantly, until slightly thickened; do not allow to boil. Add a squeeze of lemon juice and adjust the seasoning. Return the chicken, mushrooms and onions to the casserole and turn them over to coat them in the sauce.

PINTADEAU SUR NOIX

Guinea Fowl with Walnuts

The black-and-white speckled plumage of guinea fowl can still be seen in country gardens and on smallholdings in the area; a reminder that in France the birds were part of the farmyard flock. They have a much better flavour than we tend to expect, although that of the corn-fed birds now available is almost as good.

This recipe comes from a family who have kept guinea fowl for as long as any of them could remember – and the gnarled form of the walnut tree in their garden is witness to the family's longevity. The cheese for the stuffing also used to be homemade, but no longer.

Inserting a stuffing between the skin and the flesh of the breast, and perhaps the legs, of a bird has become fashionable in recent years, but it is no surprise that such an obviously good idea has been in use for many years.

SERVES 3-4
150g/5oz piece of lightly smoked bacon, cut across into strips
115g/4oz soft full-fat cream cheese
25g/1oz skinned and chopped walnuts, preferably fresh
2 small shallots, chopped
1 plump guinea fowl, dressed
2 tablespoons walnut oil
6-8 walnut or vine leaves
85ml/3fl oz good dry white Saumur
salt and freshly ground black pepper
sprigs of chervil, to garnish
55g/2oz walnuts, tossed in hot butter

Preheat the oven to 190C/375F/gas5.

Heat a heavy flameproof casserole over a fairly low heat, add the bacon and cook until the fat runs, without allowing it to colour. Remove the casserole from the heat and scoop out about 25g/1oz of it. Drain on paper towels and chop finely.

Mix with the cream cheese, nuts, 1 tablespoon of shallot and seasoning. Season the cavity of the guinea fowl, then insert the stuffing in between the flesh and skin of the breast and over the legs.

Return the casserole to the heat, stir in the remaining shallot and cook, stirring occasionally, until softened.

Rub walnut oil liberally over the guinea fowl skin then tie walnut or vine leaves over the back and breast.

Pour the wine into the casserole, allow to bubble briefly then place the bird, breast-side down, in the casserole. Cover tightly and cook in the oven for 35 minutes. Turn the bird so that the breast is uppermost, re-cover and cook for a further 30 minutes or so, until the guinea fowl is just cooked through.

Transfer the guinea fowl to a warmed plate. Check the seasoning of the cooking juices. Surround the guinea fowl with butter-tossed walnuts, spoon the sauce over the bird and garnish with chervil.

Serve accompanied by more of the Saumur, or a Saumur-Champigny.

'L'ÉTUVE' D'AGNEAU DE LAIT

Lamb with Young Loire Vegetables

(Illustrated opposite)

This is an adaptation of a dish created by Paul Le Quéré of Pavillon Paul Le Quéré (see far right) both to show off local produce to advantage, and to produce a dish which is fundamentally old-fashioned *cuisine du terroir* but modern in execution.

The mélange of vegetables chosen for the garnish will vary according to what is particularly good on any given day, bearing in mind that it must be complementary to the fine, delicate flavour of the lamb.

SERVES 6
1.5-1.75kg/3½lb young lamb chops and chopped fillet end of leg
leaves of 3 small sprigs of rosemary, chopped
leaves of 3 small sprigs of thyme, chopped
115ml/4fl oz olive oil
200g/7oz unsalted butter
3 shallots, chopped
4 large well-flavoured tomatoes, skinned, seeded and chopped
500ml/18fl oz light veal stock
seasonal vegetables to garnish
4-6 tablespoons chopped herbs such as basil, thyme, tarragon, flat-leaved parsley, chives and chervil, plus more to garnish

Place the lamb in an earthenware terrine, add the herbs and 85ml/3fl oz of the oil. Cover with a lid or foil and leave in a cool place for 2 hours.

Lift the lamb from the marinade. Heat the remaining oil and 25g/1oz of the butter in a large sauté pan, add the lamb and brown it evenly for about 5 minutes. Transfer the lamb to a pre-warmed plate and keep warm.

Pour off the fat from the pan, add another 25g/1oz butter and the shallots and cook for 2 minutes. Stir in the tomato, cook for a further minute then add the stock. Simmer for about 10 minutes. Gradually whisk in the remaining butter, adjust the seasoning and add the herbs. Add the lamb and the vegetables for the garnish to the sauce, heat for about a minute, then serve sprinkled with more chopped herbs.

PAVILLON PAUL LE QUÉRÉ

3 boulevard Foch
Angers
Tel 41 20 00 20
See recipes on pages 114, 123, and left

When Martine and her *chef-patron* husband Paul Le Quéré had their restaurant, 'Le Quéré', in Angers, they gained a reputation for the finest cooking in the area, and for offering the best and widest selection of Loire wines (these were the domain of highly respected *sommelier* Martine). However, the surroundings were not in the same league, so the couple felt that if they were to join the highest echelons of top restaurants they would have to move. After a long search they settled for a secluded but neglected listed building right in the heart of Angers. Given extensive renovation, the Pavillon Paul Le Quéré has become not only a luxurious restaurant, but has a few well-appointed guest rooms too. Martine is now involved with administration, as well as keeping an eye on all the work that is carried out both 'behind the scenes' and 'front of house'. Paul is continuing the policies of using local ingredients, specializing in Loire fish and giving precise consideration to matching all his dishes to wines on their extensive wine list.

NOTRE DAME
Place de l'Église
Béhuard
St-Georges-sur-Loire
Tel 41 72 20 17
See recipe on pages 114-15 and picture opposite

At about 3km long and with 94 residents, the island of Béhuard is one of the largest on the Loire, and also one of its most attractive and interesting, with verdant pastures, country lanes as they should be, and peaceful avenues of poplars gliding down to the river's edge. At the heart is the pre-Christian village of St-Georges-sur-Loire. A number of restaurants cluster in or near the main square, but the simple family restaurant of Notre Dame, run by the husband-and-wife team of Giselle and Gérard Choupin, is the one famed for its *fritures*. Depending on your mood, and the side of French life you want to see and be a part of, you can either eat in the bar or dine more quietly in the restaurant.

MATELOTE DES TONNELIERS

Veal Casseroled in Wine

Matelote in this instance means 'cooked in wine'. The wine used here is red to make a richly flavoured casserole from veal to satisfy hungry *tonneliers*, men who transported wine on the Loire. Saumur-Champigny has quite a delicate flavour; you can substitute a Cabernet d'Anjou for greater robustness.

SERVES 4
70g/2½oz butter, diced
16 small onions
2 small carrots, chopped
350g/12oz shoulder of veal, cut into 4cm/1½in cubes
350g/12oz veal flank, cut into cubes along the direction of the grain
2 teaspoons plain flour
400ml/14fl oz Saumur-Champigny
a bouquet garni consisting of 2 sprigs of thyme, 1 bay leaf, 2 sprigs of parsley and a sprig of chervil
salt and freshly ground black pepper

Melt half the butter in a sauté pan or large frying pan, add the vegetables and cook over a low heat for about 5 minutes.

Stir in the veal, and cook for 2-3 minutes. Sprinkle the flour over, stir for 2-3 minutes then gradually stir in the wine. Add the bouquet garni, bring just to a simmer, cover tightly and cook gently for about an hour, or until the pieces of meat are very tender.

Uncover the pan towards the end of cooking, if necessary, to evaporate off some of the liquid. If by the time the veal is tender there is still too much liquid, strain it off and boil it down until reduced and concentrated. Discard the bouquet garni, adjust the seasoning and stir in the remaining butter to finish.

CUL DE VEAU À L'ANGEVINE

Loin of Veal in Anjou or Saumur wine

In Anjou, *cul de veau* is the *quasi-entier*, that is, the whole hind loin plus the rump, but as this makes a rather large amount I have used a smaller joint.

If pork skin proves impossible to find, the dish can be made without it but the sauce will lose much of its delicious unctuousness. Braised mushrooms are a traditional accompaniment.

SERVES 6
1 large piece of fresh pork skin
2 onions, chopped
3 small carrots, chopped
1.35kg/3lb loin of veal
225ml/8fl oz dry white Anjou or Saumur wine
175ml/6fl oz veal stock
a bouquet garni, of 2 sprigs of thyme, ½ bay leaf, a sprig of chervil, 6 chives and a sprig of parsley
115ml/4fl oz crème fraîche
salt and freshly ground black pepper

Preheat the oven to 200C/400F/gas6.

Line the bottom of a heavy casserole with the pork skin, fat side down. Layer the onions and carrots on the skin. Season the veal and place it on the vegetables. Place, uncovered, in the oven and cook for 20 minutes, turning the joint over halfway through. Add the wine, stock and bouquet garni. Cover tightly and cook in the oven for about 1½ hours more, turning the meat over 2 or 3 times.

Remove the veal, cover and keep warm. Discard the pork rind, vegetables and bouquet garni. Strain the cooking liquor and skim off excess fat. Bring the liquor to the boil and reduce to concentrate the flavour. Stir in the crème fraîche and simmer until thickened. Adjust the seasoning to taste.

Carve the veal into thick slices, arrange them overlapping on a warmed plate, and pour the sauce over. Or carve the veal at the table and serve the sauce separately in a warmed jug.

(Above)
Wines for the Saumur appellations are grown on the south side of the Loire. The best known are the Champagne-style white wines, and the charming red Saumur-Champigny, their areas of production being separated by the town of Saumur: the red wines are produced east of the town, the white ones to the west.

(Left)
Gérard Choupin cooked his version of carré de veau for us at his restaurant, Notre Dame (see opposite). For his recipe, the veal and vegetables are fried to a rich brown before braising in wine and stock; to create such a dark sauce, red wine would of course be used.

SAUTÉ DE PORC AUX PRUNEAUX

Pork with Prunes

(Illustrated right)

Since Alain Seydoux of Gratien & Meyer (see page 107) demonstrated to me the excellence of the partnership between a sparkling *demi-sec* white Saumur with *porc aux pruneaux*, I always serve the two together.

Porc aux pruneaux is one of the most well-known dishes of the Val de Loire, and there are many versions. This one is based on a recipe from M. Timmerman, a Saumurois *traiteur*, who often cooks it for the guests of Gratien & Meyer when the company entertains in its private dining rooms in the cellars. It is my favourite, as it is akin to traditional family recipes in its many good flavours and in not including cream. Use large prunes that need soaking, as those that need none have been treated. M. Timmerman adds a garnish of carefully prepared seasonal vegetables.

SERVES 4
16-20 large prunes
1 bottle dry white Saumur
25g/1oz butter
1.25kg/2½lb very lean shoulder or hand of pork, chopped
225g/8oz chopped mixed carrot, onion and celery
1 bouquet garni consisting of 2 sprigs of parsley, 1 bay leaf and 3 sprigs of thyme
250ml/9fl oz veal stock
salt and freshly ground black pepper
a little lemon juice

Put the prunes in a bowl, cover with half the wine and leave to soak overnight.

Melt the butter in a sauté pan, add the pork and brown it lightly on both sides.

Drain on paper towels then place in a heavy casserole. Add the vegetables and bouquet garni to the casserole.

Stir the remaining wine into the sauté pan, bring to the boil then pour over the pork. Boil the stock then add it to the casserole. Season, cover tightly and cook over a low heat for about 1½ hours. Add the prunes and their soaking liquid, cover again and cook for a further 30 minutes.

Transfer the pork and prunes to a serving dish, cover and keep warm. Boil the cooking liquor until slightly thickened. Taste and adjust the seasoning, adding a little lemon juice if necessary, then pass through a sieve over the pork and prunes.

I strongly recommend serving a *demi-sec* sparkling white Saumur with this.

PIGEONNEAU ET PETIT CHOU FARCI

Pigeon with Small Cabbage Parcels

Serge Lebert, *chef-patron* of Le Clafoutis just outside Angers, gave me this wonderfully savoury, typical country Angevin recipe: he used Coteaux de l'Aubance wine (a sweet wine from chenin blanc grapes) from south of the Loire. Production is small and the wine is rarely found outside the area so he suggested using Coteaux du Layon instead. Bread is the only accompaniment necessary. Game birds such as partridge or pheasant could be used, but wild pigeon is the traditional choice, as there is no close season for them.

SERVES 4
8 smallish cabbage leaves
70g/2½oz unsalted butter
100g/3½oz shallots, chopped
4 young pigeons, dressed weight of each about 450g/1lb, hearts, livers and innards reserved
350ml/12fl oz Coteaux de l'Aubance, or similar medium-dry Anjou white wine
200g/7oz good-quality sausage meat
1 egg, beaten
1 tablespoon chopped chives
1 piece of caul fat (optional)
200g/7oz piece of smoked belly of pork or bacon, diced
200g/7oz onions, chopped
200g/7oz carrots, chopped
2 sprigs of thyme
1 bay leaf
500ml/18fl oz chicken stock
salt and freshly ground black pepper

Preheat the oven to 190C/375F/gas5.

Blanch the cabbage leaves in boiling salted water for 2 minutes. Drain, refresh under cold running water, drain well again and leave to dry and cool on paper towels or a clean tea towel.

Melt 15g/½oz butter in a heavy-based saucepan, add the shallots and finely chopped pigeon innards, if available. Cook gently for 2-3 minutes. Stir in 55ml/2fl oz of the wine, then boil until reduced. Season and mix with the sausage meat, egg and chives.

Spread out the cabbage leaves, cut out the central veins and divide the stuffing between the leaves. Fold the leaves over to make neat parcels then wrap these in the caul, if available.

Melt 25g/1oz butter in a flameproof casserole into which the cabbage parcels will just fit, and add half the pork or bacon, and half the onions and carrots. Cook, stirring occasionally, until lightly browned. Pack the cabbage parcels on top, making sure the seams are underneath. Tuck in the herbs, pour over 175ml/6fl oz of the wine and sufficient stock to come just over halfway up the parcels. Cook on the lower shelf of the oven for about 40 minutes. After this time pour off and reserve the cooking liquid.

Meanwhile, rub the pigeons with some of the remaining butter, season, and roast on the shelf above the cabbage, basting from time to time, for about 15 minutes. Remove the breasts and legs from the carcasses and keep warm. Chop the carcasses and return them to the roasting dish with the remaining onion and carrot and brown lightly. Stir in the remaining wine, boil until almost evaporated then stir in the liquid from the cabbage. Boil until slightly thickened. Pass through a sieve, reheat and gradually swirl in the remaining butter. Adjust the seasoning.

Transfer the cabbage parcels and the carrot and onion to warmed plates, add the pigeon breasts and legs, and pour over the sauce.

(Above)
Onions put by amongst a jumble of old-fashioned agricultural tools and implements (all probably still in use, and valued for their original purposes) will eventually be used to add savour to winter cooking.

TARTE AUX MIRABELLES

Mirabelle Tart

(Illustrated above)

Château de la Jaillière near Angers has belonged to the d'Anthènaise family for hundreds of years. In the grounds there is the most idyllic walled fruit garden – a real haven of sun, fruit, vegetables and herbs – from where the present Countess picked the small sublime mirabelles for the *tarte* she had prepared as the finale to our lunch.

This recipe for a glazed tart can be used with any suitable fruit. For a classic apple tart, peel, core and thinly slice sweet eating apples and arrange them generously, in neat overlapping rows, on the pastry case, as shown above. Peaches make an equally delicious tart.

SERVES 6-8
200g/7oz plain flour
pinch of salt
100g/3½oz unsalted butter, chopped
1½ tablespoons vanilla sugar
550-700g/1¼-1½lb mirabelle plums or greengages, halved and stoned
sugar, preferably nibbed, for sprinkling

Sift the flour and the salt into a bowl, toss in the butter, then rub in until the mixture resembles breadcrumbs. Stir in the sugar and sufficient water to bind to a dough. Cover and chill for 30 minutes.

On a floured surface, roll out the pastry and use it to line a 25cm/10in round flan tin or a 34 x 12cm/13 x 5in loose-bottomed rectangular tart tin. Press it well into the tin.

Preheat the oven to 200C/400F/gas6. Prick the base of the pastry case and chill it for 15-30 minutes. Bake it blind for about 10 minutes, until lightly coloured.

Arrange the fruit in the pastry case. Cook in the oven until the fruit is almost tender. Sprinkle with sugar to taste, then return to the oven for about 5 minutes until the sugar melts and glazes the surface. Serve warm or cold.

COUPE DE FRAISES

Strawberries in Wine

The luscious Angevin strawberries, which ripen to bright fruitiness in the clear warm sunlight of the area, marry to perfection with the many styles of good Anjou wines: crystal-honeyed white wines of the Coteaux du Layon; red wines with low tannin levels and plenty of soft fruit typified by Saumur-Champigny; and sparkling wines to suit all tastes – dry, *demi-sec*, sweet, and a light sweetish red that makes a surprisingly good match for the berries. The end result will vary according to the style of wine.

SERVES 4
450g/1lb ripe strawberries
caster sugar (optional)
1 bottle sparkling Saumur, chilled, or about 300ml/10fl oz still white or red wine

Hull the strawberries, and sprinkle with a little sugar unless a sweet wine is used.

If using sparkling wine, pour over sufficient wine almost to cover. Cover and chill lightly. Then divide the strawberries between 4 goblets and pour over more wine almost to cover.

If using still white or red wine, pour over the wine, cover and keep in a cool place for about 2 hours, then chill lightly.

BIJANE

Bread with Fruit and Wine

Bijane (you might also come across *miot*, *chicolle*, *chicolte* or *rôtie*) is one of several variations found in Touraine as well as Anjou on the theme of fruit in wine with bread, traditionally eaten as a *casse-croûte* at about four o'clock in the afternoon – an alcoholic afternoon tea!

The practice of adding bread to wine was started in the days before the fining of wines (which removes the fine particles of sediment) became so efficient, the bread serving to clarify the wine. *Bijane* is nowadays served as a dessert.

SERVES 4
550g/1¼lb ripe strawberries, hulled
about 85g/3oz vanilla sugar
about 575ml/1pt red wine
4 slices of brioche, to serve, toasted if liked

Sprinkle the sugar over the strawberries, pour on the wine, cover with a plate and leave in a cool place for 12 hours.

Serve in cold dishes, accompanied by slices of brioche to eat separately or to dunk or crumble into the wine.

LA MOUSSE DE COINTREAU, SAUCE AU MIEL

Cointreau Mousse with Honey Sauce

(Illustrated above right)

For his *gelée d'orange*, Paul Le Quéré of Pavillon Paul Le Quéré (see page 117) makes a syrup of 85g/3oz sugar and 85ml/3fl oz water, to which he adds 1½ teaspoons powdered gelatine dissolved in 125ml/4½fl oz orange juice.

SERVES 6
FOR THE CUSTARD
1 vanilla pod
250ml/9fl oz milk
3 egg yolks
55g/2oz caster sugar
FOR THE MOUSSE
grated zest of 1 orange, blanched and well drained
1 scant tbsp gelatine
4 tbsp Cointreau
300ml/½pt crème fraîche, whipped to soft peaks
flavourless oil, for greasing
gelée d'orange (*see left*)
125g/4½oz flower honey
75g/2½oz unsalted butter, chopped
red fruits, mint leaves and saffron threads, to decorate

Add the vanilla pod to the milk and bring gently to a simmer. Cover, remove from the heat and leave for about 20 minutes for the flavour to infuse.

Strain the milk and use to make a custard with the egg yolks. Leave to cool.

Add the Cointreau and orange zest and slowly stir in the gelatine dissolved in 3 tablespoons of water. Leave until beginning to set, then fold in the whipped cream.

Lightly oil six 7.5cm/3in muffin rings and place them in the centres of 6 cold plates. Divide the orange mixture between them. Chill in the refrigerator for 2 hours. Spoon the cooled *gelée d'orange* over the tops and then return to the refrigerator for a further 15 minutes. Gently melt the honey with the butter then beat well with an electric whisk. Remove the rings from the mousses, surround the mousses with honey sauce and decorate with the red fruit, mint leaves and saffron.

POIRIER

Pear Cake

A yeast dough is traditional for *poirier* (around Saumur it may be a brioche dough rather than the one given here). It can be finished after cooking by brushing with a glaze made by boiling down the syrup in which the pears were poached, boosted perhaps with *eau-de-vie de poires Williams* or Cointreau.

SERVES 4
175g/6oz strong plain flour
salt
85g/3oz vanilla sugar
½ packet easy-blend yeast
2 eggs
85ml/3fl oz milk
55g/2oz softened unsalted butter, plus more for greasing
2-3 ripe pears
115g/4oz sugar
oil, for greasing

Sift the flour and salt into a bowl, stir in the vanilla sugar and yeast and form a well in the centre. Beat together the eggs and milk and pour into the well, then stir all the ingredients together until evenly blended and the mixture forms a dough.

Turn out on a lightly floured surface and knead until smooth and elastic. Place in a lightly oiled bowl, cover with a damp cloth and leave until the dough has doubled in volume.

Turn out on to the floured surface again and punch down, then lightly knead in the butter. Form into a round about 14cm/5½in across. Place in a well-buttered 15cm/6in round cake tin, cover with a damp cloth and leave until risen.

Meanwhile, preheat the oven to 190C/375F/gas5, and peel and core the pears.

Over a low heat, dissolve the sugar in about 450ml/15fl oz water, then bring just to a simmer. Add the pears and poach until just tender; the time varies according to the ripeness of the fruit. Using a slotted spoon, lift the pears from the syrup and slice them evenly.

Bake the cake in the oven for about 15 minutes. At the end of that time, take it out and arrange the pears on top. Brush with some of the syrup and return to the oven for a further 15-20 minutes, or until the cake is lightly browned. It will be ready when a fine skewer inserted in the centre comes out clean.

Serve warm with crème fraîche.

(Left)
Traditional and well-used utensils hang in a busy restaurant kitchen.

CRÉMET D'ANGERS

Cream Cheese Dessert

(Illustrated right)

The prettiest way to serve *crémet d'Angers* is in individual portions using the heart-shaped *cœur à la crème* moulds that you can buy in good kitchenware shops or department stores; or you can make a large quantity in a muslin-lined sieve, and spoon it out generously into individual bowls. In Gratien & Meyer's private dining room in Saumur (see page 107), where our example was photographed, they serve this dessert admirably simply just with fresh strawberries, but the fruit can be currants, nectarines, peaches, apricots or raspberries.

SERVES 6
500ml/18fl oz crème fraîche
3-4 egg whites, whisked
sugar or vanilla sugar, fresh fruit (see above) and crème fraîche, to serve

Line an 850ml/1½pt mould, or 6 individual *cœur à la crème* moulds, or a sieve, with muslin or cheesecloth.

Whip two-thirds of the crème fraîche until it forms soft peaks. Whisk in the egg whites until the mixture is stiff again.

Spoon into the mould(s) or sieve, and leave in a very cool place or the refrigerator to drain for 8-24 hours: the longer the mixture is left, the firmer it becomes.

Turn out the *crémet(s)* on a cold plate or plates. Serve sugar or vanilla sugar, fresh fruit and crème fraîche separately.

TO THE SEA

THE FINAL STRETCHES OF THE RIVER AS IT FLOWS THROUGH THE PAYS NANTAIS TO THE ATLANTIC

FROM THE VICINITY OF CHAMPTOCEAUX, ON ITS SOUTH BANK, THE LOIRE LEAVES ANJOU AND STARTS THE LAST LEG OF ITS JOURNEY, THROUGH THE PAYS Nantais to the sea. The hills on either side of the river dwindle away in the south, but continue a little further downstream on the opposite shore to Mauves. The banks of the river are mainly reed-fringed, and the land a low, flat, marshy plain of alluvium, changing from mainly pasture to market gardens on the approaches to Nantes. After Nantes, the river passes by an appealingly lonely low plateau of rough pasture, vineyards, heaths, fen and little woods. Around Paimbœuf, waters that had a few kilometres earlier constituted the glorious *fleuve royal*, dissipate into oblivion and become no more than a few drops in the mass of the Atlantic Ocean.

The Atlantic is the major climatic influence here, resulting in pleasant, temperate weather ideal for growing fruits, early vegetables and vines. However, the ocean also causes a gentle

(Opposite) The smallholding was at one time the norm for produce grown in the regions of the Pays Nantais, as here near Champtoceaux; but now larger-scale, more commercially viable, market gardens are taking over.
(Above) A Nantais letterbox.

GUANES
GAVOTTES
PETIT NANTAIS
24 SABLES AU BEURRE
VINS
200 M

west wind and temperatures can vary wildly, allowing oleanders and umbrella pines to grow to the south of the Loire, but producing damaging frosts well into April.

The Pays Nantais is an administrative creation. It does not have a unified and distinct overall cuisine, as it is made up principally of three very different areas which were only recently brought together under the one name. It is, however, the home of two of the Loire's most famous products, the sauce *beurre blanc* (see pages 131 and 136) and Muscadet wine.

The food in the north and west reflects that of Brittany, while in the east there are Angevin influences. To the south, the coast and the Vendée put their stamp on the cooking; while at the heart, in sophisticated, cosmopolitan Nantes, dishes from all three areas exist alongside those owing their origins to its position as a port. From the eighteenth century, sugar, rum, spices, nuts, bananas and other fruits passed through the city, and inevitably found their way into the cooking. To supply provisions for the crews of the merchant ships, food-processing industries also grew up. The French inventor Nicolas Appert developed the canning process which enabled local fruits and vegetables to be preserved for long sea voyages; fish was also canned. There is still some food manufacturing in Nantes, but of greater gastronomic importance is France's second-largest fresh food wholesale market after Paris's Rungis, which owes its existence to the abundance and calibre of local produce, and good transport links.

Nantais poultry, such as duck, chicken, quails and guinea fowl, are not actually bred in Nantes. The name is a synonym for the better known and highly prized Challans poultry. Challans is the town where the birds are reared according to a specially designated free-range regime (Challans is not the name of a breed), but Nantes was the point from where they were dispatched to the rest of the country so the packing cases and paperwork were stamped with its name. *Poulets d'Ancenis*, which come from the small town on the northern bank of the Loire almost on the Anjou border, also have a certain standing locally.

To the south of Nantes, the mild climate, varied soil and ready access to profitable markets have spawned innumerable market gardens specializing in *primeurs*. The vegetables are mainly those traditionally associated with the area, such as carrots (there is a variety of carrot called 'Nantes'), turnips, red radishes, leeks and potatoes, as well as artichokes and asparagus. It is also the modern centre for the growing of the many types of salad leaves that have enjoyed such popularity in recent years: *frisée* (curly endive); two varieties of *mâche* (corn salad); and commercially grown *pissenlits* (dandelion leaves). Herbs, tomatoes and strawberries complete the line-up of the major market-garden produce.

For years, the marshes, ponds and streams of the Marais have provided wild food. Shiny green strands of *salicorne* (marsh samphire) are picked early in the spring, before their central spikes form. They are cooked very simply, and eaten like *haricots verts* with butter, perhaps as an accompaniment to oysters, mussels or salmon. Alternatively, they may be pickled in white wine vinegar, like *cornichons*. If they are not picked until later in the summer, the flesh has to be stripped off the spike by pulling it between the teeth.

1 *Mussels and oysters on sale on the Atlantic coast near La Baule. Mussels make the best accompaniment to a typical Muscadet.* **2** *A selection of rye breads: rye was the common grain of Brittany, and is still used to make the delicious breads that go well with the region's shellfish.* **3** *A worker packing celery on a farm outside Nantes. The city has France's second largest wholesale market, and is used particularly for its vegetables.* **4** *An architectural detail at La Cigale, a seafood restaurant in the centre of Nantes noted for its interior.* **5** *Ivy and ornamental vines on a wall near Champtoceaux.* **6** *LU is the now very large company that was first created for the production of the original* petits beurres *biscuits.* **7** Berlingots *are boiled sweets, variously flavoured and coloured, and common in the region.* **8** *Langoustines, minutes away from their watery home, plump and fine-flavoured and ready for the pot.* **9** *At a simple sign like this, the wine will most likely also be simple, although you may be lucky and find a real vinous bargain.*

1	**2**	**3**
4	**5**	**6**
7	**8**	**9**

(Above left)
SELECTION OF SEAFOOD
In the Pays Nantais seafood more or less takes over from freshwater fish; and as there are plenty of people, especially restaurants, who are willing to pay high prices for good fish, there are plenty of fishermen making a living off the shores.

(Above right)
THE LOIRE
The river peacefully nearing its journey's end.

At one time, another wild food provided in abundance by the marshes were frogs. Although today there is still a limited amount of frog farming, gone are the days when *cuisses de grenouilles* could be seen in fishmongers, hanging in pairs suspended from wooden skewers. Most of the frogs' legs used in the area now have been imported from eastern Europe, and are usually frozen stiff, although some restaurants buy in live whole frogs. The classic way of serving the legs is with *sauce poulette*, a rich, mild-tasting and pale sauce. Chef Delphin at La Châtaigneraie (see page 146) claims to be one of the only two people surviving who know the true recipe. South of Nantes, a more local accompaniment is a sauce made from the watercress that thrives on the Marais.

Further south, in the Vendée, life has been – and still is – more rural. For instance, Vendéens are fond of beans, especially the variety known as *mojettes* or *mougettes* (see page 138), so called because they are flat and white, with a black line around them, resembling a nun at prayer. *Mojettes* have such a following that a 'Confrérie de Mojettes' was formed in the mid-1980s to generate publicity and promote the beans. In the late summer, *mojettes* are eaten fresh, but they are mainly dried for use in warming *pots au feu*, often in combination with another great standby of the area, cabbage. This occupied such an important place in the local diet that the Royalist insurgents of the Vendée, and later the counter-revolutionaries of the 1790s, were dubbed '*Chouans*'.

Vendéen ham is traditionally heavily salted and often eaten raw. Light cooking in butter intensifies the saltiness and the local means of combating this is to eat it with *mojettes*. Modern less salty hams can be quite delicious, making a better marriage with ripe (locally grown, of course) charentais melon even than Parma ham.

Cattle were introduced after phylloxera decimated the vineyards in the 1870s. However, trade for the once-important cattle market at Cholet has declined. The local sheep are highly commended by chefs, and in spring there are some *pré-salé* lambs from the coast.

On the other side of the Loire, culture and food take on an altogether different feel and flavour – that of neighbouring Brittany. The most obvious evidence of the Breton presence are *galettes* (see page 147). At one time these were used as bread, being dipped into soup, used to mop up juices from a stew, or wrapped around a filling to make a meal in themselves. The custom grew up for *galettiers* to sell their wares from stalls, especially along the estuary. In a few places on market days, *galettiers* may still be seen deftly flipping over *galettes* with a wooden *rabot*, before adding an appetizing filling – sweet or savoury – as ordered by a waiting customer.

The taste of salt characterizes the cooking of the Pays Nantais, principally because the butter most usually used in cooking is salted. This probably stems from the days when the butter had to be preserved by the addition of salt to slow down the onset of rancidity during long sea voyages, coupled with the occurrence along the Breton coast of natural evaporating pans, *œillets*, for supplying salt from the sea. The first salt of the year, *fleur de sel*, is particularly fine, with a subtle taste other than just that of salt.

There are also plenty of good buttery things to be found in the region. *Pains Nantais* are butter-and-almond biscuits and Nantes is the birthplace of famed 'Petit Beurre' biscuits, although their originator, Monsieur Lefèvre, did not come from the area. He adapted a recipe which he had brought with him and the rectangular-shaped biscuit grew in popularity, eventually becoming known as '*le Véritable Petit Beurre*'. In 1987, a large purpose-built factory was opened just outside Nantes, and now each year 15 million 'le Petit Beurre Nantais' come off its production lines.

The buttery sauce you will come across time and time again near the Loire, and in Nantes, is *Beurre blanc* (see right). *Beurre blanc* was described by Curnonsky (see page 105) as a 'sauce of exquisite finesse and lightness'. The shallots which give a discreet seasoning 'must be, so to speak, volatized in the vinegar', and should be no more than a remote presence, so must therefore be chopped very finely. Another 'secret', according to locals, is to use *demi-sel* (lightly salted) butter. The inclusion of cream, however, is definitely not authentic.

Both Nantais and Angevins claim with quiet certainty that their region is the home of *beurre blanc*. However, it would be wrong to say there is a battle between the two regions over the subject, as each seems oblivious of the claims of the other. In support of their claim, Angevins say that their local shallots have to be used to obtain the necessary subtlety of flavour. I have even been told by an Angevin that *beurre blanc* made in Nantes is not true

BEURRE BLANC

Nantais claim that beurre blanc *was 'created' – albeit unintentionally – by Madame Clémence, cook to the Marquis de Goulaine at the turn of the*

century, during the preparation of a meal for a particularly important dinner party.

With so much to do, she asked one of her assistants to make the sauce béarnaise, *while she attended to other things. As the meal was being served, Madame Clémence noticed that something was amiss with the* béarnaise *– the egg yolks had been omitted! The faulty sauce tasted surprisingly good, which was fortunate as there was no time to replace it, so it was duly served. After the meal, Madame Clémence was summoned to the dining room. Up she went in trepidation, expecting a reprimand, but instead she was congratulated on the 'new sauce' and eventually* buerre blanc *became a classic.*

beurre blanc, but *beurre Nantais*, the shallots having been strained out. Nantais, on the other hand, claim that the sauce originated with a failed *sauce béarnaise* made by one Madame Clémence; her new sauce was such a success that she became a local personality, eventually opening her own restaurant. As so often happens, the sauce is more than likely to have been created in both regions, as both Nantais and Angevin cooks had access to the same ingredients, and because a buttery, slightly sharp sauce is the obvious accompaniment to the dryish, fairly bland river fish that it classically accompanies.

There are some small producers of goats' cheese, but the best-known cheese is Curé-Nantais, created in the last century by a priest in an effort to provide food for the poor. Curé-Nantais, resembling St-Paulin both in appearance and flavour, is a flat disc with a golden rind and a paste that is pale straw-coloured, smooth and punctured by small holes. Production of this subtle, rounded and distinctively flavoured cheese is now limited, but look for the cheese from a small farm near Pornic.

Although there is some freshwater fish in the cooking of the Pays Nantais, with the proximity of the estuary and the coast the fruits of the sea are more in evidence. There is a wealth of sea fish, such as line-caught turbot from the inshore waters of the Atlantic, and seafood, such as scallops, lobsters, a variety of crabs, langoustines, and oysters from the lower stretches of the river and along the estuary. Mussels usually come from further south along the Vendée coast. There is an increasing amount of fish-farming, but small fishing ports are still the home of small-scale fishermen. The town of Paimbœuf – which I think acts as a marker for the demise of the Loire – is, for example, a thriving little place, despite the roadstead being partly silted up. The tiny harbour, complete with lighthouse, is busy with boats chugging about laying or hauling in their nets and traps, unloading eels, enormous lampreys, mullet and shad by the netful, while their owners bargain on the quayside. Tall reeds rustle at the water's edge and cafés and bars line the waterfront, while petrol-tankers head up-river from the huge refineries at Donges on the opposite shore.

At the dead of a very dark night or in the early morning from the end of February to early April, when the spring flood-tide washes up the estuary, if you happen to look out across the river near the estuary and see lights bobbing eerily on the water, it will be a flotilla of barges and small boats, each lit with a single lantern. From the boats will be suspended buckets or large carboy-like containers of thick glass attached to cords, in the eager expectation of catching a haul of wriggling, transparent *piballes* or *civelles* (elvers). These immature eels may look as fragile as glass rods, but they will have swum over 3,200 kilometres (2,000 miles) from the Sargasso Sea. Provided they elude the buckets and other traps, they will force their way up the Loire until they reach the streams. Here they will stay for up to 9 years, to grow into full-size eels, before returning along the river – again having to dodge the hopeful efforts of fishermen to stop them – back to the Atlantic and across to the Sargasso Sea to spawn and die. The favourite local way with *piballes* is to fry them briefly in hot oil until they turn white, then to serve them sizzling hot with salt and pepper.

MARQUIS DE GOULAINE
The family of Robert, Marquis de Goulaine have lived in the same château for 1,000 years. Today the vineyards are large by Muscadet standards and are divided into two distinct areas – the Château de Goulaine with nearby Clos de Montys, and Château de la Grange.

Both Muscadet and Gros Plant are produced, with most of the wines being bottled *sur lie*. Made by traditional vinification methods combined with modern scientific knowledge and meticulous attention to detail, Marquis de Goulaine's Muscadet can be worthy of consideration as a 'serious' full-bodied wine.

(Opposite)
GEESE FARMING
The rearing of geese is not traditional in the Loire regions, so this sight of a flock of farmed geese is a rare one. Duck are more commonly bred for the lucrative foie gras and other related products.

(Below)
NEWLY-PLANTED VINES
While an older generation turns to more reliable crops, a band of eager younger vignerons is keen to embrace the vine. Newly-planted vines need protecting from the attentions of rabbits.

(Below right)
WINE TASTING
Most cost-effective for a small farmer-vigneron is to sell his production direct to the public; driving through the region you will often see simple, hand-made signs inviting you for a roadside dégustation (tasting).

WINES

By far the most important wines of the Pays Nantais are Muscadet and Gros Plant, with the former being about treble the latter in volume produced. Muscadet is not a region, but a grape variety that was introduced in the mid-eighteenth century. Before that, most of the wines were red. In 1709 a frost so severe that the coastal waters froze destroyed the existing vines. A move towards white wine production had already started, so the vines chosen for replanting were of a white variety and included the melon de Bourgogne. In its new home it came to be known as '*muscadet*', literally 'small musky one'.

There are three Muscadet *appellations*: simple, regional Muscadet, which can come from the largest area but which accounts for only about 10% of the output, then slightly better but scarcer (about 5%) Muscadet des Coteaux de Loire, and lastly the most severely delimited – and most expensive – Muscadet de Sèvre-et-Maine.

About 85% of the Muscadet vineyards lie south-east of Nantes, where the climate is so mild that oleanders and fig trees flourish. The vine has characteristic rounded leaves and

the grapes ripen early, making them susceptible to late frosts, as was the case at the end of April 1991, when nearly all of the flowers were destroyed in some places. The *vendange* is correspondingly early, usually taking place in September, or even as early as August.

The light structure, restrained alcohol and naturally low acidity of Muscadet make it liable to oxidation. To keep it fresh, it is bottled by the method unique to the Pays Nantais, known as *sur lie*. When fermentation has stopped, the wine is not transferred to other vats or wooden *fûts*, which could allow contact with air, but instead is left to rest on its lees (sediment) during the following winter, and bottled without racking before 30 June (racking could also give exposure to air and destroy the slight 'prickle' of natural carbon dioxide that makes Muscadet tingle pleasantly on the tongue). This system extracts the maximum flavour from the grapes, adding character to the wine. Unfortunately, as it can be a tricky process to carry out well, it also adds to the price.

Muscadet is always dry and light in flavour and alcohol (uniquely, the maximum level, 12 degrees, is laid down in the *appellation* – although this may be increased in exceptional years). Well-made Muscadet is crisp and clean, an easy quaffing wine which needs chilling, making pleasant summer drinking on its own or with mussels or oysters. Poorly made wines, however, are thin and acidic. Top wines of good years can last up to 5 years, or even 10, but although delicious, they will not taste quite like normal Muscadet.

As in the other Loire regions, the Pays Nantais is an area mainly of small growers, and much of the vinification – as well as about 50% of the marketing and selling – is done by the numerous *négociants*. Muscadet began to 'take off' in Britain after the Second World War, and by the late 1980s its combination of easy drinking and low price (and familiarity) made it the top-selling white wine in the UK. Either through a desire to 'progress' and try out new techniques, or because of concern about the number of vastly improved cheap wines being made further south in France, Spain and Italy, some growers have been experimenting with *macération pelliculaire* (a process which leaves the fermenting juice in contact with the skins for longer, so more aromatic compounds are extracted – but at the risk of harmful oxidation and excessive acidity), and ageing the young wine in new oak barrels. Both of these techniques change the essential *typicité* of Muscadet, and are frowned upon by Muscadet lovers – *vignerons* and drinkers alike.

The 'second' wine of the Pays Nantais is Gros Plant. It can be made more or less anywhere in the region and only warrants VDQS status; it too can be bottled *sur lie*. Gros Plant is made from the folle blanche, a large greenish grape that produces a simple, light, dry, sometimes rather acidic, wine.

The area around the small town of Ancenis, on the north bank of the Loire, also produces a small amount of wine, the majority of which (90%) is red. Light, smooth, fruity and slightly aromatic, Coteaux d'Ancenis red wines are best when young and served lightly chilled. The grapes can be gamay à jus blanc, cabernet franc and cabernet sauvignon. The rosés are lightly fruity, the whites fresh and dry.

LOUIS MÉTAIREAU

Louis Métaireau runs what is often regarded as the most prestigious Muscadet wine business, yet he started with just 1½ hectares (4 acres) of vines. The driving force responsible for his success, apart from his dynamic personality, is his passionate belief in the *typicité* of Muscadet, and its quality. In 1957 he formed a group, unique in France, of nine Muscadet *vignerons* who together agree to co-operate in the marketing of their wines. Each grower joins with the others to select their joint fourteen best *cuvées*. At three blind tastings

throughout the year, they eliminate any wines that do not reach a pass mark, and the chosen wines are sold under the Métaireau label. Apart from the kudos of coming first among peers, there is the incentive of 40,000 francs for the producer of the top wine.

JARDINS DE LA FORGE *
1 bis place Piliers
Champtoceaux
Tel 40 83 56 23
See recipe far right

People who have known of this one-time forge for a while will know it as Auberge de la Forge, but when chef-proprietor Paul Pauvert added a pâtisserie for the sale of his excellent cakes and pastries, and set aside a small area where they could be enjoyed *in situ* with cups of coffee or tea, he had to change the name as he had changed the restaurant's status. Set on an unusually high spot overlooking the Loire as it begins its final run to the sea, Champtoceaux

commands a wonderful panoramic view of the river. And it seems most appropriate that you can be assured of dining well on dishes made from the best of the particular season's river, sea and shellfish.

BEURRE BLANC

White Butter Sauce

From Nantes to Orléans, nearly every chef and cook to whom I have spoken has their own version of *beurre blanc*. The most frequent variable is the liquid that is used. Some use all white wine vinegar (which tends to make the sauce rather sharp), some specify that the vinegar should derive from Muscadet wine, and others use a combination of wine and vinegar. Mme Métaireau, wife of the Muscadet *vigneron* (see page 135), uses a bottle of Muscadet for 4 people, which does produce the most well-balanced sauce and is the one I use for special occasions. At other times I use as much Muscadet as I feel fit and add just a touch of white *vinaigre d'Orléans*. (See also page 131).

SERVES 4
2 shallots, preferably grey, very finely chopped
about 175ml/6fl oz Muscadet (see above)
1 tablespoon or more white vinaigre d'Orléans
175g/6oz very cold lightly salted butter, diced
salt and freshly ground white pepper

In a small, thick-bottomed, non-aluminium pan over a fairly low heat, simmer the shallots in the wine and vinegar until the shallots have almost dissolved and there is hardly any liquid left.

Remove the pan from the heat for about 30 seconds to cool it slightly, then place over a very low heat. Using a small balloon whisk, whisk in the butter one piece at a time, making sure each piece is incorporated before adding the next, to give a smooth sauce with the consistency of thick whipped cream. It should not be too firm, but have distinct body. If at any time the mixture seems to be becoming too warm, with the butter showing signs of melting, remove the pan from the heat to cool down, but keep whisking.

As the last piece of butter disappears into the sauce, remove the pan from the heat and whisk for a few more seconds. Season to taste.

Serve as soon as possible, either with the food it is to accompany, or in a sauce boat warmed to the same temperature as the sauce (which should be only warm, not hot). The sauce can be kept warm for a few minutes before serving by placing the saucepan in a pan of warm water.

SOUPE DE CRUSTACÉS GLACÉE AUX COQUILLAGES

Cold Mixed Seafood Soup

(Illustrated right)

When Paul Pauvert of Les Jardins de la Forge (see left) makes his wonderfully clear-flavoured soup he adds 100g/3½oz lobster shells with the langoustine shells. This does give a better flavour, but as it is neither absolutely necessary nor very realistic for most domestic cooks, I have not included them in the recipe here.

SERVES 4-6
20 live langoustines
900g/2lb fish bones, preferably from fish such as turbot, sole and red mullet
3 onions, chopped
2 slim young leeks, sliced
500ml/18fl oz Muscadet
a bouquet garni consisting of sprigs of parsley, celery leaves, fennel leaves, thyme and a bay leaf
20 mussels, 20 cockles and 40 clams
salt and freshly ground white pepper
chopped basil, chopped parsley and parsley sprigs, to garnish

Drop the langoustines into boiling water and cook for 4-7 minutes until the shells turn red. Drain and leave to cool before removing the shells and dark intestinal tract. Reserve the langoustines and 115g/4oz of the shells.

In a large heavy casserole, sweat the fish bones, onions, leeks and reserved langoustine shells without any fat or liquid for 4-5 minutes, shaking the casserole occasionally to move them around. Stir in the wine, then boil until well reduced. Add 500ml/18fl oz water and the bouquet garni. Bring to the boil, skim the surface to remove any scum, then leave to simmer for 20-30 minutes, skimming frequently during that time.

Meanwhile, separately steam the mussels, cockles and clams in covered pans containing a little boiling water for 5-7 minutes until the shells open. Drain well, remove the flesh from the shells and cool.

Pass the soup through a sieve lined with muslin. Leave to cool, then season with salt and white pepper. Chill lightly.

Divide all the shellfish between 4 or 6 cold soup plates, scatter over the herbs and then carefully ladle over the soup. Drink a good Muscadet de Sèvre-et-Maine *sur lie* with this.

MOJETTES SUR CANAPÉS

Vendéen Beans on Toast

Mojettes are softer than many dried beans when cooked, so it is not surprising that they gave rise to this recipe, recalled by Mme Thai-Thuc of an old Vendéen family. In the absence of *mojettes*, try the recipe with well-cooked butter beans, but do use a good salted butter.

MAKES 1 SLICE
thinnish slice of pain de campagne
salted butter
about 2 spoonfuls of mojettes, *cooked until tender*

Bake the bread in an oven until just becoming crisp, or toast it slowly. Spread with butter followed by the beans, squashing them as you do so.

For *mojettes au beurre blanc* simply spoon *beurre blanc* (page 136) over the cooked beans.

(Below)
The humble cabbage is a favourite vegetable all along the Loire.

LANGOUSTINES POÊLÉES EN SALADE

Langoustine and Spinach Salad

(Illustrated opposite)

I was discussing with Louis Métaireau (see page 135) how he matched his wines with food. When it came to the cuvée *Cadre Noir* he said it was perfect with langoustines, especially warm langoustines. A *salade tiède* perhaps? But no, because the acidity of the vinaigrette is an enemy of wine. I put forward the idea of using Muscadet in place of vinegar, as it has a high acidity. Not really, the alcohol would be wrong, and wine would be too dilute. The solution: boil the wine to drive off the alcohol and concentrate the flavour. Christian Thomas-Trophime, *chef-patron* of La Manoir de la Comète in the southern outskirts of Nantes, was telephoned, and this is the recipe he produced for our lunch; its full title is *Langoustines poêlées et jeunes pousses d'épinards en salade à la réduction d'échalotes au Muscadet*. With it we drank Louis Métaireau's L.M. 1989.

SERVES 4
about 1.5-1.8kg/3½-4lb live langoustines
4 small heads of young spinach leaves
40g/1½oz shallots, preferably grey, finely chopped
575ml/1pt Muscadet
salt and freshly ground black pepper
1 tablespoon olive oil

Cook the langoustines in well-salted boiling water for about 3-4 minutes, drain, and leave to cool completely before removing their shells and their dark intestinal tracts.

Boil the Muscadet until it has reduced by three-quarters, then add the shallots and seasoning. Keep warm on the side of the stove, or over a very low heat, using a heat diffuser if necessary.

Arrange the spinach leaves on 4 plates. Briefly sauté the shelled langoustines with a touch of olive oil, season and place on the spinach. Pour the Muscadet dressing over and serve warm.

CHOUÉE

Cabbage with Butter

The essential elements of this apparently simple dish are the taste of fresh, lightly cooked cabbage, fresh butter, and, most important, the melting of the butter in the heat of the cabbage, not of the stove. Some people add a drop or so of a local white wine vinegar when the cabbage is served; I find that lemon juice makes a good alternative.

Dartrée de choux verts is just another name for what seems to be the same dish, but versions of *chouée* that fricassée the cabbage in butter until it is soft are different altogether.

SERVES 4
4 small green piochon *or* piochou *cabbages or*
4 small cabbage hearts, halved
115g/4oz fresh salted butter, diced
salt and freshly ground black pepper
mild white wine vinegar or lemon juice (optional)

Cook the cabbages in boiling salted water until tender, then drain well. The cabbage may be turned into a serving dish immediately, or mashed and then reheated.

Sprinkle the cabbage with seasoning and add the butter.

Serve with mild white wine vinegar or lemon juice trickled over, if liked.

ESTOUFFADE DE TURBOT AU MUSCADET

Turbot with Loire Vegetables and Muscadet

This recipe won first prize for M. Delphin of La Châtaigneraie (see page 146) in the *Coupe de la Ville de Nantes* competition.

SERVES 4
4 young carrots, cut into cubes
100g/3½oz unsalted butter
2 shallots, finely chopped
2 young leeks, finely chopped
4 turbot fillets, cut across into slices
½ bottle of Muscadet
150ml/5fl oz crème fraîche
white grapes, seeded, peeled and warmed in butter
lightly cooked asparagus spears, tossed in butter

Blanch the carrots in boiling salted water for 5 minutes. Drain well.

In a flameproof casserole, melt 55g/2oz of the butter, add the shallots, leeks and carrots and cook until softened.

Place the turbot on top, pour over wine to come part of the way up, and poach for 5 minutes. Take out the fish and vegetables and keep warm. Add any remaining wine to the cooking juices and boil until almost all has evaporated. Stir in the crème fraîche and simmer until thick. Remove from the heat and whisk in the remaining butter. Season.

Arrange the turbot and garnish on 4 warmed plates and pour the sauce over.

(Below)
Turbot as cooked for us at La Châtaigneraie, served with red fruits as a garnish.

TURBOT À LA LIGNE AUX CÈPES

Turbot with Ceps

Fishermen still go out from the coast to catch turbot by rod and line rather than in a net, because it is known locally how much better the fish will taste, and many will pay a premium for fish caught this way. The distinguished texture and flavour marry beautifully with those of ceps.

SERVES 4
1.8kg/4lb turbot, filleted
200ml/7fl oz crème fraîche
85g/3oz slightly salted butter, diced, plus more for sautéing
85g/3oz unsalted butter, diced
2 tablespoons chopped fresh chervil, chives and savory
juice of 1 lemon
fleur de sel (see page 131) or sea salt, for sprinkling
1kg/2¼lb ceps, thickly sliced
salt and freshly ground black pepper

Season the turbot very lightly.

Boil the crème fraîche until reduced by half. Over a low heat, gradually whisk in the two butters, one piece at a time, making sure each piece is fully incorporated before adding the next. Keep it warm.

Dry-fry the turbot in a non-stick pan until lightly coloured on each side. Sprinkle with *fleur de sel* or sea salt.

Quickly sauté the ceps in butter until lightly browned (or 'given the colour of autumn' as the original French recipe states). Add the herbs, seasoning and lemon juice to taste. Pour the sauce over 4 warmed plates, place the fish on top and scatter with ceps.

ALOSE GRILLÉE, SAUCE L'OSEILLE

Grilled Shad with Sorrel Sauce

(Illustrated below)

The best shad I have ever eaten was plainly grilled over a fire of vine prunings built on the river bank. Crusty bread and a bottle of Loire Sauvignon completed the feast. (The fish below was photographed at Beau Rivage, see right.)

Normally I would follow tradition and serve shad with sorrel, either wrapping the fish in the leaves or making a stuffing or sauce (see page 98).

SERVES 4-6
900g/2lb shad, cleaned and scaled
350ml/12fl oz dry white Anjou wine
1 shallot, finely chopped
250g/9oz unsalted butter, chilled and diced
about 150g/5oz sorrel, torn into shreds
salt and freshly ground black pepper

Season the fish both inside and out and then place over a hot barbecue or under a preheated hot grill for about 10 minutes on each side, or until the fish is browned and the flesh flakes easily when tested with the point of a knife.

Meanwhile, simmer the wine and shallots until reduced to about 3 tablespoons. Heat 25g/1oz of the butter in another saucepan, add the sorrel and leave to cook, stirring occasionally, until wilted.

Lower the heat to its lowest setting and gradually beat in the remaining butter, making sure each piece is fully incorporated before adding the next. Beat in the sorrel and adjust the seasoning.

BEAU RIVAGE

Clermont-sur-Loire
Le Cellier
Tel 40 25 46 40
See recipe this page

The tiny hamlet of Le Cellier is down a small road off the N23 between Nantes and Angers. The Beau Rivage is at the end of the road, overlooking the Loire, just downstream from Champtoceaux on the opposite bank. The restaurant now belongs to Jacques Grelet and his wife Marie-Christine. Although M. Grelet spent much of his working life as a *pâtissier* in Paris, he now draws more upon the diverse knowledge and experience gained during his childhood at his parents'

restaurant in Orléans, to include all types of dishes – and particularly the classic Loire fish – on his menu.

POULET MARAÎCHER

Chicken with Vegetables

This is a dish for the late spring when colourful *primeurs* from the many *maraîchers* (market gardeners) are at their best.

SERVES 4-6
115g/4oz unsalted butter
1 free-range chicken, dressed weight about 1.35kg/3lb, cut into portions
8 small carrots
8 small leeks
8 small turnips
2 tablespoons chopped mixed herbs, including parsley, thyme, chervil and fresh bay
115ml/4fl oz good-quality Muscadet
150ml/5 fl oz chicken stock
salt and freshly ground black pepper

Melt half the butter in a wide, shallow pan. Add the chicken portions in a single layer and cook gently, uncovered, for about 15 minutes, turning them occasionally, until golden. Meanwhile, melt the remaining butter in another pan. Add the vegetables and cook, shaking the pan occasionally, for about 8 minutes.

Add the vegetables and cooking juices to the chicken. Season, cover the pan and cook gently for about 30 minutes, until the chicken and vegetables are tender. Sprinkle over the herbs, shake the pan well and cook for a further 3-4 minutes. Transfer the chicken and vegetables to a warmed serving plate and keep warm.

Skim the fat from the cooking juices, stir in the wine and deglaze the sediment. Bring to the boil and reduce to about 2 tablespoons, then add the stock and reduce by about half. Check the seasoning.

Serve the sauce in a warmed jug with the chicken and vegetables.

CANARD NANTAIS AU MUSCADET

Duck in Muscadet

This recipe is based on an old family recipe of Mme Métaireau, wife of one of the leading Muscadet *vignerons* (see page 135). The acidity of Muscadet helps to counteract the richness of the duck. Wine grapes should be used when they are available, but during the rest of the year dried currants, not grapes, are substituted as they have a better combination of sweetness and sharpness than dessert grapes.

SERVES 4-5
Up to 1l/1¾pt good-quality Muscadet
450g/1lb breast or knuckle of veal
450g/1lb onions, halved
450g/1lb carrots, halved
1 bouquet garni
salt
85g/3oz dried currants
1 large duck, preferably free-range and a special breed, such as Lunesdale, dressed weight at least 2.7kg/6lb
150g/5oz unsalted butter, diced

The day before the duck is required, slowly simmer together half the Muscadet, the veal, onions, carrots, bouquet garni, salt and 500ml/18fl oz water for 4 hours. Strain and leave until cold. Remove the fat from the surface. Soak the currants in a little of the remaining Muscadet.

Next day, preheat the oven to 160-180C/325-350F/gas3-4. Place the duck on a rack in a roasting tin and cook in the oven for 20 minutes.

Heat the remaining Muscadet in a large flameproof casserole, then add the duck and cook, covered, over a low heat for about 1¼-1½ hours, the time depending on the quality and size of the bird.

Strain the currants very well.

Heat the cold stock without allowing it to boil. Using a fork, gradually whisk the butter into it, making sure each piece is fully incorporated before adding the next. When all the butter has been added, add the currants.

Cut the duck into portions and place on a hot serving plate. Pour over the sauce.

CUL DE LAPIN À LA NANTAISE

Rabbit with Mushrooms and Shallots

SERVES 4
1 young wild rabbit, dressed and cut into pieces
550ml/18fl oz Muscadet
1 small carrot, sliced
3 shallots, preferably grey, finely chopped
2 sprigs of thyme
100g/3½oz lightly salted streaky pork or bacon, sliced across into strips and blanched
225g/8oz mushrooms, wild if possible
100g/3½oz lightly salted butter, diced
salt and freshly ground black pepper
finely chopped parsley, to garnish

Season the rabbit with pepper and a little salt. Put it in a bowl with the wine, carrot, shallots and one of the sprigs of thyme, and leave the meat and herbs to marinate for about 24 hours in a cool place.

Remove the rabbit from the marinade, allowing excess to drain off, and pat it dry. Reserve the marinade and shallots. Heat the pork or bacon in a heavy-based pan until they begin to colour and the fat runs. Remove with a slotted spoon and reserve.

Increase the heat, add the rabbit pieces to the pan and cook until lightly browned. Remove and reserve. Lower the heat again, add the mushrooms and shallots and cook gently, shaking the pan occasionally, for 4-5 minutes.

Remove with a slotted spoon and reserve. Strain the marinade into the pan. Boil for 2-3 minutes. Lower the heat so the liquid is barely simmering, then add the rabbit, half the reserved mushrooms, the pork or bacon and the second sprig of thyme. Cover and cook slowly, turning the rabbit occasionally, until tender (about 1 hour). Transfer the rabbit to a warmed plate, cover and keep warm.

Boil the liquid until reduced by half, lower the heat and gradually swirl in the butter, making sure each piece is fully incorporated before adding the next.

Return the rabbit to the sauce, along with any juices that have collected on the plate and the mushrooms and shallots. Heat through without boiling. Adjust the seasoning according to taste and sprinkle with the parsley to serve.

(Left)
At Les Maraîchers in Nantes, rabbit joints are served surrounded by delicious wild mushrooms, with a sauce made from the cooking juices served separately. The recipe given above can be served in this way simply by not returning the rabbit to the sauce at the end.

PÊCHES DES VIGNES

White Peaches in Wine

One of my most memorable culinary experiences was eating a white peach freshly plucked from the tree, its flesh still warm from the sun. That year had been dry with plenty of sunshine, and the fruit, never very large, was particularly small, and packed with wonderful flavour.

White peach trees (it is the peaches that are white, not the trees) do particularly well in the Pays Nantais climate and were once a common sight in the Muscadet vineyards. They were not planted to act as an early indication of disease, as is the case with roses in Bordeaux, but simply, I was assured by Pierre Luneau of La Grange, because they grow in the same conditions and can be treated in the same way as the vines (and, perhaps most importantly, because the *vignerons* like eating them). Vineyard white peach trees are sadly not as common as they once were because they get in the way of modern ploughs, tractors and other machinery.

This is how Madame Luneau prepares their *pêches des vignes* for the *vendangeurs*.

SERVES 4
6 ripe pêches des vignes, or white-fleshed peaches
about 3 tablespoons caster sugar, preferably vanilla-flavoured
350-425ml/12-15fl oz white wine, preferably Coteaux du Layon

Peel the peaches (if really ripe, there should be no need to pour boiling water over the fruit). Cut them into halves and remove the stones.

Put the peach halves into a bowl and sprinkle with sugar according to the sweetness of the fruit. Leave until the sugar has dissolved, then pour over the white wine to cover.

Place a plate on top to prevent the peaches floating and leave overnight in a very cool place, or in the refrigerator. Serve at this temperature.

GALETTES NANTAISES

Nantais Butter Biscuits

Rich, buttery *galettes Nantais* are very similar to *galette* or *gâteau bretonne*, except that the dough is cut into small biscuits rather than being baked in a large circle.

MAKES ABOUT 18
115g/4oz unsalted butter
85g/3oz vanilla sugar
3 egg yolks, beaten
225g/8oz plain flour
pinch of salt
egg yolk beaten with cold water, for glazing

Beat the butter and sugar together until soft, then work in the egg yolks. Using a spatula, gently fold in half the flour and the salt. When just evenly mixed, fold in the remaining flour. Using a round-bladed knife, lightly form into a dough, then knead until it no longer sticks to the fingers. Cover and chill. Using a lightly floured rolling pin on a lightly floured surface, roll out the dough thinly. Cut out circles with a diameter of about 5cm/2in. Brush with egg. Carefully transfer to a baking sheet, taking care not to distort the shapes. Chill for about 30 minutes.

Preheat the oven to 190C/375F/gas5 and bake the *galettes* for about 10 minutes. Leave to cool slightly on the baking tray, then carefully transfer to a wire rack to cool completely.

BOURDAINES

Apples in Pastry

(Illustrated opposite)

Bourdaines is the most common name for this apple dessert, but *bourdanes* or *bambolles* may also be used. Enclose a peeled pear or a peach (not too ripe and soft) instead of the apple for *bourdaines à la poire*, or *pêche* – in which case the cooking time can be reduced by about 20 minutes, depending on the firmness of the fruit.

SERVES 4
225g/8oz plain flour
pinch of salt
115g/4oz unsalted butter, diced
2 teaspoons caster sugar
4 large apples, peeled and cored
4 teaspoons quince or plum conserve
milk, cream or beaten egg, for glazing

Mix the flour and salt and rub the butter into it until the mixture resembles breadcrumbs. Stir in the sugar, then, using a round-bladed knife, lightly bind to a soft but not sticky dough with 2-3 tablespoons of water. Cover and chill for 30 minutes.

Preheat the oven to 180C/350F/gas4.

Divide the dough into 4 pieces. On a floured surface, roll out each piece to a square large enough to enclose an apple.

Sit an apple in the centre of each square and place a teaspoonful of the conserve in each apple cavity. Dampen the edges of the pastry and fold around the apples to make pyramid shapes, sealing the edges together well. Brush lightly with milk, cream or beaten egg. Place on a buttered baking tray. Bake for about 45 minutes, or until the apples are tender. Cover the pastry if it becomes too brown.

La Châtaigneraie **

156 route Carquefou
Sucé-sur-Erdre
Tel 40 77 90 95
See recipes on this page and page 140

La Châtaigneraie opened in its idyllic setting, overlooking the river Erdre and 16km from the

centre of Nantes, on 9 November 1988. Joseph Delphin had already gained a name for himself at his restaurant closer to Nantes, after moving there in 1961. When his son, Jean-Louis, joined him there, however, larger premises were needed to allow them both to utilize and develop their individual talents more fully. Mme Delphin is also actively involved. The restaurant is now in a classified manor house, built in 1872 out of tufa and situated in beautiful parkland with its own lake. Full advantage is taken of the variety and quality of fish and shellfish from the river, estuary and coast, as well as local frogs' legs.

Sorbet au Muscadet

Muscadet Sorbet

(Illustrated above)

This recipe was supplied to me by Joseph Delphin of La Châtaigneraie (see left).

SERVES 6-8
200g/7oz sugar
juice of 1 lemon
1 bottle of Muscadet
edible leaves, to decorate
crisp biscuits, such as tuile d'amandes, *to serve*

In a heavy-based saucepan, heat the sugar in 225ml/8fl oz water, stirring until dissolved. Then bring to the boil and simmer for 2 minutes. Leave to cool. Strain in the lemon juice and add the wine. Chill, then transfer to an ice-cream maker, or pour into a metal container and place in the freezer or the frozen food compartment of a refrigerator set to the lowest setting. Freeze until half frozen, then turn into a chilled bowl and whisk to break up the ice crystals. Return to the container and freeze until firm, repeating the whisking twice more.

Decorate with edible leaves and serve with crisp biscuits.

GALETTES

Buckwheat pancakes

(Illustrated above)

Buckwheat *galettes* are usually served with a savoury filling; among the most delicious is grated Cantal or goats' cheese.

Buckwheat is sold in some health food stores, but if it is unavailable – or if you intend to use a sweet filling – use all plain flour. To make richer *galettes*, replace half to three-quarters of the water with milk.

MAKES 6
115g/4oz buckwheat flour
115g/4oz plain flour
pinch of salt
55g/2oz clarified butter, melted, plus more for greasing and serving

Stir the flours and salt together and form a well in the centre. Gradually stir in 150ml/5fl oz water, keeping the mixture smooth, and beat well. Stir in a further 150ml/5fl oz water and beat well. Still beating, add 150ml/5fl oz, or a little more, of water to give a batter with the consistency of thick cream. Finally beat in the butter.

Rub a large crêpe pan or heavy frying pan with a piece of well-buttered paper, and heat until a drop of batter sizzles immediately it is dropped into it.

Pour 2 or 3 spoonfuls of the batter into the pan, tipping it so the batter coats the base. Cook over a high heat until he *galette* is set and lightly coloured underneath. Turn and cook the other side.

Dot butter over it immediately without allowing it to cook further. Fold in four, add a filling, and serve very hot.

FAR BRETON

Prune Batter Pudding

Traditionally a *far breton* is made in large rounds and served cut into wedges while still lukewarm. When cold it will be more solid. The mixture may also be cooked in individual ramekin dishes. The cooking of Brittany is a significant influence on that of the Pays Nantais, and you will find many Breton specialities, such as this, all over the region.

This version has more eggs but less flour than some, so it is richer, lighter, more tender – and quite delicious.

SERVES 4
200g/7oz prunes
4 tablespoons rum (optional)
25g/1oz unsalted butter
55g/2oz plain flour
40g/1½ oz sugar
4 eggs, beaten
450ml/16fl oz milk
icing sugar, for dusting

Soak the prunes in rum or the same quantity of warm water for 2 hours.

Put the butter into a shallow baking dish and place in the oven while heating it to 200C/400F/gas6.

Mix the flour and sugar together in a bowl, then gradually stir in the eggs, followed by the milk, stirring constantly to keep it smooth. Drain the liquid from the prunes and stir it into the batter.

Put the prunes into the hot butter in the dish. Carefully pour the batter over and bake for about 1 hour or until the pudding is well risen, just set in the centre and golden brown on the top.

Leave to cool slightly, then serve warm, dusted with icing sugar.

A Visitor's Guide

To provide a comprehensive guide to all the restaurants and places of interest in such a wide area is beyond the scope of this book, but listed below is a compilation of various recommendations. It includes a wide range of restaurants where it is felt you will have an enjoyable meal.

All the major towns, as well as many smaller places, have an *office de tourisme* or *syndicat d'initiative*, which will provide current information about local fairs and festivals, and opening times of places of interest; some also have information on restaurants and shops.

Wild mushroom-gathering, shooting and fishing may appear to be ubiquitous, but beware. Stay off private land and keep a watchful eye open for signs stating *chasse privé* or *champignons interdit*, which expressly forbid hunting and mushrooming. As in Britain, there are close seasons for game, but they are not always the same as ours, or even the same everywhere along the Loire, so check at the local town hall or police station. There are also seasons governing fishing which apply to particular stretches of water (classified as Category A or Category B). Detailed advice can be obtained from a local fishing tackle shop, which will also often sell permits. Fishing permits are issued for use within a *département*, and are valid for a year.

If you gather wild mushrooms, only pick those you are certain are safe and if you are in any doubt at all, check them against the colour charts displayed at chemists' shops; the chemist will also identify species for you.

PLEASE NOTE THAT WHILE EVERY EFFORT HAS BEEN MADE TO PROVIDE ACCURATE INFORMATION, ALL ADDRESSESS, TELEPHONE NUMBERS AND OPENING TIMES ARE LIABLE TO CHANGE.

VINEYARD VISITING

In the wine producing areas there are many signs indicating wine tastings (*dégustations*) and visits, so unless you are particularly interested in specific wines it is not necessary to make any arrangements beforehand. However, remember that most will close between midday and 2pm for lunch, and do not expect to be greeted with much enthusiasm if you visit during the *vendange*. Some visits and tastings are free, sometimes a charge is made.

The *maison des vins*, and sometimes the *syndicat d'initiative*, will have up-to-date details of places where visitors are welcome, whether just for a tasting, for a guided tour or both, and whether English is spoken. They will also know if an appointment is necessary, and should arrange it for you.

Auvergne, Nivernais and Bourbonnais

Restaurants

LA BRUSCADE
place de la Résistance
Antraigues Tel 75 38 72 92
Closed Wednesday, from June – September closed Tuesday and Wednesday

LO PODELLO
Antraigues Tel 75 38 71 48
Closed 1 October – 31 March, June, Thursday

LE PRÉ BOSSU *
Moudeyres
Tel 71 05 10 70
Closed first weekend November – Easter, Tuesday lunch and Wednesday off-season

AUBERGE JEAN LE DINDON
Le Bourg
Chaudeyrolles
Tel 71 59 56 82
Closing days not fixed, best to call ahead

LA MARMITE
61 rue des Lacs
St-Flour Tel 71 60 03 06
Open daily all year

CHEZ GUITOU
Saint-Poncy
Massiac Tel 71 73 11 62
Closed 21 – 28 December, 2 – 21 January

AUBERGE DU MOULIN DE CIVADOUX
Sauxillanges
Tel 73 96 81 94
Closed January, Tuesday evening and Wednesday

LE BOUT DU MONDE
Saint-Georges
Tel 71 60 15 84
Closing days not fixed, best to call ahead

AUBERGE DES CIMES
Saint-Bonnet-le-Froid
Tel 71 59 93 72
Closed 15 November – Easter, Wednesday, Sunday evenings in the off season

MARC ET CHRISTINE
29 avenue Marc-Seguin
Annonay Tel 75 33 46 97
Closed 2 – 24 January, Monday (except holidays), Sunday eves

LE PATIO
29 avenue Marc-Seguin
Annonay Tel 75 67 58 41
Closed August

PIERRE GAGNAIRE
7 rue de la Richelandière
Saint-Étienne
Closed Sunday, Monday

AUBERGE DES TERRASSES
Saint-Symphorien-de-Lay
Tel 77 64 72 87
Closed January, one week in August, Sunday eves, Monday

LA RENAISSANCE **
N7 Magny-Cours
nr. Nevers Tel 86 58 10 40
Closed late February – late March, August, Sunday evenings, Monday

HÔTEL DU PONT DU CHER
2 avenue de la Gare
Orval Tel 48 96 00 51
Closed Sunday evenings, Monday

LE MOULIN DE CHAMÉRON
route de Sancoins
Bannegon Tel 48 61 83 80
Closed 15 November – 1 March, Tuesday off-season

Markets

Le Monastier-sur-Gazeille: *Tuesday*
Fay-sur-Lignon: *Wednesday*
Saugues: *Monday, Friday*
Le-Puy-en-Velay: *Wednesday, Saturday*
Siaugues-Saint-Marie: *Sunday*
Langeac: *Tuesday, Thursday*
Tence: *Tuesday*
Le Chambon-sur-Lignon: *Saturday*
Yssingeaux: *Thursday, Saturday*
Montfaucon-en-Velay: *Wednesday*
Riotord: *Friday*
Monistrol-sur-Loire: *Friday*
Saint-Didier-en-Velay: *Wednesday*
Annonay: *Wednesday, Saturday*
Saint-Genest-Malifaux: *Thursday, Sunday*
Aurec-sur-Loire: *Wednesday, Friday, Sunday*
Firminy: *Tuesday, Thursday*
Saint-Étienne: *daily*
Andrézieux-Bouthéon: *Tuesday, Thursday, Friday*
Montbrison: *Saturday*
Montrond-les-Bains: *Thursday*
Balbigny: *Monday*
Violay: *Tuesday, Sunday*
Roanne: *Tuesday, Friday, Saturday, Sunday*
Ambierle: *Thursday*
Marcigny: *Monday*
Lapalisse: *Thursday*
Saint-Pourçain: *Saturday*
Le Donjon: *Tuesday*
Paray-le-Monial: *Friday*
Digoin: *Friday, Sunday*
Bourbon-Lancy: *Saturday*
Decize: *Friday*
Saint-Amand-Montrond: *Wednesday*
Orval: *Friday*
Sancoins: *Wednesday*
Guerche-sur-l'Aubois: *Tuesday*
Nevers: *Saturday*
Guerigny: *Friday*
La Charité-sur-Loire: *Saturday*

Places of interest

CHÂTEAU DU MONASTIER
Le Monastier-sur-Gazeille
Tel 71 03 80 01
Closed Saturday and Sunday lunchtimes

FERME DES FRÈRES PERREL
Moudeyres Tel 71 05 12 13
Closed 16 September – 7 July, lunchtimes

MUSÉE POPULAIRE DU MASSIF-CENTRAL
Saint-Didier-en-Velay
Tel 71 66 22 61
Closed 2 September – 1 July, mornings

MAISON DE LA BÉATE, MUSÉE DES ARTS ET TRADITIONS PAYSANNES
Marlhes
Saint-Genest-Malifaux
Tel 77 51 24 76
Open Sunday afternoons only, 16 September – 15 July

LA JASSERIE DU COQ NOIR
Col des Supeyres
Saint-Anthème
Tel 73 82 03 11
Closed last Sunday June – last Sunday September

MAISON SAUVAGNARDE
Sauvain
Saint-Georges-en-Couzan
Tel 77 76 81 83
Closed 26 September – 5 June, Sunday, mornings

MUSÉE ALICE-TAVERNE
Ambierle Tel 77 65 60 99
Closed 1 December – 1 February, lunchtimes

MUSÉE DE CHARROUX ET DE SON CANTON
rue de la Poulaillerie
Charroux
Chantelle Tel 70 56 85 25
Closed 1 October – 30 June, mornings

MUSÉE DE LA VIGNE ET DU VIN
Cour des Bénédictins
Saint-Pourçain-sur-Sioule
Tel 70 45 32 73
Closed January – February, and mornings 16 September – 14 June

MUSÉE RURAL DE LA SOLOGNE BOURBONNAISE
Mairie de Beaulon
Beaulon
Chevagnes Tel 70 42 70 89
Open Sunday and holiday afternoons in summer

MUSÉE DU PLAIX
Lignières Tel 48 60 00 18
Open Sunday afternoons in summer

AU BURON
(see Cantal being made)
Salilhes
Thiézac Tel 71 47 52 16
Closed lunchtimes and Sunday afternoons

SYNDICAT D'INITIATIVE
(will arrange visits to burons)
place Tissandier-d'Escous
Salers Tel 71 40 70 68

Specialities of the region

ALAIN COMTE
43 Fixe-St-Geneys
Tel 71 57 02 12

AU NÉGUS
96 rue du Commerce
Nevers Tel 86 61 06 85
Closed Sunday, Monday mornings, lunchtimes

PÂTISSERIE-CONFISERIE EDE
75 rue du Commerce
Nevers Tel 86 61 02 97
Closed Sunday afternoons, Mon

Festivals/Fairs

Saugues: *(mid-July)* 'Foire aux Bestiaux' Animal Fair
(early October) 'Foire aux Champignons' Mushroom Fair
Aiguilhe: *(last weekend in September)* 'Foire au Miel' Honey Fair
Yssingeaux: *(late December)* 'Marché au Foie Gras Frais de Canard' Fresh foie gras market
Saint-Bonnet-le-Froid: *(early November)* 'Foire aux Cèpes' Wild Mushroom Fair
Annonay: *(early December)* 'Rôtie Monstre de Châtaignes' Chestnut-roasting Festival
Sauvain: *(mid-August)* 'Fête de Myrtilles' Bilberry Festival
Montbrison: *(early October)* 'Journées de la Fourme' Montbrison cheese days
Panissières: *(early April)* 'Fête du Printemps' Spring Festival
(late June) 'Fête de la Saint Jean'
Thiers: *(September 14)* 'Foire au Pré' Traditional Fair
(December 7) 'Saint-Eloi des Goges' Food Festival
Roanne: *(5-10 October)* 'Foire Froide'
Saint-Pourçain-sur-Sioule: *(last weekend in February)* 'Foire aux Vins'
(last weekend in August) 'Foire des Vins'
Bruère-Allichamps: *(end of September)* 'Foire aux Fromages' Cheese Fair
Clamecy: *(early August)* 'Fête de l'Andouille' Chitterling Sausage Festival

SOLOGNE AND ORLÉANAIS

Restaurants

AUBERGE ALPHONSE MELLOT
16 Nouvelle Place
Sancerre Tel 48 54 20 53
Closed mid-December – mid-January, Wednesday

LA TOUR
place Halle
Sancerre Tel 48 54 00 81
Closed 4 – 15 March, 16 December – 10 January, Monday evenings, Tuesday

L'ÉTOILE
2 quai de la Loire
Sancerre Tel 48 54 12 15
Closed mid-November – February, Wednesday

RIVAGE *
1 quai Nice
Gien Tel 38 67 20 53
Closed early February – early March

AUBERGE DES TEMPLIERS **
N7 Les Bézards
Tel 38 31 80 01
Closed mid-January – mid-February

GUILLAUME DE LORRIS
8 Grande Rue
Lorris Tel 38 94 83 55
Closed Wednesday, Tuesday evenings

LE VIEUX RELAIS
2 route d'Isles
Vannes-sur-Cosson
Tel 38 58 04 14
Closed 7-15 September, 22 December – 15 January, Sunday evenings and Monday (except 15 June – 31 August)

ROBERT PESSON
54 rue du General de Gaulle
Meung-sur-Loire
Tel 38 44 75 14
Closed Sunday and Monday

AUBERGE DU CHÂTEAU
Talcy Tel 54 81 03 14
Closed Monday evenings, Tuesday

BERNARD ROBIN **
1 avenue Chambord
Bracieux Tel 54 46 41 22
Closed 23 December – 30 January, Tuesday evenings, Wednesday

HÔTEL SAINT-HUBERT **
rue Nationale
Cour-Cheverny
Tel 54 79 96 60
Closed Tuesday evenings and Wednesday

GRAND HÔTEL DU LION D'OR **
69 rue Georges Clemenceau
Romorantin-Lanthenay
Tel 54 76 00 28
Closed early January – mid February

MOULIN DE VILLIERS
Nouan-le-Fuzelier
Tel 54 88 72 27
Closed January – end March, and first two weeks September. Closed Tuesday and Wednesday in November and December

HÔTEL DE LA PLAGE
42 rue du Pont
Chabris Tel 54 40 02 24
Closed 23 December – early February, Sunday evenings, Monday off-season

GRAND HÔTEL ST-AIGNAN
7 quai Jean Jacques Delorme
St-Aignan-sur-Cher
Tel 54 75 18 04
Closed Sunday eves, Monday, 15 December – 1 February

Markets

Bourges: *Wednesday, Thursday, Friday, Saturday, Sunday*
Menetou-Salon: *Sunday*
Sancerre: *Saturday, Tuesday (March-November)*
Pouilly-sur-Loire: *Friday*
Cosnes-sur-Loire: *Wednesday, Sunday*
Aubigny-sur-Nère: *Saturday*
Gien: *Saturday, Wednesday*
Lorris: *Thursday*
Montargis: *Wednesday, Saturday*
Orléans: *Tuesday, Wednesday, Thursday, Saturday*
La Ferté-Saint-Aubin: *Thursday*
Lamotte-Beuvron: *Friday*
Beaugency: *Saturday*
Vendôme: *Friday, Sunday*
Mer: *Thursday*
Blois: *Tuesday, Wednesday, Thursday, Saturday, Sunday*
Bracieux: *Thursday*
Contres: *Friday*
Romorantin-Lanthenay: *Wednesday, Saturday*
Selles-sur-Cher: *Sunday*
Noyers-sur-Cher: *Sunday*
Montrichard: *Monday, Friday*

Places of interest

MUSÉE DU BERRY
4 rue des Arénes
Bourges Tel 48 70 41 92
Closed Tuesday, Sunday mornings, holidays, lunchtimes

FAIENCERIE DE GIEN (*earthenware*)
78 place de la Victoire
Gien Tel 38 67 00 05
Closed holidays

MUSÉE INTERNATIONAL DE LA CHASSE
place du Château
Gien Tel 38 67 69 69
Closed December – January

MUSÉE DES TANNEURS
Ilot des Tanneurs
1 rue du Château
Montargis Tel 38 95 10 00
Open Saturday afternoons, first Sunday every month

MUSÉE DE L'ARTISANAT RURAL ANCIEN
Clos Rolland du Roxcoat
Tigy Tel 38 58 00 42
Open Sunday and holiday afternoons, Easter, last Sunday October, Saturday in summer, every day for groups

MUSÉE DE LA TONNELLERIE (*cooperage*)
La Cour des Muids
1 rue de Patay
Checy Tel 38 62 72 45
Open Saturday afternoons, Sunday, Easter, holidays

DOMAINE DE CIRAN
Le Ciran
Menestreau-en-Villette
La Ferté-Saint-Aubin
Tel 38 76 90 93
Closed Tuesday, lunchtimes

MUSÉE DUNOIS
2 place Dunois
Beaugency Tel 38 44 55 23
Closed Tuesday

MUSÉE DE LA CORBILLIÈRE
Mer Tel 54 81 10 98
Open afternoons July and August

MUSÉE MUNICIPAL DE VENDÔME
Cour du Cloître
Vendôme Tel 54 77 26 13
Closed Tuesday, holidays, lunchtimes

CHÂTEAU DE CHAMBORD
(wild game park)
Chambord Tel 54 20 31 32
Closed holidays

MUSÉE DE SOLOGNE
Hôtel de Ville
1 rue Faubourg-Saint-Roch
Romorantin
Tel 54 76 07 06
Closed Tuesday, Sunday mornings, lunchtimes

MUSÉE D'HISTOIRE ET TRADITIONS LOCALES
Cloître de l'Ancienne Abbaye
Selles-sur-Cher
Tel 54 97 40 19
Open in summer Tuesday and Thursday afternoons, weekends

LOCATURE DE LA STRAIZE
Gy-en-Sologne
Tel 54 83 82 89
Closed mid-November – end March, lunchtimes, Tuesday

MUSÉE DE L'AGRICULTURE ET DE LA VITICULTURE
La Presles-d'Oisly
Contres Tel 54 79 52 69
Open in summer, Tuesday and Saturday afternoons

Specialities of the region

Many good artisanal food shops in and around Romorantin-Lanthenay and on the Grand rue and rue Gambetta in Jargeau.

À LA RENOMÉE
5 mail Ouest
Pithiviers Tel 38 30 00 24

PÂTISSERIE BEAUFORT
23 rue de l'Amiral Gourdon
Pithiviers Tel 38 30 00 21
Closed Monday, lunchtimes, August

CHOCOLATERIE ROYALE
(M. Chavanette)
51 rue Royale
Orléans Tel 38 53 93 43
Closed Sunday, Monday mornings, lunchtimes

AUX DÉLICES
(Philippe Berteault)
52 avenue de l'Hôtel-de-Ville
Lamotte-Beuvron
Tel 54 88 10 08
Closed Monday

HÔTEL TATIN
5 avenue de Vierzon
Lamotte-Beuvron
Tel 54 88 00 03
Closed last three weeks in January, Sunday evenings, Monday

ÉTABLISSEMENT GUENARD
(Huileries du Berry)
ZI du Greletier
42 rue de Tours
Noyers-sur-Cher
Tel 54 75 09 09
Closed weekends, 2 weeks in winter, three weeks in summer

LA MAISON DU SAFRAN
21 route des Pativiers
Boyne
Tel 38 33 13 84, 38 33 13 05
Open 1 April – 11 November

BERGERIES DE SOLOGNE *(products from Sologne breed of sheep)*
Ferme de Gaugeny
Fontaines-en-Sologne
Tel 54 46 45 61
Open every day

Vineyard Visiting

DOMAINE VACHERON
Caves Saint-Pierre
1 rue de Puits Poulton
Sancerre Tel 48 54 09 93
Closed end September – October

M. GAUMIER
route de Lury-sur-Arnon
Lury-sur-Arnon
Quincy Tel 48 51 31 55
Open by appointment Monday – Friday

L'UNION VITICOLE SANCERROISE
16 bis avenue Nationale
Sancerre Tel 48 54 03 51

CLAUDE LAFOND
Le Bois St Denis
Reuilly Tel 54 49 22 17
Open by appointment

SYNDICAT VITICOLE DE POUILLY
Les Loges
Pouilly-sur-Loire
Tel 86 39 12 65

DOMAINE GUY SARGET
route Nationale 7
Pouilly-sur-Loire
Tel 86 39 16 37
Closed Christmas and New Year

Festivals/Fairs

Pouilly-sur-Loire: *(15 August)* 'Foire aux Vins'
Menetou-Salon: *(15 August)* 'Journée caves ouvertes' Cellar open-days
(10 October) 'Exposition des Champignons Sauvages' Wild mushroom exhibition
Sancerre: *(first weekend in May)* 'Foire aux Fromages' Cheese Fair
(Pentecost weekend) 'Foire aux Vins'
(last Sunday in October) 'Foire aux Huîtres' Oyster Fair
Verdigny: *(last Sunday in July)* 'Fêtes des Grappes Nouvelles' Grape Festival
Tigy: *(third Sunday in May)* 'Foire aux Asperges' Asparagus Fair
Jargeau: *(end April)* 'Concours des Vins de la Région Centre' Wine contest
(second Sunday in June) 'Foire aux Andouilles' Chitterling Sausage Fair
(mid-October) 'Foire aux Châtaignes' Chestnut Fair
Saint-Denis-de-l'Hôtel: *(30-31 May)* 'Foire aux Fromages' Cheese Fair
Orléans: *(first week in May)* 'Fête de Jeanne d'Arc' Joan of Arc Festival
Romorantin: *(late October)* 'Journées Gastronomiques' Food Festival
Millançay: *(last weekend in September)* 'Fête à la Citrouille' Pumpkin Festival
Mennetou-sur-Cher: *(first weekend in May)* 'Foire aux Andouillettes' Chitterling Sausage Fair
Selles-sur-Cher: *(first Sunday after Easter)* 'Foire aux Vins'
Saint-Aignan: *(last Saturday in October)* 'Foire de St Simon'
Céré-la-Ronde: *(last Sunday in October)* 'Foire aux Produits de Chèvre' Goat Products Fair

TOURAINE

Restaurants

BON LABOUREUR ET CHÂTEAU
Chenonceaux
Tel 47 23 90 02
Closed 15 December – 15 February

LE MANOIR SAINT THOMAS *
1 Mail Saint Thomas
Amboise Tel 47 57 22 52
Closed 15 January – 15 March and Monday

LE CHOISEUL
36 quai Charles-Guinot
Amboise Tel 47 30 45 45
Closed 8 December – 18 January

LES HAUTES ROCHES *
86 quai de la Loire
Rochecorbon
Tel 47 52 88 88
Closed mid-January – mid-March, Sunday evenings, Monday except holidays

AUBERGE DE LA BRENNE
12 rue de la République
Neuillé-le-Lierre
Tel 47 52 95 05
Closed Tuesday evenings, Wednesday, mid-January – February

HOSTELLERIE DU COQ-HARDI
rue Nationale
Monnaie Tel 47 56 10 17
Closed Tuesday evenings and Wednesday

JEAN BARDET **
57 rue Groison
Tours Tel 47 41 41 11
Closed Sunday evenings, Monday from 1 November – 1 April, Monday lunchtimes in summer

BISTROT DES HALLES
31 place Gastron-Paillhou
Tours Tel 47 61 54 93
Open daily

LE CORNEILLE
49 rue Colbert
Tours Tel 47 66 72 55
Closed one week in February and three weeks in August

LE MOULIN FLEURI
route de Monts
Montbazon
Tel 47 26 01 12
Closed 15 – 31 October, February, Monday except holidays, Sunday evenings, Monday during winter

AUBERGE DU MOULIN DES ROCHES
Saint-Épain
Sainte-Maure
Tel 47 65 80 47
Closed Monday, early January

DOMAINE DE BEAUVOIS *
D49 Luynes
Tel 47 55 50 11
Closed 5 January – 14 March

AUBERGE DU GRAND VATEL
8 rue Brulé
Vouvray Tel 47 52 70 32
Closed Monday, first two weeks Dec, first two weeks March

LA CAVE MARTIN
La Vallée Coquette
Vouvray Tel 47 52 62 18
Closed Sunday evenings, Monday and Christmas

CHÂTEAU DE ROCHECOTTE
Saint-Patrice
Tel 47 96 90 62
Closed February

LE GRAND MONARQUE
3 place de la République
Azay-le-Rideau
Tel 47 45 40 08
Open 15 March – 6 November

L'AUTOMATE GOURMAND
La Chapelle-Saint-Blaise
Azay-le-Rideau
Tel 47 45 39 07
Closed 1 – 20 March, 13 – 20 November, Tuesday

AUBERGE DE L'ILE
l'Ile Bouchard
Tel 47 58 51 07
Closed October, February, Sunday evenings, Monday

AU PLAISIR GOURMAND *
quai Charles VII
Chinon Tel 47 93 20 48
Closed Sunday evenings, Monday, February

HOSTELLERIE GARGANTUA
73 rue Voltaire
Chinon Tel 47 93 04 71
Closed Wednesday and Thursday off-season, 15 November – March

CHÂTEAU DE MARÇAY
Marçay Tel 47 93 03 47
Closed 10 January – 10 March

AUBERGE DE TOUVOIS
Bourgueil Tel 47 97 88 81
Closed 22 December – 22 January, Monday

GERMAIN
6 rue Alain Chartier
Bourgueil
Tel 47 97 72 22
Closed 1 – 21 October, Sunday eves, Monday except holidays

AUBERGE DU PORT BOULET
Port Boulet
Chouzé-sur-Loire
Tel 47 95 15 92
Closed Sunday evenings

Markets

Amboise: *Friday, Sunday*
Vouvray: *Tuesday, Friday*
Loches: *Wednesday*
Tours: *daily, except Monday*
Joué-les-Tours: *Wednesday, Thursday, Saturday, Sunday*
Montbazon: *Friday*
Veigné: *Friday*
Sainte-Maure-de-Touraine: *Friday*
Luynes: *Saturday*
Langeais: *Sunday*
Azay-le-Rideau: *Wednesday*
Chinon: *Thursday, Saturday*
Richelieu: *Monday*
Bourgeuil: *Tuesday, Sat*

Places of interest

DISTILLERIE 'FRAISES D'OR'
62 route de Tours
Chissay-en-Touraine
Tel 54 32 32 05
Open Easter – end of September, closed lunchtimes

MUSÉE DES VINS DE TOURAINE
16 rue Nationale
Tours Tel 47 61 07 93
Closed Tuesday, holidays, January – February

L'ABBAYE DE MARMOUTIER
17 quai Marmoutier
Tours Tel 47 05 58 08
Visit by appointment

CHÂTEAU DE VILLANDRY
Villandry
Joué-lès-Tours
Tel 47 50 02 09
Garden open daily. Château closed mid-November – mid-March

MUSÉE DU TERROIR
(agriculture)
Villaines-les-Rochers
Azay-le-Rideau
Tel 47 45 43 08
Open Saturday and Sunday afternoons in summer, or by request

MUSÉE DU BOUCHARDAIS
Ancienne Gare
L'Ile-Bouchard
Tel 47 58 56 65
Open Tuesday/Friday/Sunday afternoons 1 July – 31 August

Festivals/Fairs

Chenonceaux: (*third Sunday in July*) 'Foire aux Boudins' Sausage Fair
Amboise: (*Saturday of Easter*) 'Foire aux Vins'
(*15 August*) 'Foire aux Vins'
(*first Wednesday in September*) 'Foire aux Melons' Melon Fair
Montreuil-en-Touraine: (*mid-September*) 'Foire aux Pains' Bread Fair
Saint-Georges-sur-Cher: (*Easter weekend and Monday*) 'Foire aux Vins'
Athée-sur-Cher: (*end March*) 'Foire aux Andouillettes' Chitterling Sausage Fair
Bléré: (*second Friday in September*) 'Foire aux Melons' Melon Fair
Vouvray: (*17 November*) 'Dégustation de Vin Nouveau' Vin Nouveau tasting
(*first Sunday of February*) 'Foire aux Vins'
Preuilly-sur-Claise: (*early October*) 'Foire aux Rillons' Potted Pork Fair
Tours: (*26 July*) 'Foire à l'Ail et aux Échalotes' Garlic and Shallot Fair
Neuillé-Pont-Pierre: (*mid-May*) 'Foire aux Fromages' Cheese Fair
Sainte-Maure: (*first Sunday in June*) 'Foire aux Fromages' Cheese Fair
Lignières-de-Touraine: (*mid-November*) 'Foire aux Pommes' Apple Fair
Azay-le-Rideau: (*end February*) 'Foire aux Vins'
(*first weekend in November*) 'Foire aux Pommes' Apple Fair
Crouzilles: (*early December*) 'Veillé aux Noix' Walnut Festival
Chinon: (*first weekend in March*) 'Foire aux Vins'
(*early August*) 'Marché Médiéval' Medieval Feast
Bourgueil: (*last Tuesday in July*) 'Foire à l'Ail' Garlic Fair
(*first weekend in February*) 'Foire aux Vins'

Specialities of the region

LE VIRAGE GASTRONOMIQUE
(Charcuterie Hardouin)
25 route Nationale 152
Vouvray Tel 47 52 60 24
Open daily

LA PÂTISSERIE AND LA CONFITERIE TOURANGELLE
31 and 6 rue Nationale
Tours Tel 47 05 42 00
Open daily except Mondays, closed lunchtimes

Vineyard Visiting

COMITÉ INTERPROFESSIONNEL DES VINS DE TOURAINE
(information on Touraine wines)
19 square Prosper-Mérimée
Tours Tel 47 05 40 01

MAISON DES VINS DE BLOIS
84 avenue de Verdun
Blois Tel 54 74 76 66
Closed lunchtimes and Thursday

GASTON HUET
Le Haut Lieu
Vouvray Tel 47 52 78 87
Closed lunchtimes, Sundays and Saints' Days

CAVES COOPERATIVES DES PRODUCTEURS DES GRAND VINS DE VOUVRAY
Vallée Coquette
Vouvray Tel 47 52 75 03
Closed lunchtimes

MAISON AUDEBERT ET FILS
20 avenue Jean Causeret
Bourgueil Tel 47 97 70 06
Closed lunchtimes, weekends, August

COULY CAVES
12 rue Diderot
Chinon Tel 47 93 05 84
Closed lunchtimes, Saturday afternoons, Sundays, holidays

ANJOU

Restaurants

AUBERGE DE L'ABBAYE
8 avenue des Roches
Fontevraud-l'Abbaye
Tel 41 51 71 04
Closed 6 – 29 October, Tuesday evenings, Wednesday

LA LICORNE *
31 rue Robert-d'Arbrissel
Fontevraud-l'Abbaye
Tel 41 51 72 49
Closed January – February, Sunday evenings, Monday

LE CHAPY
Allonnes Tel 41 52 02 63
Closed Monday/Tuesday/Wednesday/Sunday evenings

L'ESCARGOT
30 rue Maréchal LeClerc
Saumur Tel 41 51 20 88
Closed January, Wednesday

LES MENÉSTRALS
11 rue Raspail
Saumur Tel 41 67 71 10
Closed Sunday, Monday, last week in December

LE PRIEURÉ
Chênehutte-les-Tuffeaux
nr. Saumur Tel 41 67 90 14
Closed January – February, open all week

AUBERGE JEANNE DE LAVAL *
54 rue Nationale
Les Rosiers-sur-Loire
Tel 41 51 80 17
Closed 8 January – 17 February, Mondays except holidays

PAVILLON PAUL LE QUÉRÉ
3 boulevard Foch
Angers Tel 41 20 00 20
Open daily all year

LA SALAMANDRE
1 boulevard Maréchal-Foch
Angers Tel 41 88 99 55
Closed Sunday

LA PETIT MÂCHON
43 rue Bressigny
Angers Tel 41 86 01 13
Closed Saturday lunchtimes, Sunday, August

AUBERGE D'EVENTARD
route de Paris
Saint-Sylvain-d'Anjou
Tel 41 43 74 25
Closed Sunday evenings, Monday, first two weeks Feb

LE CLAFOUTIS
route de Paris
Saint-Sylvain-d'Anjou
Tel 41 43 84 71
Closed Tuesday evenings, Wednesday, Sunday

LE RELAIS DE BONNEZEAUX
Thouarcé Tel 41 54 08 33
Closed Wednesday, second half December, second week Feb

NOTRE DAME
place de l'Église
Béhuard
Saint-Georges-sur-Loire
Tel 41 72 20 17
Closed Wednesday

Markets

Fontevraud-l'Abbaye: *Wednesday*
Saumur: *Tuesday, Wednesday, Thursday, Sat*
Gennes: *Tuesday*
Les Rosiers: *Monday*
Baugé: *Monday*
Beaufort-en-Vallée: *Wednesday*
Mazé: *Friday*
Thouarcé: *Tuesday*
Angers: *daily*
Saint-Sylvain-d'Anjou: *Sunday*
Châteauneuf-sur-Sarthe: *Friday*
Rochefort-sur-Loire: *Wednesday*
Saint-Georges-sur-Loire: *Thursday*
Montjean-sur-Loire: *Thursday*
Cholet: *Tuesday, Wednesday, Thursday, Saturday*

Places of interest

ABBAYE DE FONTEVRAUD
Fontevraud-l'Abbaye
Tel 41 51 71 41
Closed 1 – 11 November, 1 January, 1 May

MUSÉE DU CHAMPIGNON
La Houssay
St-Hilaire-St-Florent
Saumur Tel 41 50 31 55

CHÂTEAU DE MONTGEOFFROY
Mazé Tel 41 80 60 02
Open all year

VILLAGE TROGLODYTIQUE DE ROCHEMENIER
Louresse-Rochemenier
Doué-la-Fontaine
Tel 41 59 18 15
Open 1 April – 15 November

COINTREAU
rue de la Croix Blanche
ZI Saint-Barthélémy
(industrial park)
Saint-Barthélémy-d'Anjou
Tel 41 43 25 21
Open daily by appointment

MUSÉE DE LA VIGNE ET DU VIN D'ANJOU
place des Vignerons
Saint-Lambert-du-Lattay
Tel 41 78 42 75
Closed 1 November – 31 March

MUSÉE DES VIEUX MÉTIERS
Saint-Laurent-de-la-Plaine
Chalonnes-sur-Loire
Tel 41 78 24 08
Closed 1 November – 1 April

Specialities of the region

LE VAL HULIN
(Pommes Tapées)
Turquant
nr. Saumur Tel 41 51 48 30
Open every day from June – September, phone for rest of year

LES CAVES DE MARSON
(Fouaces)
Marson
nr. Saumur Tel 41 67 10 12

HUILERIE CROIX VERTE
29 rue Bouju
St-Lambert-des-Levées
Tel 41 67 43 00

Vineyard visiting

MAISON DES VINS DE L'ANJOU
(information centre for Anjou and Saumur wines)
5 bis place Kennedy
Angers Tel 41 88 81 13

MAISON DES VINS DE SAUMUR
(information centre for Saumur wine producers)
25 rue Beaurepaire
Saumur Tel 41 51 16 40

COULÉE DE SERRANT
Château Roche aux Moines Tel 41 72 22 32
Closed Sunday and holidays

GRATIEN-MEYER
rue Beaulieu
Saumur Tel 41 51 01 54
Open daily all year

BUVET LADUBAY
rue de l'Abbaye
St-Hilaire-St-Florent
Saumur Tel 41 50 11 12
Open daily all year

Festivals/Fairs

Saumur: *(date to be decided)* 'Foire du Vin' Wine weekend
Villebernier: *(last weekend in May)* 'Fête des Fraises' Strawberry Festival
Chacé: *(first weekend in September)* 'Foire au Champigny' Champigny Wine Fair
Souzay-Champigny: *(June)* 'Fête à la Friture' Deep-fried Fish Festival
Vernoil: *(May)* 'Foire au Asperges' Asparagus Fair
Mouliherne: *(19-20 October)* 'Foire aux Pommes' Apple Fair
Beauné: *(first Saturday in September)* 'Foire aux Rillauds' Potted Pork Fair
Coutures: *(third weekend in September)* 'Foire aux Artichauts' Artichoke Fair
Saint-Gemmes-sur-Loire: *(third weekend in June)* 'Fête à la Tomate' Tomato Fair
Brissac-Quincé: *(16 November)* 'Concours d'Anjou Rouge' Red Anjou competition
(end September) 'Foire aux Aulx' Garlic Fair
Angers: *(January)* 'Foire au Miel' Honey Fair
Vauchrétien: *(last weekend in July)* 'Foire aux Lumas' Snail Fair
Thouarcé: *(first Sunday in June)* 'Foires aux Vins et aux Fromages' Wine and Cheese Fair
Saint-Aubin-de-Luigné: *(third weekend in July)* 'Fête aux Vins'
Saint-Lambert-du-Lattay: *(second Sunday in July)* 'Fête à la Vinée' Coteaux-du-Layon wine competition
La Poueze: *(Saturday closest to 24 August)* 'Foire aux Melons' Melon Fair
Chalonnes-sur-Loire: *(last weekend in February)* 'Foire aux Vins'
(last weekend in August) 'Foire aux Melons' Melon Fair
Angrie: *(second Sunday in August)* 'Fête des Moissons' Harvest Festival

Pays Nantais

Restaurants

LES JARDINS DE LA FORGE *
1 bis place Piliers
Champtoceaux
Tel 40 83 56 23
Closed 8 – 23 October, Sunday and Tuesday evenings, Wednesday

BEAU RIVAGE
Clermont-sur-Loire
Le Cellier Tel 40 25 46 40
Closed Sunday evenings, Monday, second half of August

LE ROSERARIE
3 avenue de la Gare
Mauves-sur-Loire
Tel 40 25 50 21
Closed Tuesday

CLÉMENCE
La Chebuette
Saint Julien de Concelles
Tel 40 54 10 18
Closed first three weeks of December, Sunday evenings, Monday

MON RÊVE
route des Bords de Loire
Basse-Goulaine
Tel 40 03 55 50
Closed November, February, Tuesday evenings, Wednesday

LE COLVERT
14 rue Armand-Brossard
Nantes Tel 40 48 20 02
Closed Sunday

LES MARAÎCHERS
21 rue Fouré
(Champ de Mars)
Nantes Tel 40 47 06 51

VIÉ
quai de l'Erdre
Sucé-sur-Erdre
Tel 40 77 70 06
Closed first half of January, Sunday evenings

LA CHÂTAIGNERAIE **
156 route Carquefou
Sucé-sur-Erdre
Tel 40 77 90 95
Closed 29 July – 12 August, January, Monday, Sunday evenings

LES VOYAGEURS
place de l'Eglise
Paulx Tel 40 26 02 26
Closed 2 – 8 January, 10 – 23 September, Sunday evenings, Monday

DOMAINE D'ORVAULT *
Chemin des Marais du Cens
Orvault (n. of Nantes)
Tel 40 76 84 02
Closed Monday lunchtimes, February

MANOIR DE LA COMÈTE
21 rue de la Libération
St-Sébastien (s. of Nantes)
Tel 40 34 15 93
Closed first week of January and first two weeks of August, Sunday

Markets

Ancenis: *Thursday*
Vallet: *Sunday*
Basse-Goulaine: *Wednesday*
Haute-Goulaine: *Tuesday*
Saint-Sébastien-sur-Loire: *Tuesday, Thursday, Friday*
Nantes: *daily (Saturday is best)*
Carquefou: *Thursday*
La Chapelle-sur-Erdre: *Wednesday, Friday, Sunday*
Sucé-sur-Erdre: *Tuesday*
Nort-sur-Erdre: *Tuesday, Friday*
Orvault: *Friday*
Bourgneuf-en-Retz: *Saturday*
Le Croisic: *Thursday*

Places of interest

MUSÉE PIERRE-ABÉLARD
Le Pallet
Vallet Tel 40 26 42 15
Closed weekdays except holidays and closed 1 November – Easter

MUSÉE D'ARTS POPULAIRES DE BRETAGNE
Château des Ducs de Bretagne
Nantes Tel 40 47 02 42
Closed Tuesday, holidays

MUSÉE DE PAYS DE RETZ
Bourgneuf
Tel 40 21 40 83
Closed December – Easter

Specialities of the region

MICHEL HOYET
(L'Hermine d'Or)
19 rue Paul-Bellamy
Nantes Tel 40 48 15 20
Closed 1 October – 31 April, Sunday, Monday

Vineyard Visiting

LOUIS MÉTAIREAU
La Février
Maisdon-sur-Sèvre
Tel 40 54 81 92
Open all year by appointment

CHÂTEAU DE GOULAINE
Haute-Goulaine
Tel 40 54 91 42
Closed Tuesday afternoons

SAUVION ET FILS
Château de Cléray
Vallet Tel 40 36 22 55
Open weekdays Easter – end of September

MAISON DES VINS
Belle rue
La Haie-Fouassière
nr. Nantes
Tel 40 36 90 10

Festivals/Fairs

Vallet: *(14-16 March)* 'Foire aux Vins'
Nantes: *(mid-October)* 'Fête des Châtaignes et du Vin' Chestnut and Wine Festival
Nozay: *(early October)* 'Fête des Boudins' Sausage Festival
Saint-Nazaire: *(15 September)* 'Foire aux Oignons' Onion Fair

UK Wine Merchants with Good Loire Wine Lists

THE OLD STREET WINE COMPANY
309 Old Street
London EC1V 9LA
Tel 071 729 1768

ADNAMS WINE MERCHANTS
The Crown
High Street
Southwold
Suffolk IP18 6DP
Tel 0502 724222

LAY & WHEELER
6 Culver Street West
Colchester
Essex C01 1JA
Tel 0206 764446

YAPP BROTHERS
The Old Brewery
Mere
Wiltshire BA12 6DY
Tel 0747 860423

LIST OF RECIPES

Page numbers in bold refer to illustrations

STARTERS

Pumpkin and Chestnut Soup 22, **23**
Carrot Soup 22
Fishermen's Soup 110
Cold Mixed Seafood Soup 136, **137**
Pounti 24, **25**
Swiss Chard Ribs with Eggs and Cheese 80
Crayfish in an Aromatic Broth 25
Langoustines and Spinach Salad 138, **139**
Friture 114, **115**
Salade de Rillons 76, **76**
Rillettes 76, **66**
Boudins Blancs, Pommes en l'Air 78, **79**
Rabbit and Herb Terrine 22
Buerre Blanc 136

SNACKS

Potato Pastries 46, **46**
Baked Jacket Potatoes with Wild Mushrooms 46
Tomato Tart 110, **110**
Rillettes Tart 77
Poached Eggs in White Wine 111
Vendéen Beans on Toast 138

VEGETABLE DISHES

Tapinaude 26, **26**
Potato Pie 47
Buttered Cabbage 112, **113**
Cabbage with Butter (*Chouée*) 138
Pounti 24, **25**
Shallots with Vinegar and Honey 48, **50**
Cardoons with Mushrooms 80
Swiss Chard Ribs with Eggs and Cheese 80
Peas with Lettuce Hearts and Cream 112
Artichokes with Mushrooms 112, **113**
Green Puy Lentils in the Auvergne Style 26
Red Haricot Beans in Young Red Wine 47
Haricot Beans with Walnut Oil 111
Broad Beans with Ham 80, **87**

SHELLFISH AND FISH

Crayfish in an Aromatic Broth 25
Langoustines and Spinach Salad 138, **139**
Friture 114, **115**
Loire Salmon with Radish 49, **49**
Carpe à la Chambord 81
Perch Fillets with Nettle Purée 82
Pike with Hazelnut Sauce 48
Roast Pike with Walnuts 85, **84**
Stuffed Courgette Flowers 82, **83**
Stuffed Pike-perch with a Sauce of Red Anjou Wine 114, **114**
Grilled Shad with Sorrel Sauce 141, **141**
Matelote 85
Turbot with Vegetables and Muscadet 140
Turbot with Ceps 140

MEAT, POULTRY AND GAME

Neck of Lamb with Beans and Mushrooms 51, **50**
Lamb with Young Loire Vegetables 116, **117**
Kid with Sorrel 28
Beef and Vegetable Stew 28
Pork with Prunes 120, **120**
Veal Casseroled in Wine 118
Loin of Veal in Anjou or Saumur Wine 118
Coq au Vin 27
Chicken with Lime Blossom 86
Poached Chicken 86, **87**
Chicken in White Anjou Wine 116
Chicken with Vegetables 142
Guinea Fowl with Walnuts 116
Wild duck with Quince 55, **54**
Duck in Muscadet 142
Partridge Pâté Baked in a Pastry Crust 51
Pheasant with Ceps 53
Pigeon with Small Cabbage Parcels 120
Stuffed Wild Rabbit 55
Rabbit with Mushrooms and Shallots 143, **142-3**
Hare with Redcurrant Jelly 28, **23**
Venison in Red Sancerre 52

PUDDINGS AND DESSERTS

Tarte Tatin 56, **56**
Bourdaines 144, **145**
Pear Tart 90, **91**
Poirier 124
Raspberry Pancakes 58, **59**
Poached Peaches with Raspberry Sauce 88, **89**
Mirabelle Tart 122
Strawberries in Wine 122
Bread with Fruit and Wine 123
White Peaches in Wine 144
Far Breton 147
Cointreau Mousse with Honey Sauce 123, **123**
Crémet d'Angers 124, **125**
Muscadet Sorbet 146, **146**
Chestnut Conserve 29, **29**

BREADS, CAKES AND BISCUITS

Brioche au Fromage Frais du Chèvre 91, **79**
Galettes 147, **147**
Gâteau de Pithiviers 57, **32**
Pain d'Épices 57, **41**
Almond Cakes from Sully 57
Macaroons 88, **89**
Nantais Butter biscuits 144

INDEX

Page numbers in bold refer to illustrations

Académie des Gastronomes 105
Alfred Gratien Champagne 107
aligot 17, 20
almonds
  Almond Cakes from Sully 57
  Gateau de Pithiviers 57, **32**
  Macaroons 88, **89**
Alose Grillée, Sauce l'Oseille 141, **141**
Ancenis wines 135
andouillettes 66
Anjou region 93-109
  beurre blanc debate 131-3
  goats' cheeses 106
  wines 11, 12, 106-9
AOC see *appellation d'origine contrôlée*
appellation d'origine contrôlée
  Anjou wines 108
  Loire wines 11
  Touraine cheeses 73
  Touraine wines 73-4
Appert, Nicolas 129
apples
  Anjou region 99-100, **93, 95**
  Apples in Pastry 144, **145**
  fried, with boudins blancs 78, **79**
  Orléanais region 38
  Pommes Tapées 99, 100, 102, **99**
  Tarte Tatin 37-8, 56, **56**
artichokes
  Artichokes with Mushrooms 112, **113**
  Touraine region 63, **62**
asparagus
  Anjou region 103
  Sologne region 34
  Touraine region 67
Auberge de la Forge 136
Auberge du Grand Vatel 71, 152
Auberge des Templiers 32, 150
Auvergne region 15-20
  cheeses 17-18

barbel 37
Bardet, Jean 82-3, 84, 85, 152
Baron de Ladoucette 44
Barrat family 48
Bartlett pear 100
  see also Bon Chrétien
bateliers 11
beans
  Anjou region 103
  Broad Beans with Ham 80, **87**
  Haricot Beans with Walnut Oil 111
  Neck of Lamb with Beans and Mushrooms 51, **50**
  Pays Nantais (Vendéen) region 130
  Red Haricot Beans in Young Red wine 47
  Touraine region 68
  Vendéen Beans on Toast 138
Beau Rivage 141, 155
beef
  Beef and Vegetable Stew 28
  see also cattle
Bellanger, Edith & Philippe 77
Belon, Pierre 69
Berlingots **128**
Berry region
  cheeses 42
  wines 43-4
beurre blanc
  creation of 131
  recipe for 136
Beurré Hardy 38, 100
Bijane 123
bilberries 18-19, **16**
biscuits
  butter-and-almond 131
  Nantais Butter Biscuits 144
  petits beurres **129**
black puddings 37, 66
black radish 68
blackcurrants 103
bleak
  Anjou region 99
  Sologne region 37
  Touraine region 65
blettes 80
Bleu d'Auvergne cheese 17-18, **16**
Blois 69, 70, 72

boar 18
boats (Loire boats) 11, 105, **4-5, 33, 64**
  Auguste Poulain's steam tug 70
  for fishing 65
  steamboats 11, 70
  varnishing of 105
Bœuf aux Herbes 28
Bon Chrétien (pear) 100
  introduced from Italy 69
  Orléanais region 38
Bondaroy au foin 43
Bonnezeaux wine 108
boudins blancs 66
  Boudins Blancs, Pommes en l'Air 78, **78**
boudins noirs 37
  Touraine region 66
Bourbonnais region 21
Bourdaines 144, **145**
Bourgueil wines 12, 74-5
bourprudinier 37
Boynes 41
breads and pastries
  Auvergne region 19-20
  Bread with Fruit and Wine 123
  Brioche au Fromage Frais de Chèvre 91, **79**
  Galettes de Pommes de Terre 46
  rye bread **128**
  Sologne region 37
  Touraine region 71-2
  see also pain d'épices
bream 97
Brioche au Fromage Frais de Chèvre 91, **79**
briprunelloise 37
broad beans *see* beans
Brochet aux Noisettes 48
Brochet Rôti au Four, au Vin de Noix 85, **84**
brown trout 18
Buisse, Paul 73
burons (stone houses) 17
butter sauce 136

cabbage **138**
  Anjou region 103, **94**
  Buttered Cabbage 112, **113**
  Cabbage with Butter 138
  Pays Nantais region 130, 138
  Pigeon with Small Cabbage Parcels 120-1
  in soups 19
Cabernet d'Anjou 107
Caillé, Gilles 37-8
cakes
  Auvergne region 20, **16**
  Orléanais region 41
Canal de la Sauldre 34
Canard Nantais au Muscadet 142
Canard Sauvage aux Coings 55, **54**
Cantal cheese 17-18, **16**
cardons à la moelle 67-8
Cardons Tourangeaux au Gratin 80
cardoons 67-8
  Cardoons with Mushrooms 80
carp
  Carp with Red Wine 81
  Sologne region 37
  Touraine region 65, 97
Carpe à la Chambord 81
carrots
  Anjou region 104
  Carrot Soup 22
  Pays Nantais region 129
cassemuses/casse museaux 71
cattle
  Charolais 20
  Pays Nantais region 131
  Salers 17, **16**
  Sologne region 37
Cave Martin, La 76, 77, 152
celery 67
ceps *see* mushrooms, wild
cerises d'Olivet **33**
chalands (Loire boats) 32, 70, **33**
Challans poultry 129
Champagne 107
champignons de Paris 103
Champtoceaux 136, **127**
Chapelle, La (river port) 63
Chaptal, Jean-Antoine 72
Chapy, Le 111, 153
Charentais melons 100, **100**
Charolais cattle 20
Châtaigneraie, La 140, 146, 155, **1**
Château d'Amboise 66
Château de Chambord 81, 151
Château de Chenonceau 71, **70**
Château de Cheverny **31, 33, 35**
Château de la Grange 133
Château de la Jailliere 122
Château de Moncontour 74, **74**
Château de Plessis-les-Tours 69
Chaumont 63-4
Chavignol cheese 42
cheeses
  Auvergne region 17-18
  Berry region 42
  Cream Cheese Dessert 124, **125**
  Orléanais region 42-3
  pâte de fromage 37
  see also goats' cheeses
cherries
  Anjou region 104
  Orléanais region 38
chestnuts
  Auvergne region 19
  Chestnut Conserve 29, **29**
  Pumpkin and Chestnut Soup 22, **23**
  rolls with chestnuts 37
Chevreuil au Sancerre Rouge 52-3
chicken
  Chicken with Lime Blossom 86
  Chicken in Red Wine 27
  Chicken with Vegetables 142
  Chicken in White Anjou Wine 116
  introduction of incubators 66-7
  jambon de volaille 66
  Poached Chicken 86, **87**
chicolle/chicolte 123
Chinon wines 12, 74-5
Chocolat Poulain 70, 72, **70**
Chou au Beurre 112, **113**
Chouée 103, 138
Choupin, Giselle & Gerard 115, 118
Cigale, La **128**
civelles 133
Clafoutis, Le 120, 154
Clémence, Madame 131, 133
Clement, Didier 48
Cointreau
  Cointreau Mousse with Honey Sauce, 123, **123**
  liqueur firm 104
Cointreau, Edouard & Adolph 104
Collier d'Agneau Mère Giffard 51, **50**
Comte, Alain 19
Confiture de Marrons 29, **29**
Copin, Bernard 71
Coq au Vin 27
cordes 71
Cormery Abbey 88
corn salad 129
Coteaux d'Ancenis wines 135
Coteaux du Layon wines 12, 108
Côtes de Blette au Gratin 80
cotignac 32, 39, **33**
Coulée de Serrant 108-9, **108-9**
Coupe de Fraises 122
Courgette Flowers, Stuffed 82-3, **83**
Courgettes Fleurs Farcies 82-3, **83**
Covifruit 36
crayfish
  Auvergne region 18
  Crayfish in an Aromatic Broth 25
Cream Cheese Dessert 124, **125**
Créme Nivernaise 22
Crémet d'Angers 124, **125**
Creuse (river) 63
Crottin de Chavignol 42
Cul de Lapin à la Nantais 143, **142-3**
Cul de Veau à l'Angevine 118-19
Curé-Nantais (cheese) 133
Curnonsky 104-5, 131

dairy products
  Auvergne region 17-18
  Bourbonnais region 21
  Sologne region 34
damascenes/damsons 71
dandelion leaves 129
d'Anthenaise family 122
dartrée de choux verts 138
deer
  Auvergne region 18
  Sologne region 37
Delphin, Jean-Louis 146
Delphin, Joseph 130, 140, 146
Delphin, Mme 146
Depezay, Charles 34
Domaine Vacheron 43
Doyenné du Comice (pear) 100
Dray, Jean-Claude 26, 27

drinks
  hydromel 20
  see also eau-de-vie; wines
duck
  Anjou region 94, **94**
duck *continued*
  Auvergne region 18
  Duck in Muscadet 142
  Sologne region 34, 37
  Wild Duck with Quince 55, **54**

eau-de-vie
  Anjou region 103, 104
  de poire Williams 36
  Guignolet 104
  Orléanais region 36
  quince-flavoured 39
Échalotes d'Orléans 48, **50**
Écrevisses à la Nage 25
eels 37, 98-9
  elvers 133
  Fish in Wine 85
eggs
  Egg and Vegetable Loaf 24-5, **25**
  in Nivernais cooking 20
  Poached Eggs in White Wine 111
  Swiss Chard Ribs with Eggs 80
  see also omelettes
elvers 133
endive 129
Estouffade de Turbot au Muscadet 140, **140**
Evelyn, John (diarist) 71, 74

faire chabrot 19
Faisan aux Cèpes 53
Far Breton 147
farcidure 20
Fetchoulette 28
Fèves a la Tourangelle 80, **87**
Filets de Perche à la Purée d'Orties 82
Financiers de Sully 57
fish
  Anjou region 97-9
  Auvergne region 18
  Deep-fried Small Fish 114-15, **115**
  Fish in Wine 85
  Fishermen's Soup 110
  Pays Nantais region 133
  Sologne region 37
  Touraine region 63-4, 97
  see also individual fish
Flaubert 9
flowers *see* wild flowers
foie gras farming 94, **94, 106**
Foire aux Violettes 18
Fontaines-en-Sologne 37
Fontevraud Abbey 112

fouaces (pastries) 71-2, 154
fouasses 20
Fourme du Cantal 17-18, **16**
François de Paul, Saint 69
Fricassée de Poulet Angevine 116
fridules 37
Frinault cheeses 43
Friture 114-15, **115**
frogs' legs 36, 130
fromage de chèvre *see* goats' cheese
fruit
  Anjou region 99-103, 98
  Auvergne region 18
  Bread with Fruit and Wine 123
  Orléanais region 38-9

gabares (Loire boats) 32, **33**
gages 69
galettes 131
  Galettes 147, **147**
  Galettes de Pommes de Terre 46, **46**
  Galettes Nantaises 144
Gamay de Touraine 74
game
  Auvergne region 18
  Partridge Pâté Baked in a Pastry Crust 51-2
  Pheasant with Ceps 53
  Sologne region 37
  Venison in Red Sancerre 52-3
Gâteau de Pithiviers 57, **32**
geese
  geese farming 133, **132**
  Sologne region 34
gelée d'orange 123
Géline Lochoise 86, **87**
goats
  Auvergne region 17
  farming for cheese 42
  Kid with Sorrel 28
  Touraine region 61, **62**
goats' cheeses 106, 32, **32**
  Anjou region 106
  Brioche with Goats' Cheese 91, **79**
  Crottin de Chavignol 42
  Maturation process 73, 106
  Pays Nantais region 133
  Sologne region 42-3
  Swiss Chard Ribs with Eggs and Cheese 80
  Touraine region 72-3, **62, 72**
goujons 114
Goulaine , Marquis de 133
Grand Hotel du Lion d'Or 48, 150
Gratien & Meyer 107, 124
Gratien, Alfred 107
gratin à l'auvergnate 20
greengage 69
Gregory (Armenian bishop) 39
Grelet, Jacques & Marie-Christine 141
grey mullet 63
Gros Plant 133, 134, 135
gudgeon
  Anjou region 99
  Sologne region 37
  Touraine region 63
Guignolet 104
guinea fowl
  Guinea fowl with Walnuts 116
  Sologne region 34

hams
  Auvergne region 17
  Broad Beans with Ham 80, **87**
  drying mountain hams 19
  jambon de volaille 66
  jambons de montagne 19
  Morvan 20
  Nivernais region 20
  Sologne region 37
  Touraine region 66
  Vendéen ham 131
Hare with Redcurrant Jelly 28, **23**
haricot beans
  Anjou region 103
  Haricot Beans with Walnut Oil 111
  Red Haricot Beans in Young Red Wine 47
  Touraine region 68
Haricots Rouges au Vin Rouge 47
Harrault, Annick & Jean-Claude 111
hazelnuts
  Roast Pike with Hazelnut Sauce 48
herbs 17, 18, **16**
honey
  Auvergne region 20
  Cointreau Mousse with Honey Sauce 123, **123**
  Shallots with Vinegar and Honey 48, **50**
  Sologne region 37
Hosten et Restaurant Langeais **65**
Hôtel-Terminus Tatin 37
Huet, Gaston 75
Huilerie Croix-Verte 111
hunting
  lark shooting 41
  Sologne region 37
  see also Château de Chambord; Château de Cheverny
hydromel 20

incubators (chicken) 66-7

Jardins de la Forge, Les 136, 155
Jargeau 36, 151
Jean Bardet (restaurant) 82-3, 84
Joly, Madame 109
Journées Gastronomiques (Sologne region) 36, 151

Ladoucette wines 44
lamb
  Lamb with Young Loire Vegetables 116-17, **117**
  Neck of Lamb with Beans and Mushrooms 51, **50**
Lamotte-Beuvron 37
Langeais
  Hosten et Restaurant **65**
  melons 71
langoustines **128**
  Langoustine and Spinach Salad 138, **139**
Langoustines Poêlées en Salade 138, **139**
Lapin de Garenne à la Sologhote 55
lark shooting 41
Lebert, Serge 120
leeks 104
Lefèvre, Monsieur 131
Lentilles Vertes du Puy 18
  recipe 26-7
lentils
  Green Puy Lentils in the Auvergne Style 26-7
  Le Puy region 18
"L'Étuve" d'Agneau de Lait 116-17, **117**
Lièvre à la Duchambais 28, **23**
Lion d'Or, Grand Hotel du 48, 150
liqueurs
  Anjou region 103, 104
  Auvergne region 17, **16**
liqueurs *continued*
  Cointreau 104
  eau-de-noix des Pères Chartreux 85
  Poire William 36
  see also eau-de-vie
Luneau, Pierre 144

Macarons de Cormery 88, **88-9**
Macaroons 88, **88-9**
Maison Poirault (Tours) 63, **62**
Manoir de la Comète, La 138, 155
mariniers 11
Marmite, La 24, 148
marsh samphire 129
Martin, Jean-François 39
Martin, M. 39
Martin-Pouret 39
Matelote 85
Matelote des Tonneliers 118
melons
  Anjou region 100, 103, **100**
  Charentais 100, **100**
  Touraine region 71
Menetou-Salon wines 44
Métaireau, Louis 135, 136
Meyer, Jean 107
Michelin stars 12
michou 20
Miot 123
Mirabelle Tart 122
moelle végétale 67
mojettes 130
Mojettes sur Canapés 138
Montlouis wines 74
mougettes 130
Moulins 21
Mourges, M. 24
Mousse de Cointreau, Sauce au Miel 123, **123**
mulberries 18
mullet (grey) 63
Muscadet 133, 134-5
  Duck in Muscadet 142
  Muscadet Sorbet 146
  salad dressing 138
  Turbot with Loire Vegetables 140
Musée du Safran 41
mushrooms (cultivated) 103, **103**
  Artichokes with Mushrooms 112, **113**
  Cardoons with Mushrooms 80
  Rabbit with Mushrooms and Shallots 143, **142-3**
mushrooms (wild)
  Auvergne region 17, 19
  Baked Jacket Potatoes with Wild Mushrooms 46
  Pheasant with Ceps 53
  Touraine region **68**
  Turbot with Ceps 140
mussels 133, **128**

Nantes 11, 128
nautoniers 11
nettles
  Perch fillets with Nettle Puree 82
Nivernais region 20
Notre Dame (restaurant) 118, 154, **119**
nuts 19
  see also individual nuts
œufs au jambon 20
Œufs Poches Saumurois 111
Olivet cheeses 42-3
omelettes
  omelette à l'Auvergnate 24, **24**
  omelette Nivernaise 20
onions 103
  see also shallots
Orleanais region 31, 38-41
  cheeses 42-3
  Olivet cheeses 42-3
  wines 44
Orléans 31, 39
oysters **128**

Paimbœuf 133
pain d'épices
  Auvergne region 20
  Orléanais region 39, 41
  Pain d'Épices 57, **41**
Pains Nantais 131
pancakes
  Buckwheat Pancakes 147, **147**
  Raspberry Pancakes 58, **59**
Pannequets de Framboises 58, **59**
partridge 18
  Partridge Pâté in a Pastry Crust 51
Passe-crassane (pear) 100
pastry
  Pâte Brisée (method) 77
  Pâte Sucrée (method) 90
  Potato 46
  Sologne region 37
  see also breads and pastries

pâte de fromage 37
pâte des fruits 61, **61**
pâtés
foie gras 34
Pâté au Trauffaude 47
pâte d'alouette 41
Pâté de Perdrix en Croûte 51-2
Sologne region 37
pâtes de pommes de terre 37
Pauvert, Paul 136
Pavillon Paul Le Quéré 114, 117, 153
Pays Nantais region 127-35
goats' cheeses 133
wines 11, 134-5
peaches
bourdaines à la pêche 144
Poached Peaches with Raspberry Sauce 88, **88-9**
White Peaches in Wine 144
pears
Anjou region 99-102
Bon Chrétien 38, 69, 100
bourdaines à la poire 144
eaux-de-vie de poire Williams 36
Orléanais region 38
Pear Cake 124
Pear Tart 90, **90-1**
Touraine region 69, **68-9**
peas
Peas with Lettuce Hearts and Cream 112
Touraine region 68
Pêches des Vignes 144
Pêches Tourangelles à la Royale 88, **88-9**
peignes à myrtilles 19
perch
Perch Fillets with Nettle Purée 82
Touraine region 65, 97
Petits Beurres biscuits 131, **128**
petits pois 68
pheasants 37
Pheasant with Ceps 53
piballes 133
Pigeon with Small Cabbage Parcels 120-1
Pigeonneau et Petit Chou Farci 120-1
pigs
Auvergne region 17
Nivernais region 20
Touraine region 65, 67, **67**
see also ham
pike 37
Anjou region 97
Pike with Hazelnut Sauce 48
Roast Pike with Walnuts 85, **84**
Touraine region 63, 97
pike-perch 97
Stuffed Courgette Flowers 82-3, **83**
Stuffed Pike-perch with a Sauce of Red Anjou Wine 114
Touraine region 63
Pinguet, Noel 75
Pintadeau sur Noix 116
pissenlits 129
Pithiviers 39
plums 69, 71
Plum Tart **68**
poirée à carde 80
Poirer, Daniel 77
Poirier 124
Pois à la Mode de l'Abbaye Fontevraud 112
pollen (dried) 20
Pommes à la Forestière 46-7
Pommes Tapées 99, 100, 102, **99**
Porc aux Pruneaux 120, **120**
pork
Pork with Prunes 120, **120**
in soups 19
see also hams; pigs
potatoes
Anjou region 104
Auvergne region 20, **20**
Baked Jacket Potatoes with Wild Mushrooms 46-7
Creamy Potatoes with cheese 26, **26**
Potato Pastries 46, **46**
Potato Pie 47
Sologne region 37
Potée (Auvergne region) 19, **24**
Potironée aux Châtaignes 22, **23**
Pouilly-sur-Loire 11, 31
wines 43-4
Poulain, Auguste 70
Poulain (chocolate company) 70, 72, **70**
Poulet au Tilleul 86
Poulet Maraîcher 142
Poulets d'Ancenis 129
Pouligny-St-Pierre (cheese) 73
poultry
jambons 66
Pays Nantais region 129
Sologne region 34
see also chicken
Pounti 24-5, **25**
Pouret, M. 39
preserves
quince 39
pressure cooker 72
prunes 71
Pork with Prunes 120, **120**
Prune Batter Pudding 147
Pruniers-en-Sologne 37
psalliotes 103
pumpkins 36
Pumpkin and Chestnut Soup 22, **23**

Quarts-de-Chaume wine 108
Quéré, Le, Paul and Martine 114, 117, 123
Quéré, Le, (restaurant) 117, 153
quinces
Orléanais region 38-9
quince paste (*cotignac*) 32, 39, **33**
Wild Duck with Quince 55, **54**
Quincy wines 44

rabbit 18
Rabbit and Herb Terrine 22
Rabbit with Mushrooms and shallots 143, **142-3**
Sologne region 37
Stuffed Wild Rabbit 55
radish (black) 68
Ragoût d'Artichauts Saumurois 112, **113**
raspberries
Anjou region 103
Auvergne region 18
Poached Peaches with Raspberry Sauce 88, **88-9**
Raspberry Pancakes 58, **59**
reine-claude 69
Renaissance, La 26, 27, 148
Reuilly wines 44
Richelieu 66
rillettes 65-6, **66**
Rillettes (recipe) 76-7, **66**
Rillettes Tart 77
rillons (*rillauds/rillots*) 65
Salade de Rillons 76, **76**
roach 65
Roche-aux-Moines, La (*cru*) 108
Romorantin-Lanthenay 36, 151, **33**
Rosé d'Anjou 107
rôtie 123
russeroles 71
rye bread **128**

saffron 41
Sailland, Maurice Edmond (Curnonsky) 104-5, 131
salad leaves 129
Salad, spinach, with Langoustines 138, **139**
Salade de Grenots à l'Huile de Noix 111
Salade de Rillons 76, **76**
salicorne 129
salmon 97
Loire Salmon with Radish 49, **49**
with red wine sauce 81
Sancerre 11
Sandre Farci, Sauce à l'Anjou Rouge 114, **114**
Saumon de Loire 49, **49**
Saumon à la Chambord 81
Saumur 10
wines 107-8, 119, **119**
sausages
Sologne region 36, 37
Touraine region 66
White Sausages with Apple Slices 78, **78**
Sauté de Porc aux Pruneaux 120, **120**
Savennières wines 108
seafood **130**
Seafood Soup 136-7, **137**
Selles-sur-Cher (cheese) 73
Seydoux, Alain 107, 120
shad 97-8
Grilled Shad with Sorrel Sauce 141, **141**
shallots
Anjou region 94, 103-4, **95**
Shallots with Vinegar and Honey 48, **50**
sheep
Auvergne region 17
Pays Nantais region 131
Sologne region 37
shoots *see* hunting
slate, Trélazé 97, 100
Sologne region 31-8
Sorbet au Muscadet 146, **146**
sorrel 98
Grilled Shad with Sorrel Sauce 141, **141**
Kid with Sorrel 28
Soupe de Crustacés Glacée aux Coquillages 136-7, **137**
Soupe des Pêcheurs 110
soups
Auvergne region 19
Carrot Soup 22
Fishermen's Soup 110
Pumpkin and Chestnut Soup 22, **23**
Seafood Soup 136-7, **137**
St-Benoit/St-Benoist cheese 43
St-Catherine-de-Fierbois (plum) 71
St-Nicholas-de-Bourgueil wines 74-5
Ste-Eulalie 18
Ste-Maure (goats' cheese) 72-3, **62, 72**
Ste-Maure (town) 72
steamboats 11, 70
strawberries
Anjou region 94, 102-3, **95, 100**
Auvergne region 18, **16**
Sologne region 34
Strawberries in Wine 122
sucrins 71
Swiss chard 80
Sylviane, Alain & Sylvie 102

Tapinaude 26, **26**
Tarte aux Mirabelles 122
Tarte aux Poires 90, **90-1**
Tarte à la Tomate 110-11, **110**
Tarte Tatin 37-8, 56, **56**
Tarte Tourangelle 77
Tatin, Stéphanie and Caroline 37
tench 37
Terrine de Lapin aux Herbes 22
Thai-Thuc, Mme. 138
Thomas-Trophime, Christian 138
Thoureil, Le 99
Timmerman, M. 120
tobacco 63, **63**
Tomato Tart 110-11, **110**
toués (Loire boats) 65
Touraine Gourmande 71
Touraine region 61-75
goats' cheeses 72-3, **62, 72**
wines 11, 73-5

Touraine Sauvignon 73-4
tourism (in Touraine) 63
Tours 65, **10, 62-3**
transhumance 17, 28
trauffades 47
Trélazé 97, 100
treuffes 47
tripoux 17, **16**
trompe-bonhomme 103
trout 37
  brown trout 18
truffade 17
truffiats 47
turbot 133
  Turbot with Ceps 140
turbot *continued*
  Turbot with Loire Vegetables and Muscadet 140, **140**
Turbot à la Ligne aux Cèpes 140
turnips 104

Vacheron, Jean 43
Valençay (cheese) 73
veal
  Loin of Veal in Anjou or Saumur wine 118-19
  Veal Casseroled in Wine 118
vegetables
  Anjou region 102, 103-4
  Bourbonnais region 21
  Pays Nantais region 129
Venison with Red Sancerre 52
Villandry 61, **60**
vinaigre d'Orléans 39
violets 18
Vouvray wines 12, 74, 75
walnuts **32**
  Guinea Fowl with Walnuts 116
  Haricot Beans with Walnut Oil 111
walnuts *continued*
  Roast Pike with Walnuts 85, **84**
  Touraine region **68-9**
wild boar 18
  Sologne region 37
wild flowers
  Auvergne region 17, 18, **16**
wild mushrooms *see* mushrooms
Wilde, Oscar 9
Williams pear 100
  liqueur from 36
  see also Bon Chrétien
wines
  Anjou 11, 12, 106-9
  Domaine Vacheron 43
  importance of Orléans 39
  Ladoucette wines 44
  Loire wine areas 11-12
  méthode champenoise 106, 108
  Orléanais region 44
  Pays Nantais region 11, 134-5
  Pouilly wines 43-4
  Sancerre wines 43-4
  Touraine region 11, 73-5
  wine tasting 134, **134**

Acknowledgments

Author's Acknowledgments

Many people have helped me during the life of this book, and to all of them I am sincerely grateful. There were many formal and pre-arranged introductions, but while I was doing 'on the ground' research, I was helped spontaneously so often that people's generosity with their time, and money, began to cease to surprise me. The list of shopkeepers, stall holders, restaurateurs, chefs, cooks, friends and relatives of contacts of mine, and people I just happened to come across, is too long to include everyone. Where possible I have mentioned them in the book, but to all the others who are not included there or below and to anyone else who has helped me, 'Thank you very much'.

M. & Mme Benoist, Château du Plessis; M. & Mme Berthoumier, St-Avertin, near Tours; Brittany Ferries; Mme Cabanes, Relais & Châteaux, Paris; Philip Doumerc, Le Prieuré, Chenehutte-les-Tuffeaux; Food & Wine From France; Didier Garnier, St Quentin Group, London; Mme Garnier, Angers; M. & Mme Goupil de Bouillé, Châteaux de Reaux; Martin Hollis and all the staff at World Wide Wine Tours; Louis Métaireau; P & O Ferries; Alison Cryer at Representation Plus; Michel Sébéo, St-Aignan; Alain Seydoux, Gratien & Meyer, Saumur; M. Taupin, Domaine du Beauvois, Luynes; M. & Mme de Valbray, Château des Briotieres; Comte and Comtesse de Voguë, Château de la Verrerie.

Finally, I thank my editor, Sarah Pearce, for her hard work, efficiency and understanding.

Researcher's Acknowledgments

Sally Anne Scott would like to thank all the chefs and restaurateurs who gave so much of their time to the book, particularly those who sadly could not be featured.

Publisher's Acknowledgments

Studio photography
(pages **23, 29, 50-1, 54, 78-9, 87, 88-9, 113, 139, 145**)
Home Economist — Meg Jansz
Photographer's assistant — Leonor Silva

Visitors' Guide research
Jane Sigal

Index
Karin Woodruff